ASHLEY WOOD'S ART OF **METAL GEAR SOLID**

ART AND DESIGN BY **ASHLEY WOOD,** FOR 7174 PTY. LTD.

Special thanks to Hideo Kojima and the entire Metal Gear Solid team at Konami, and Rick Privman.

ISBN: 978-1-61377-053-5   15 14 13 12   3 4 5 6

Ted Adams, CEO & Publisher
Greg Goldstein, Chief Operating Officer
Robbie Robbins, EVP/Sr. Graphic Artist
Chris Ryall, Chief Creative Officer/Editor-in-Chief
Matthew Ruzicka, CPA, Chief Financial Officer
Alan Payne, VP of Sales

www.IDWPUBLISHING.com

Ashley Wood's **Art of**
METAL GEAR SOLID

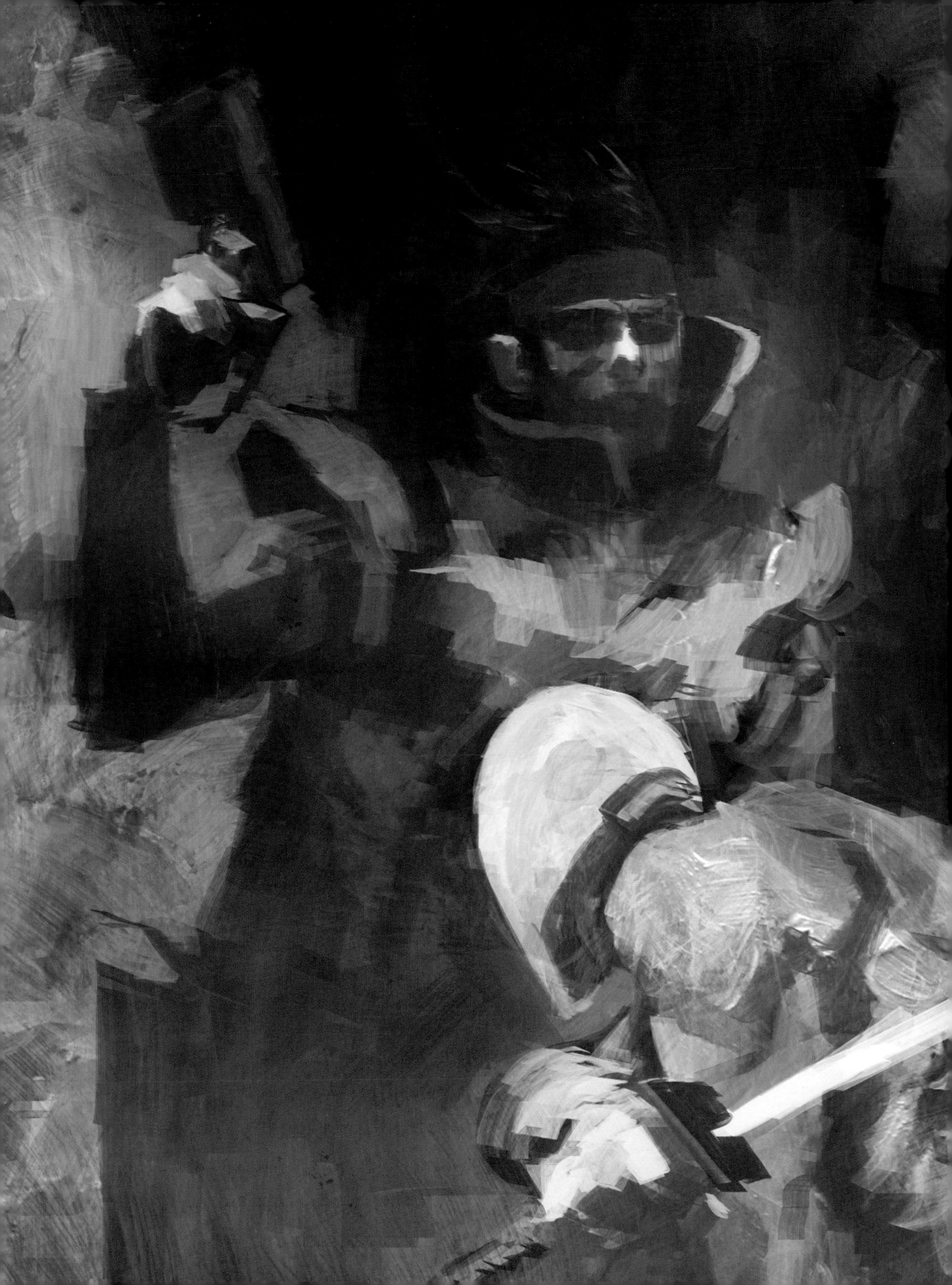

Happy to have been a small part of MGS

Ashley Wood

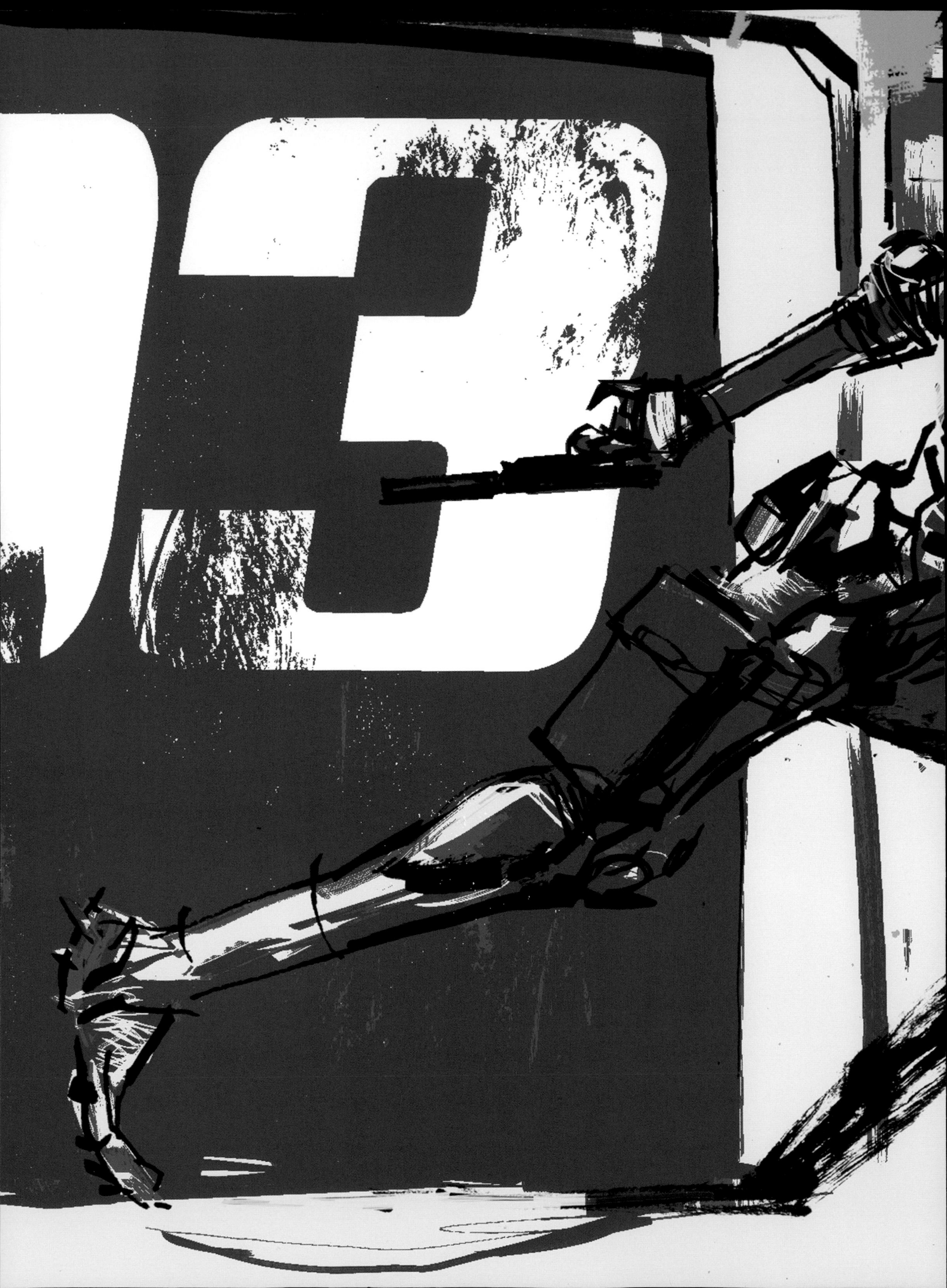

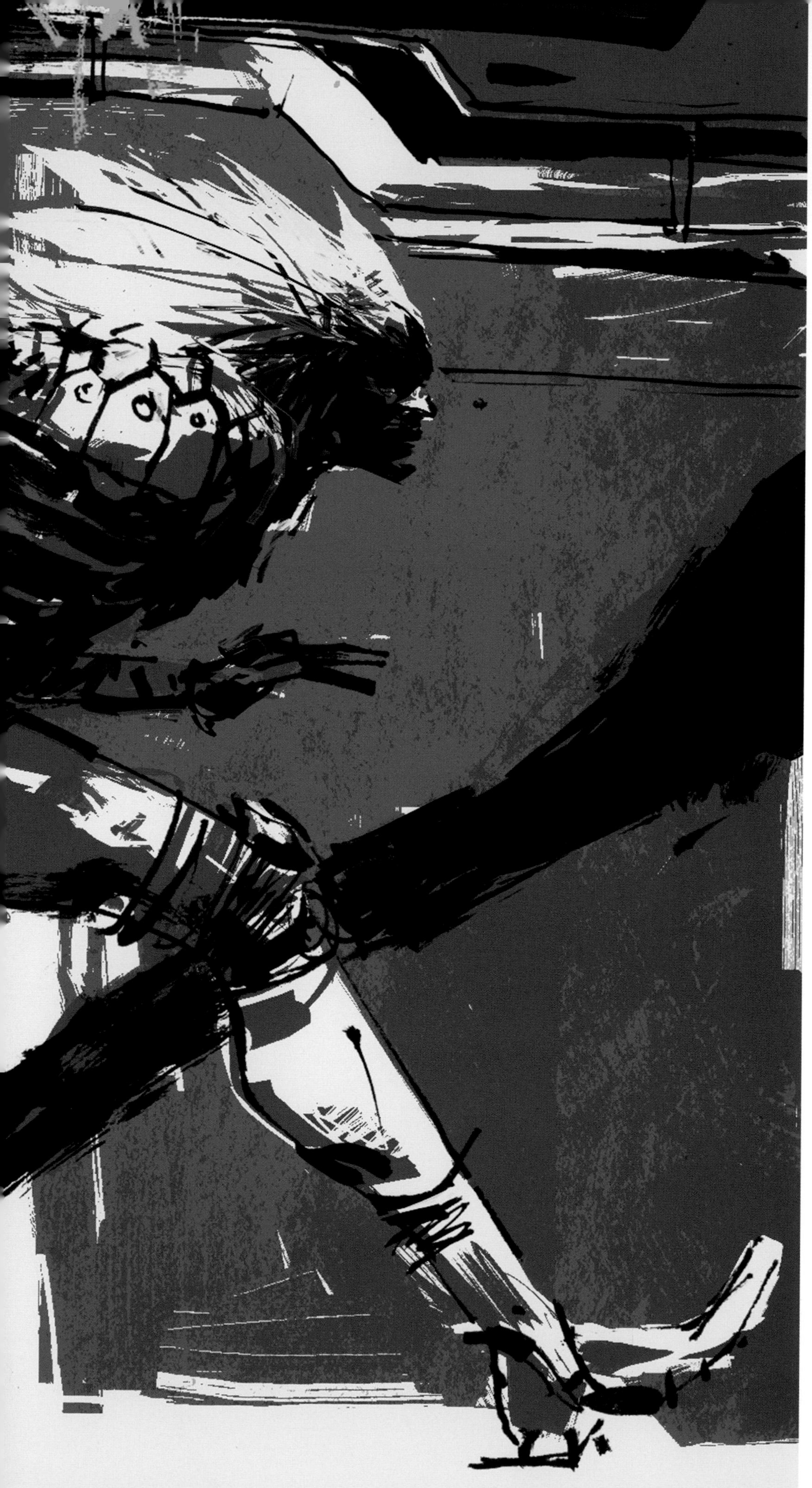

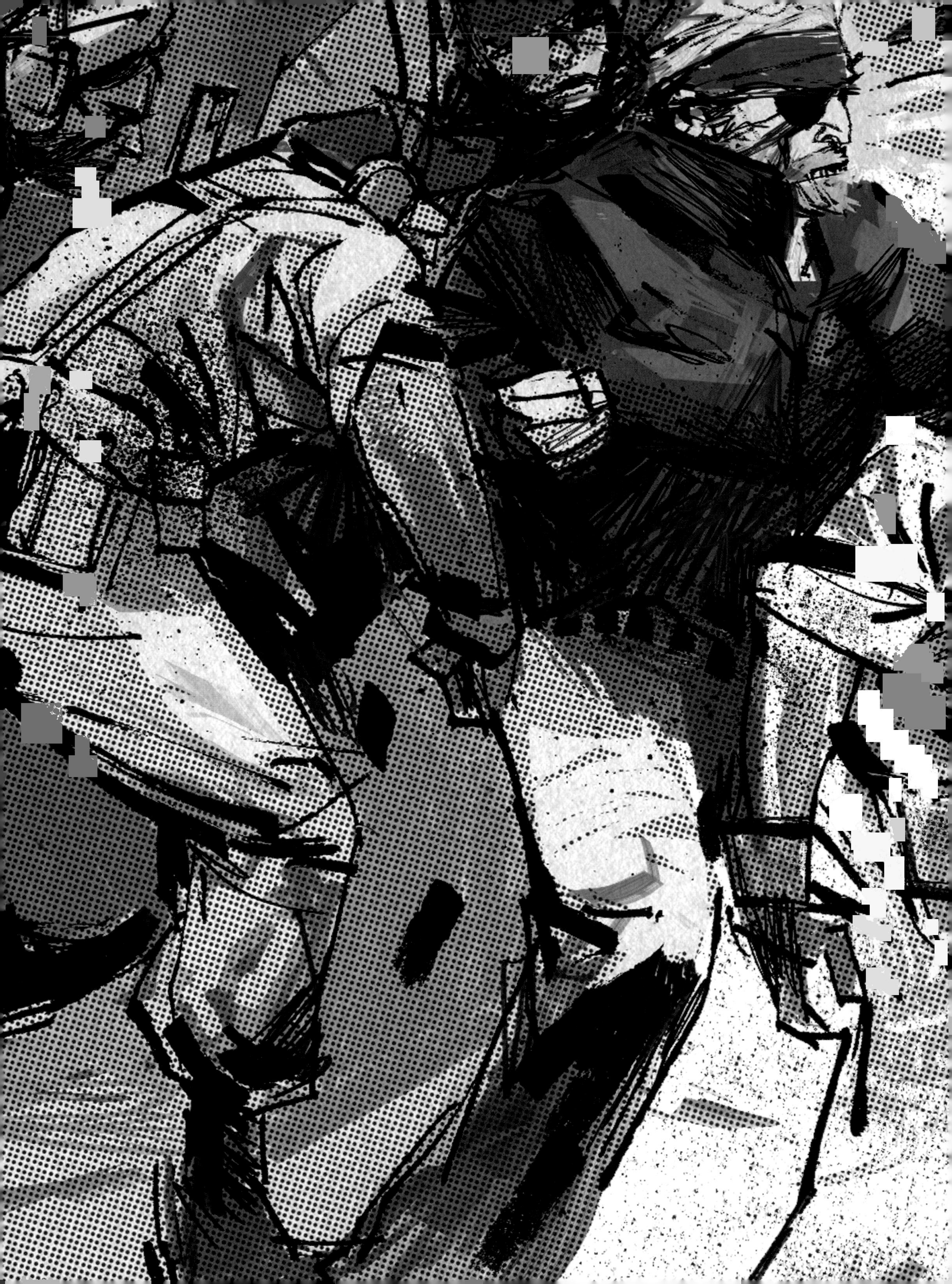

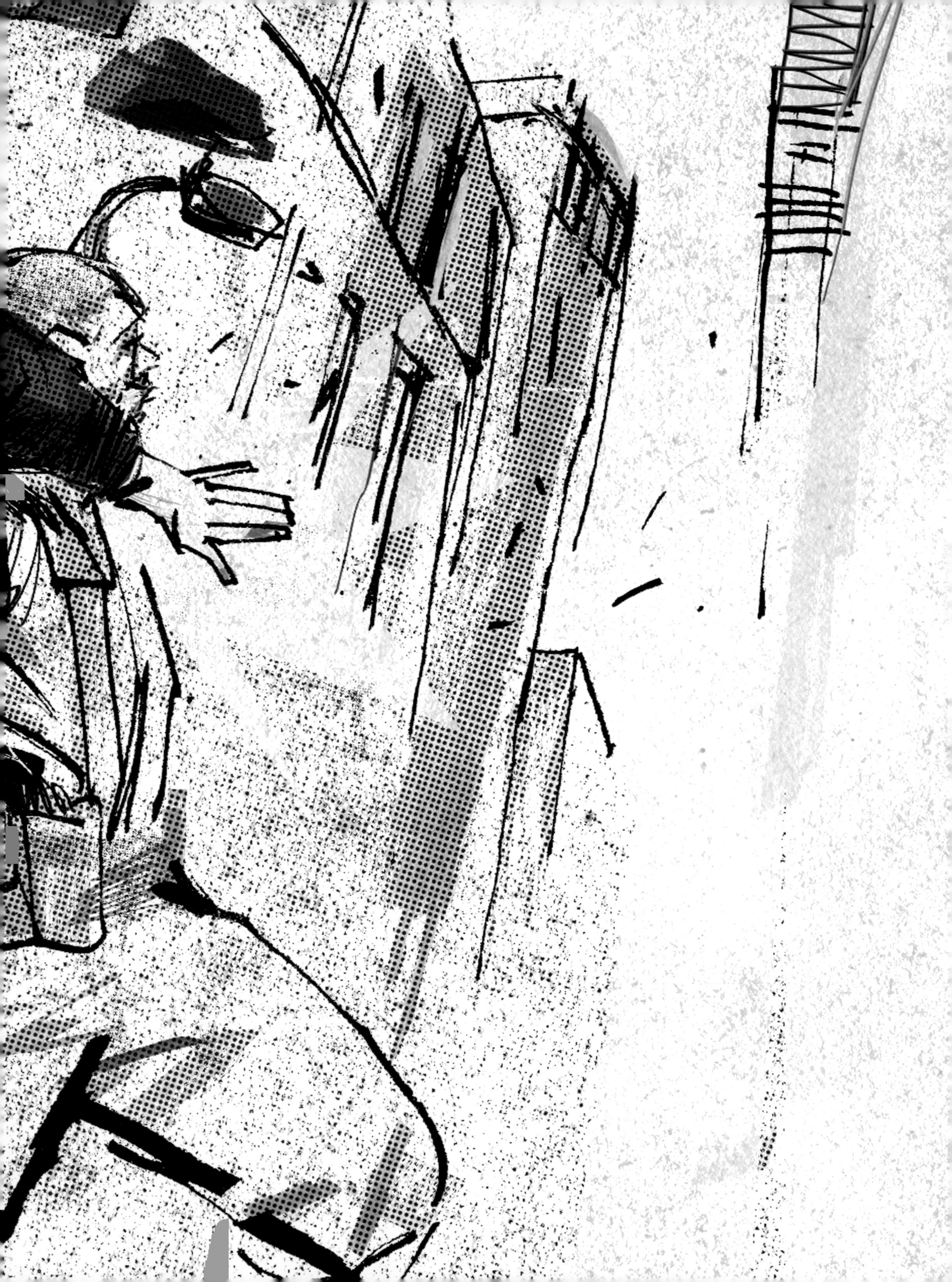

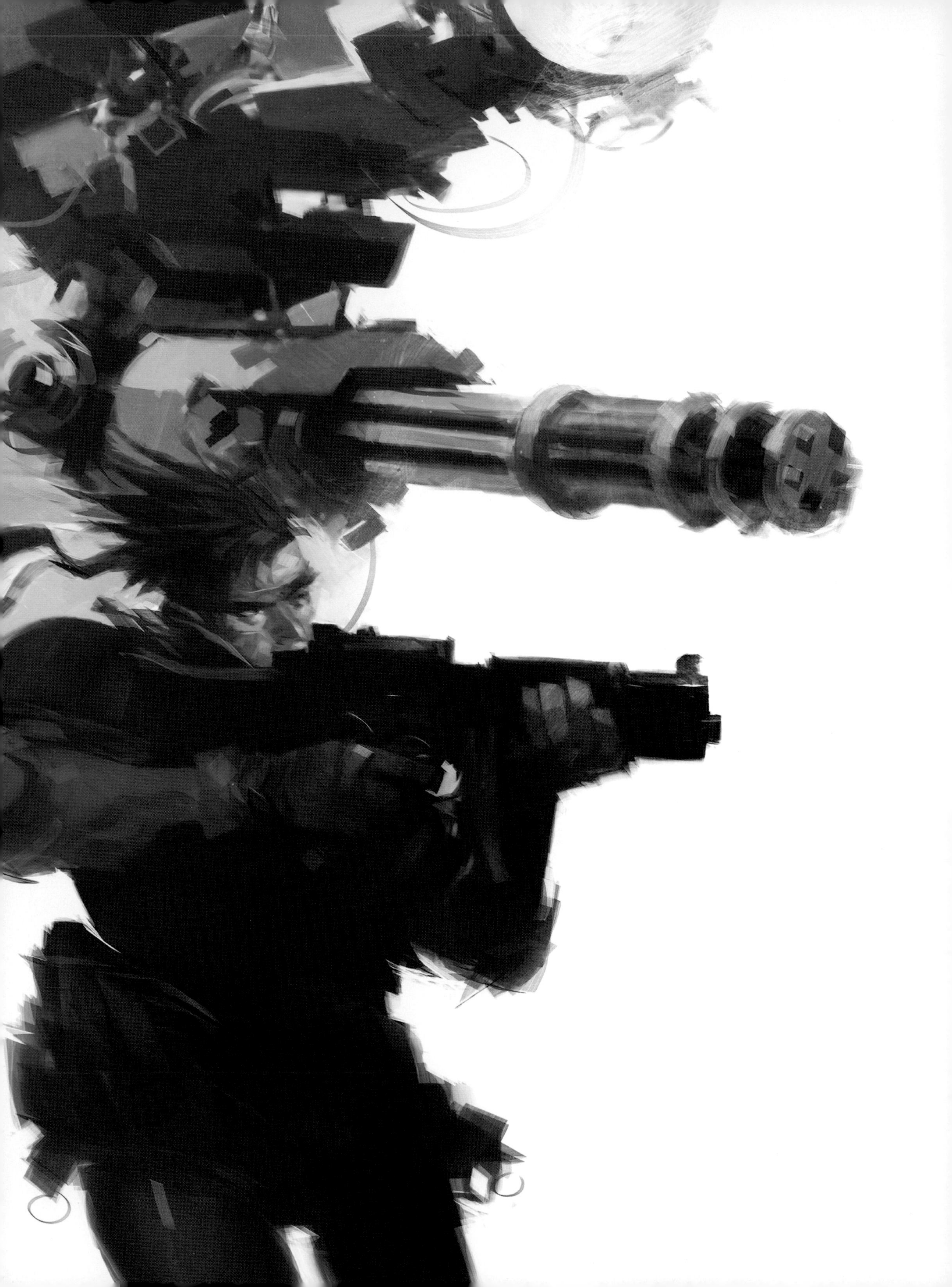

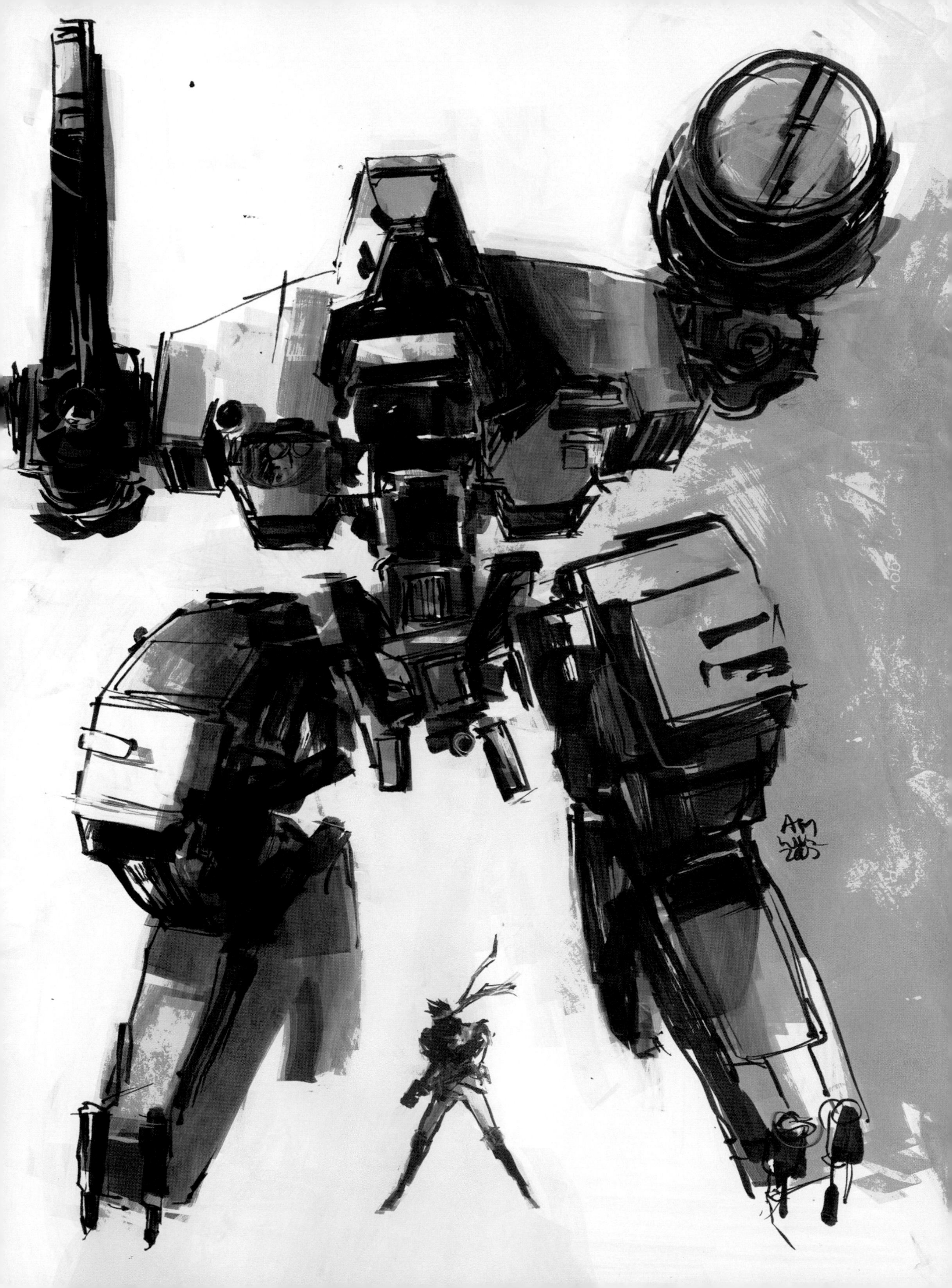

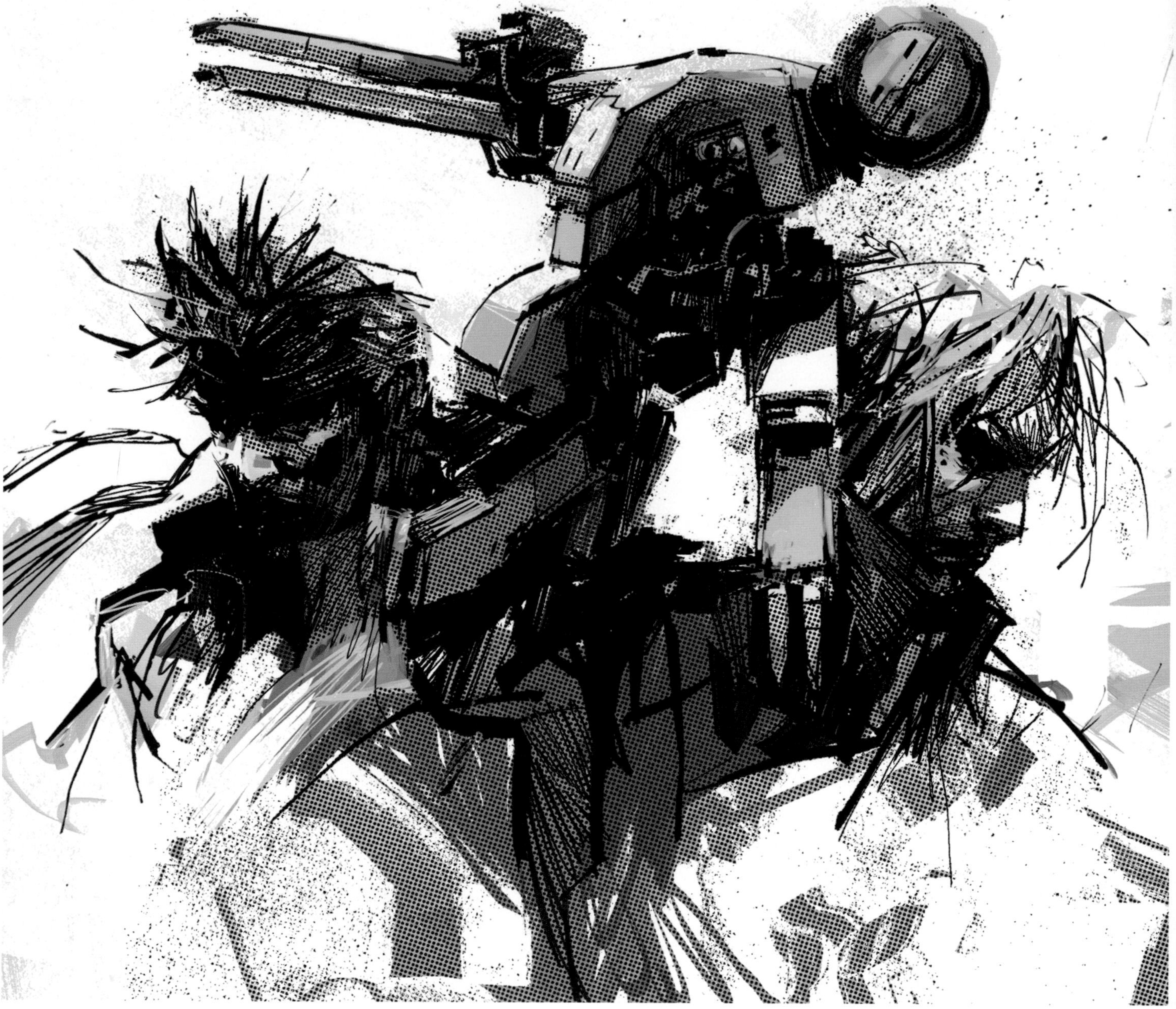

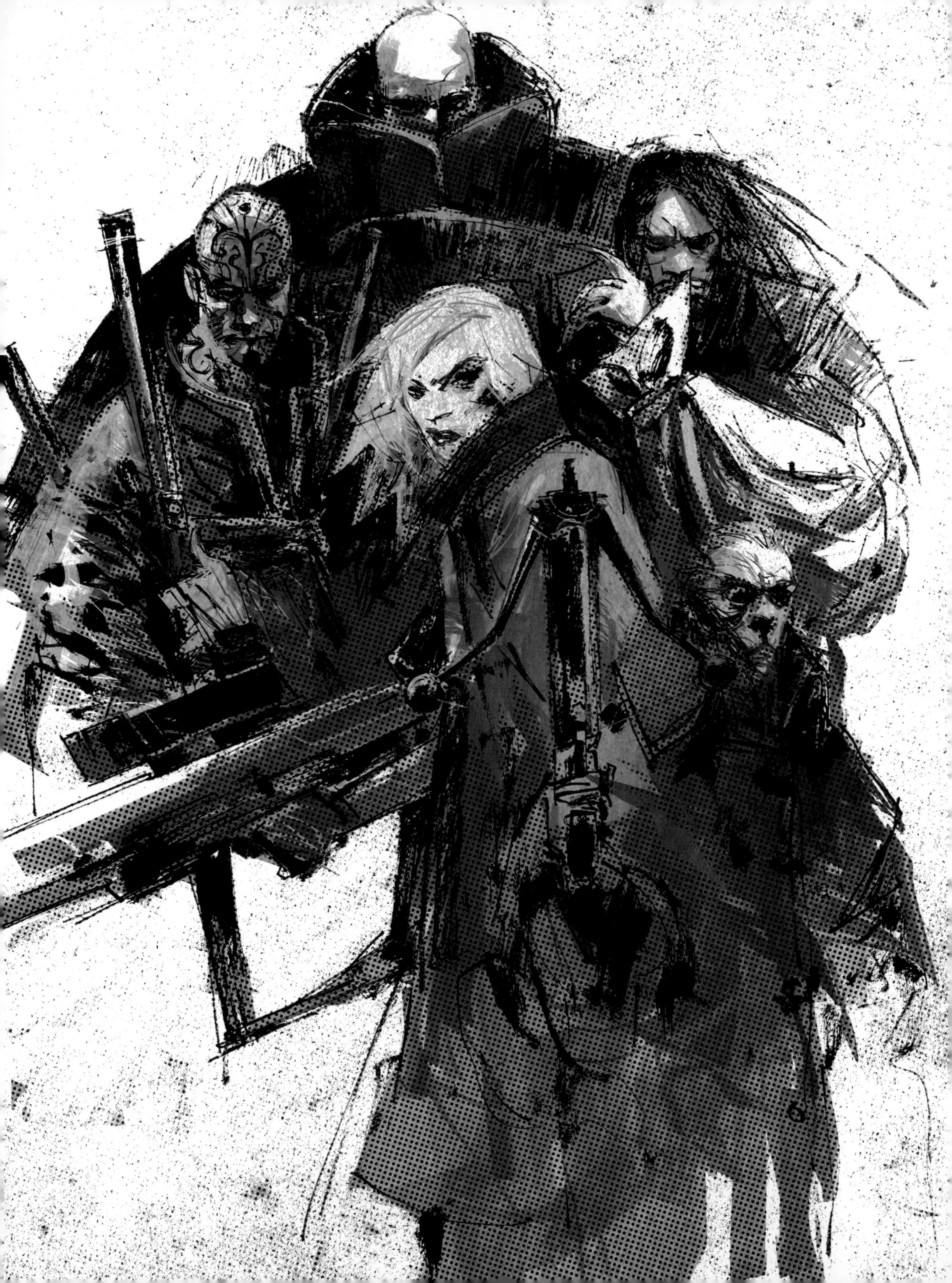

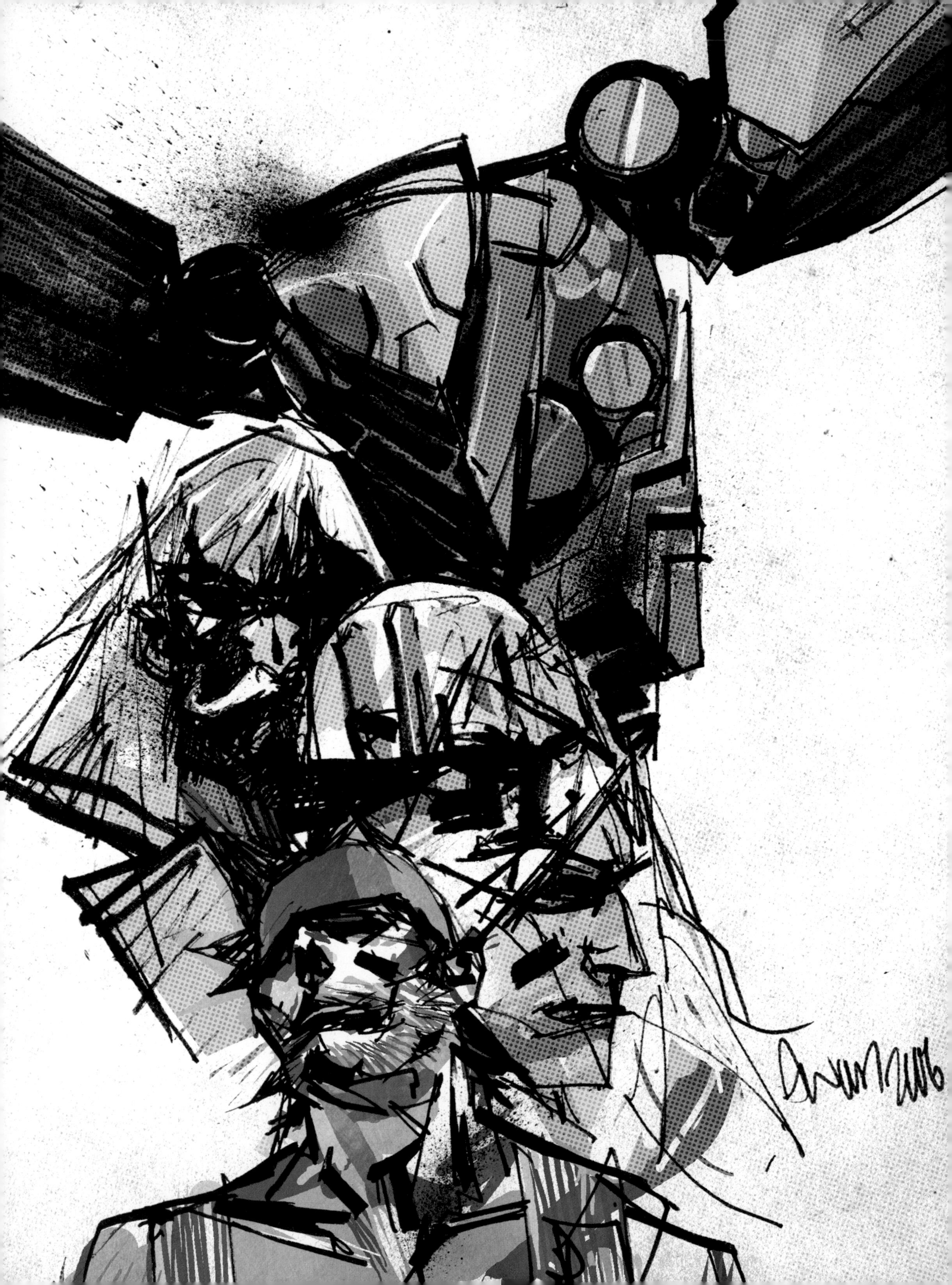

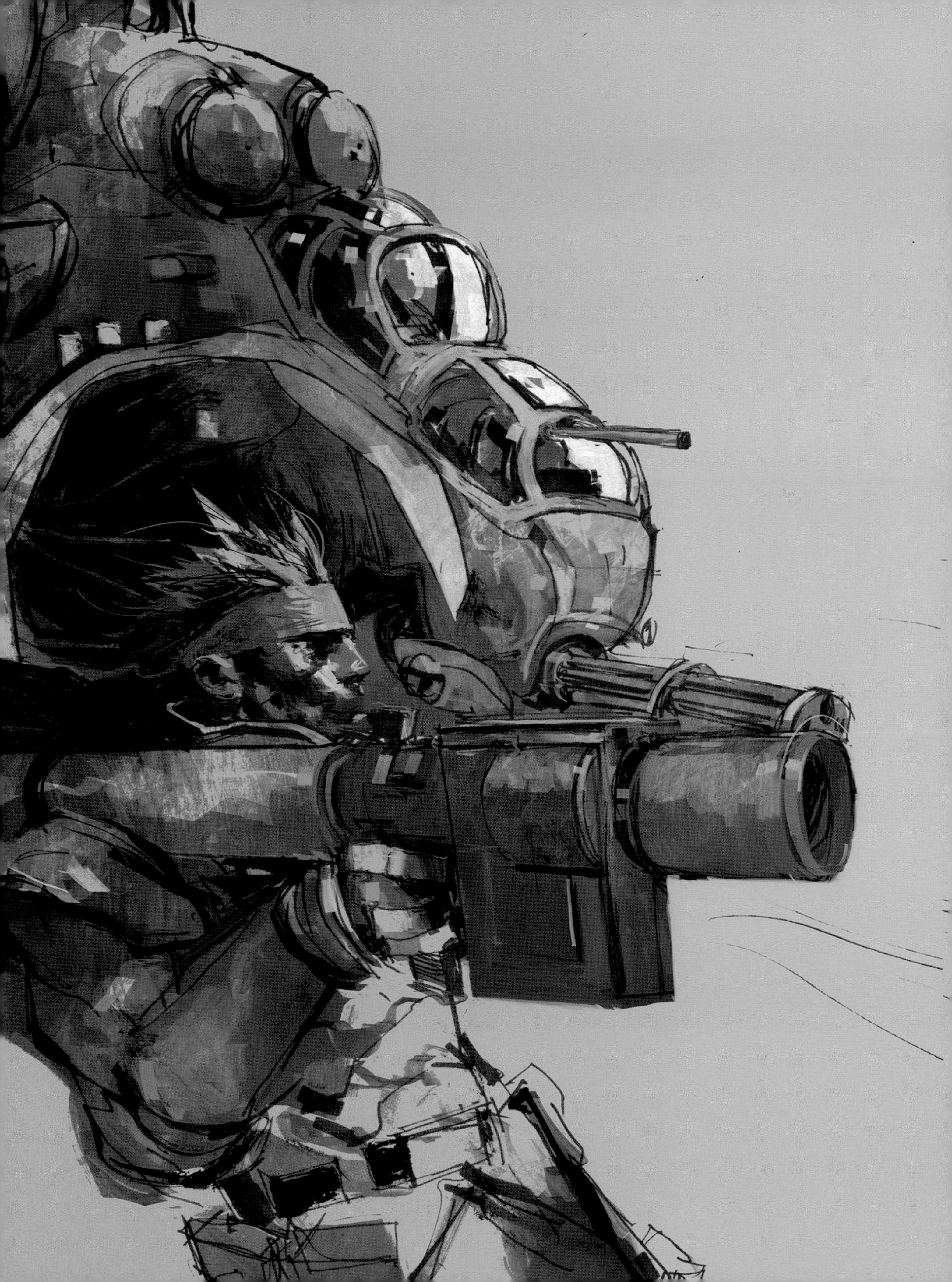

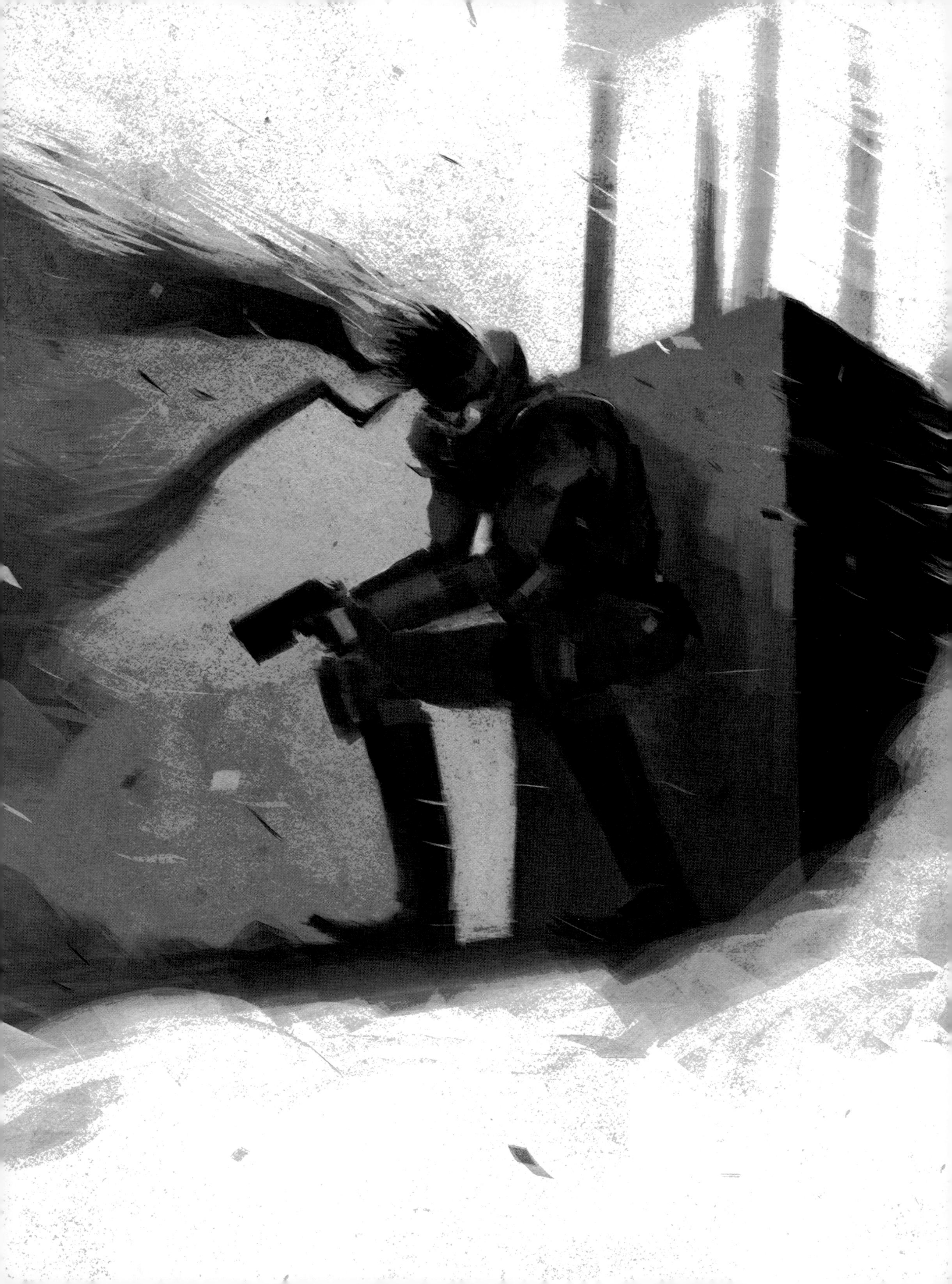

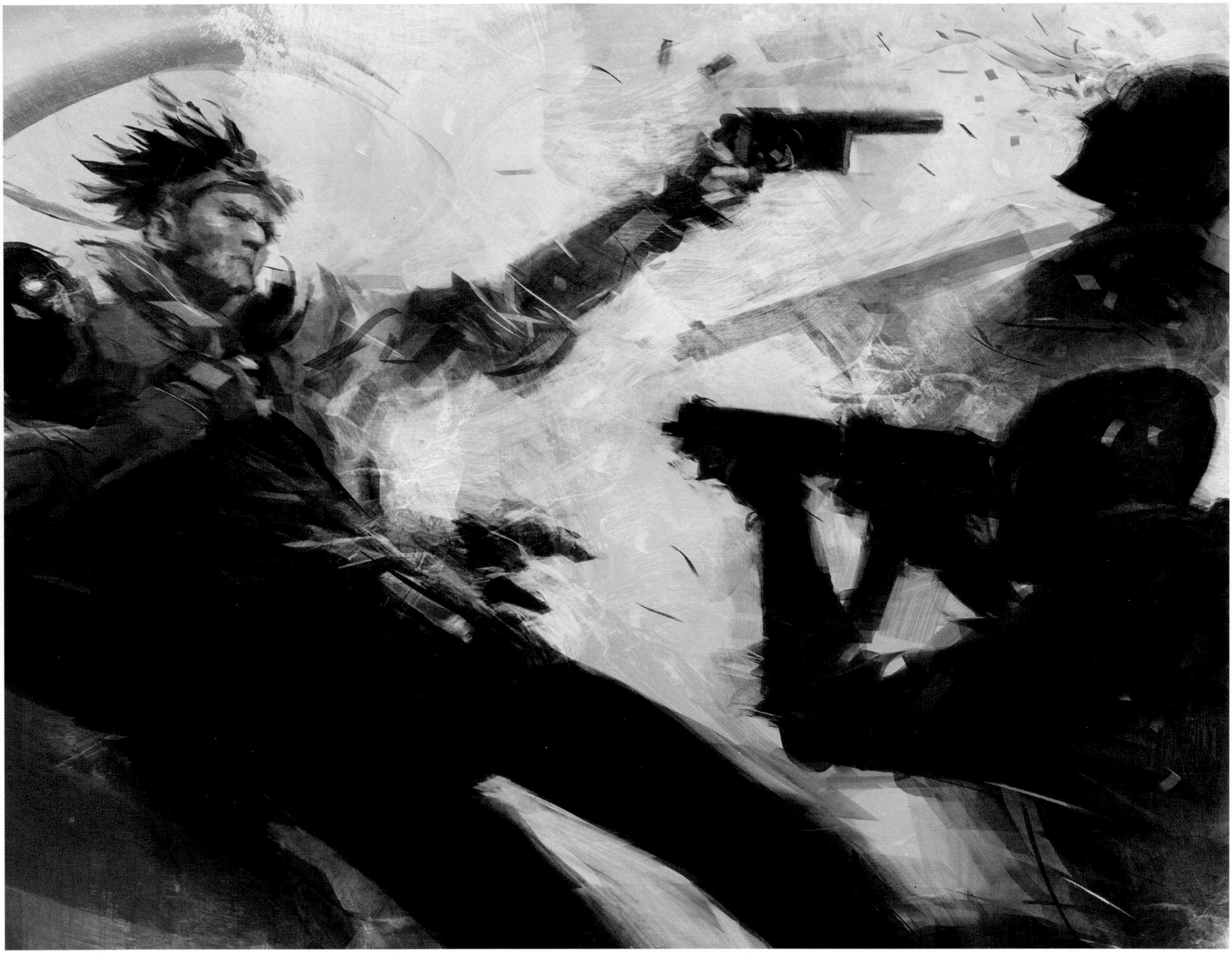

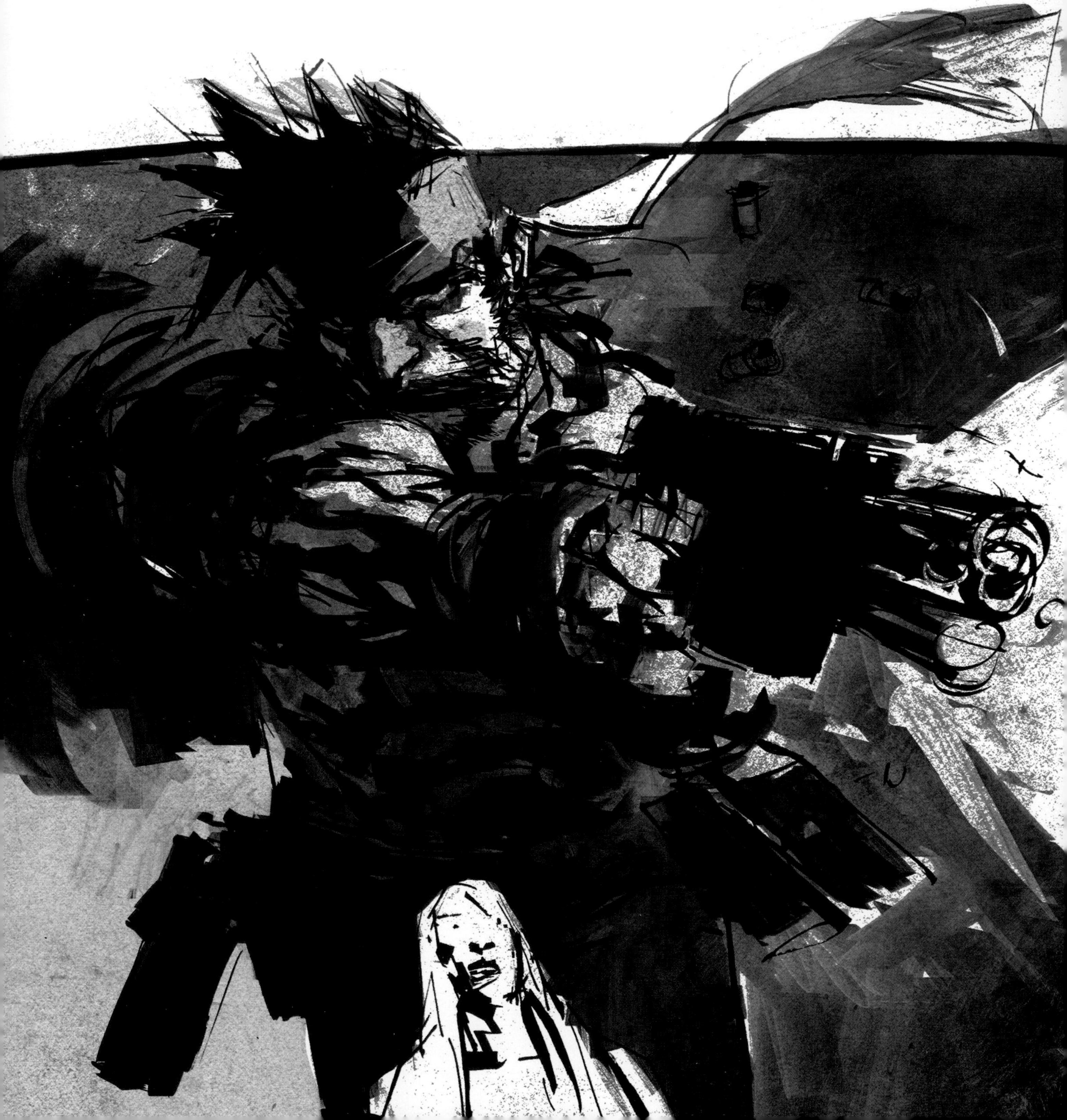

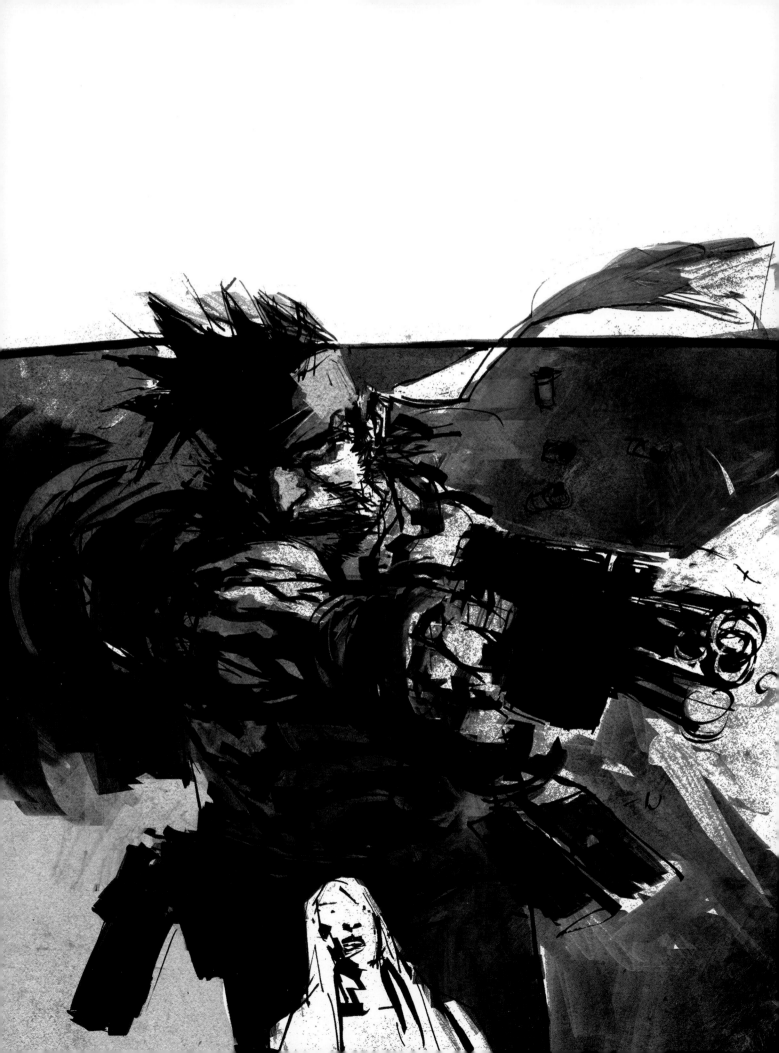

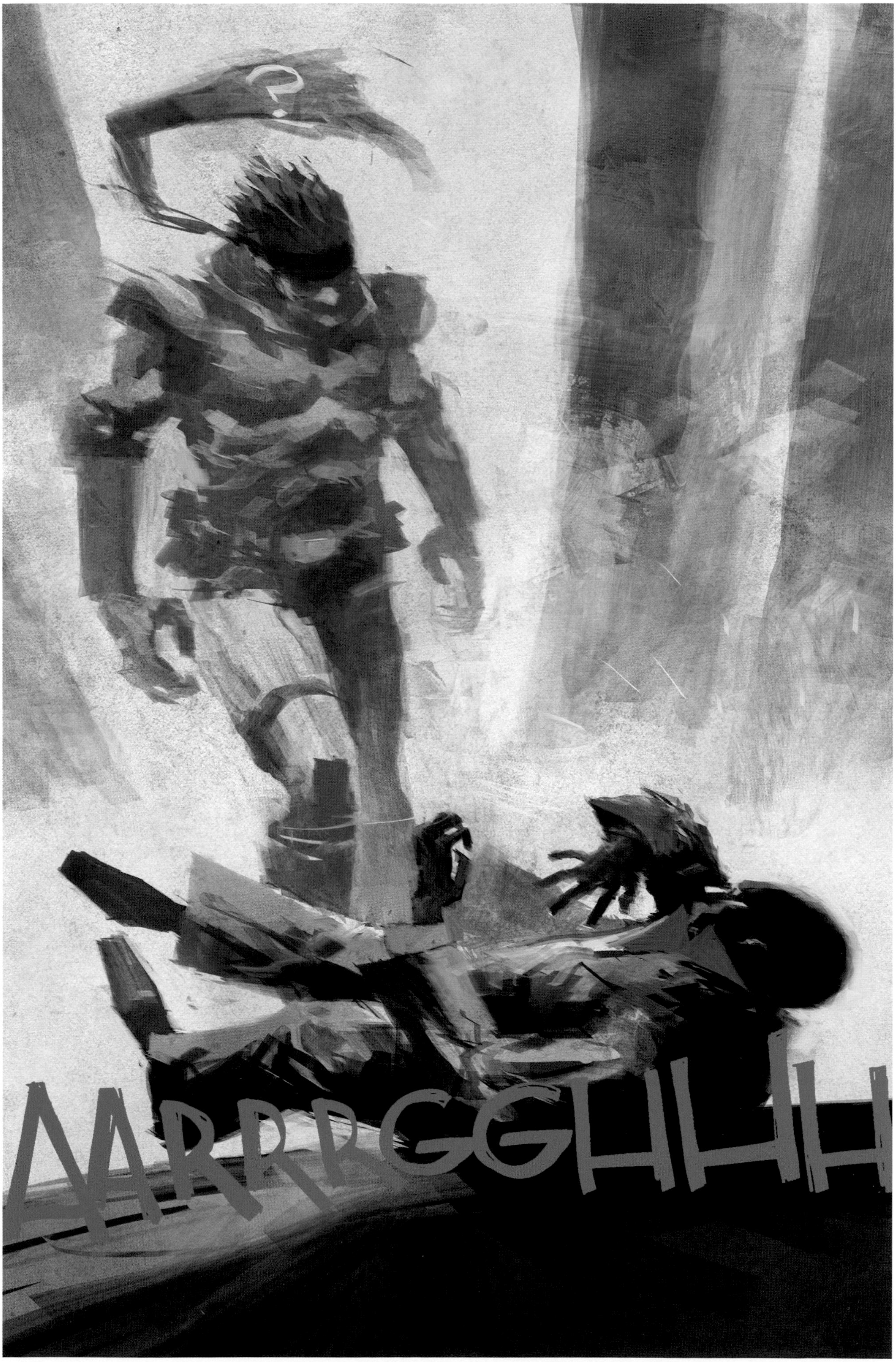
AARRRGGHHH

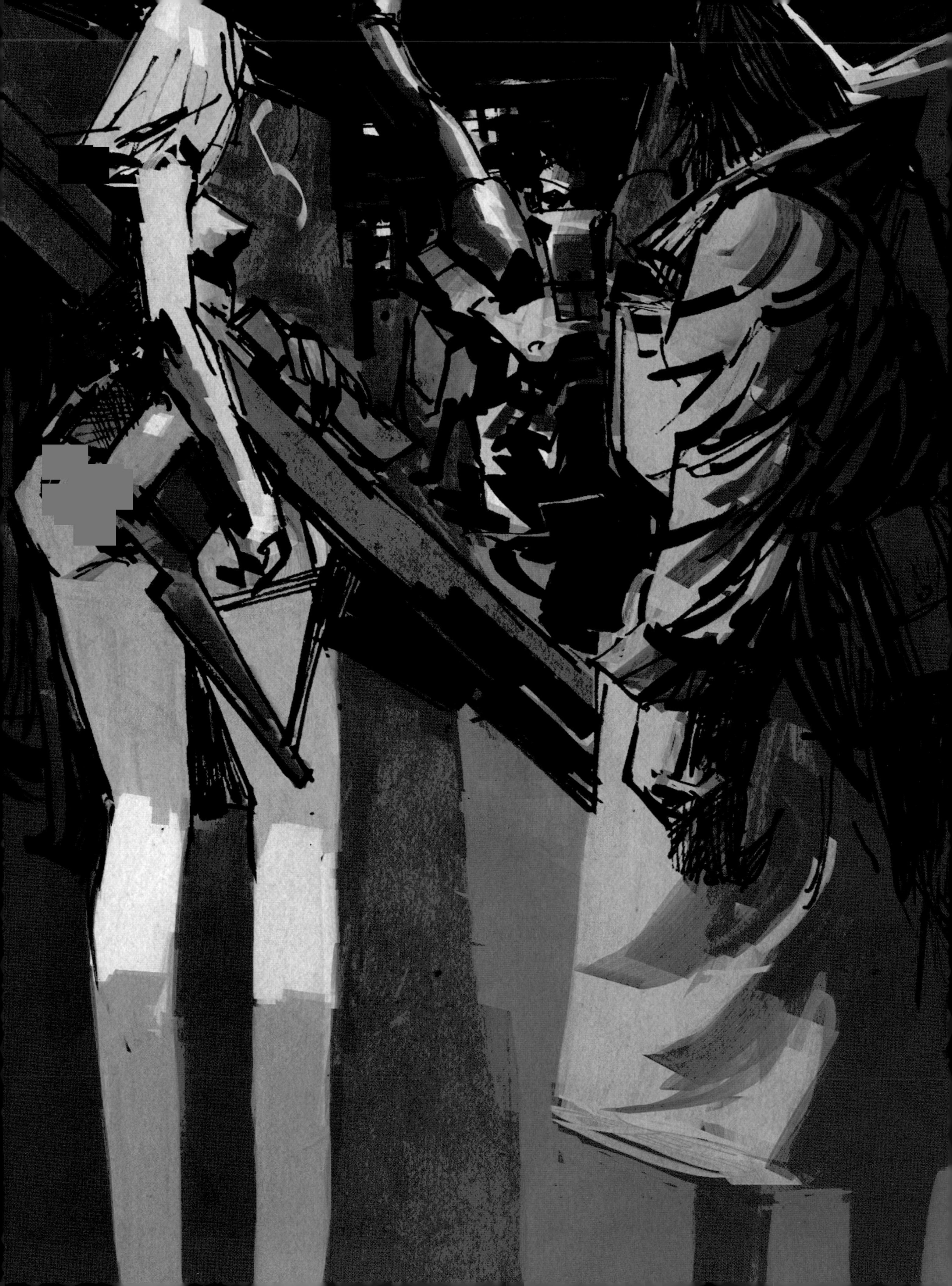

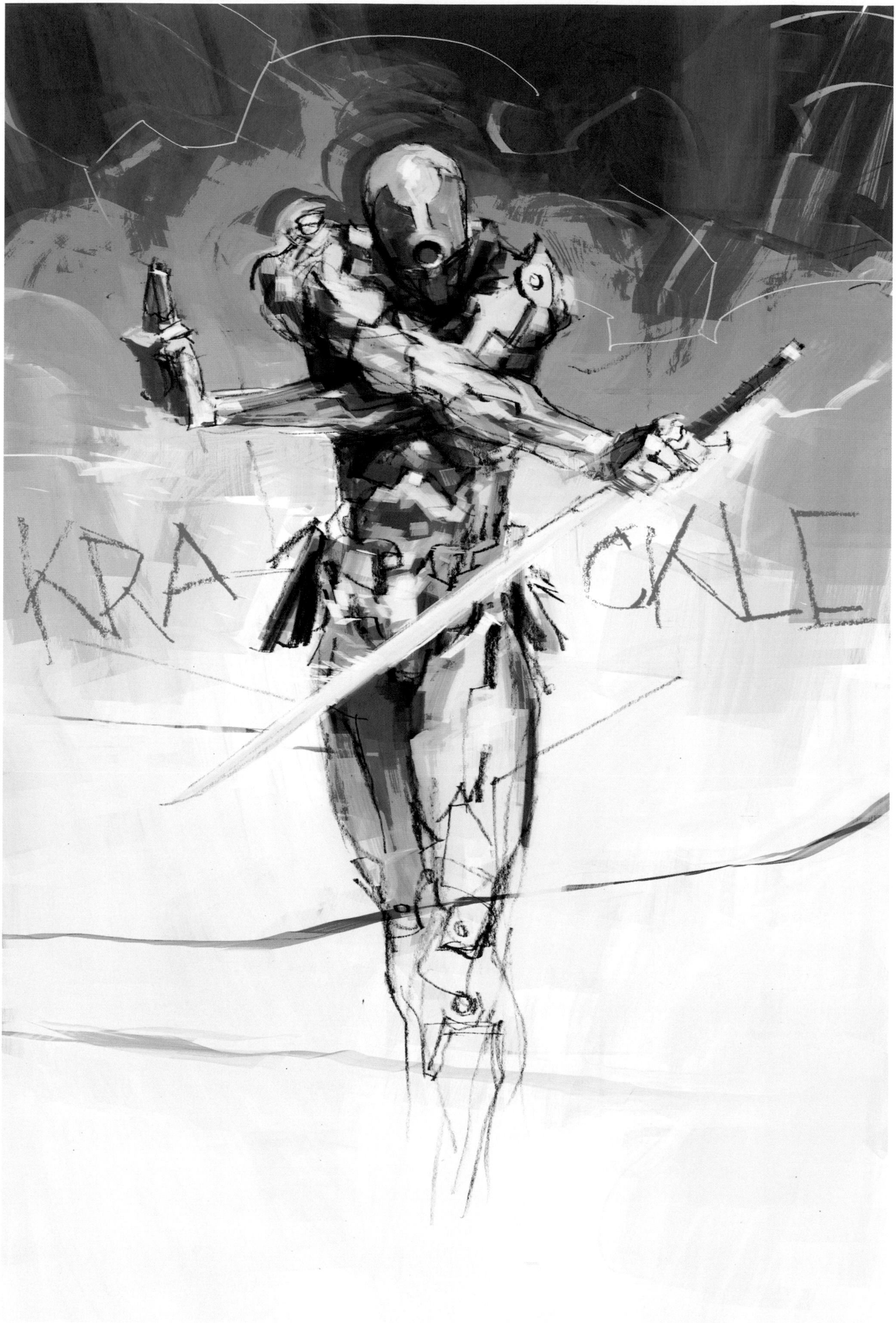
KRA
CKLE

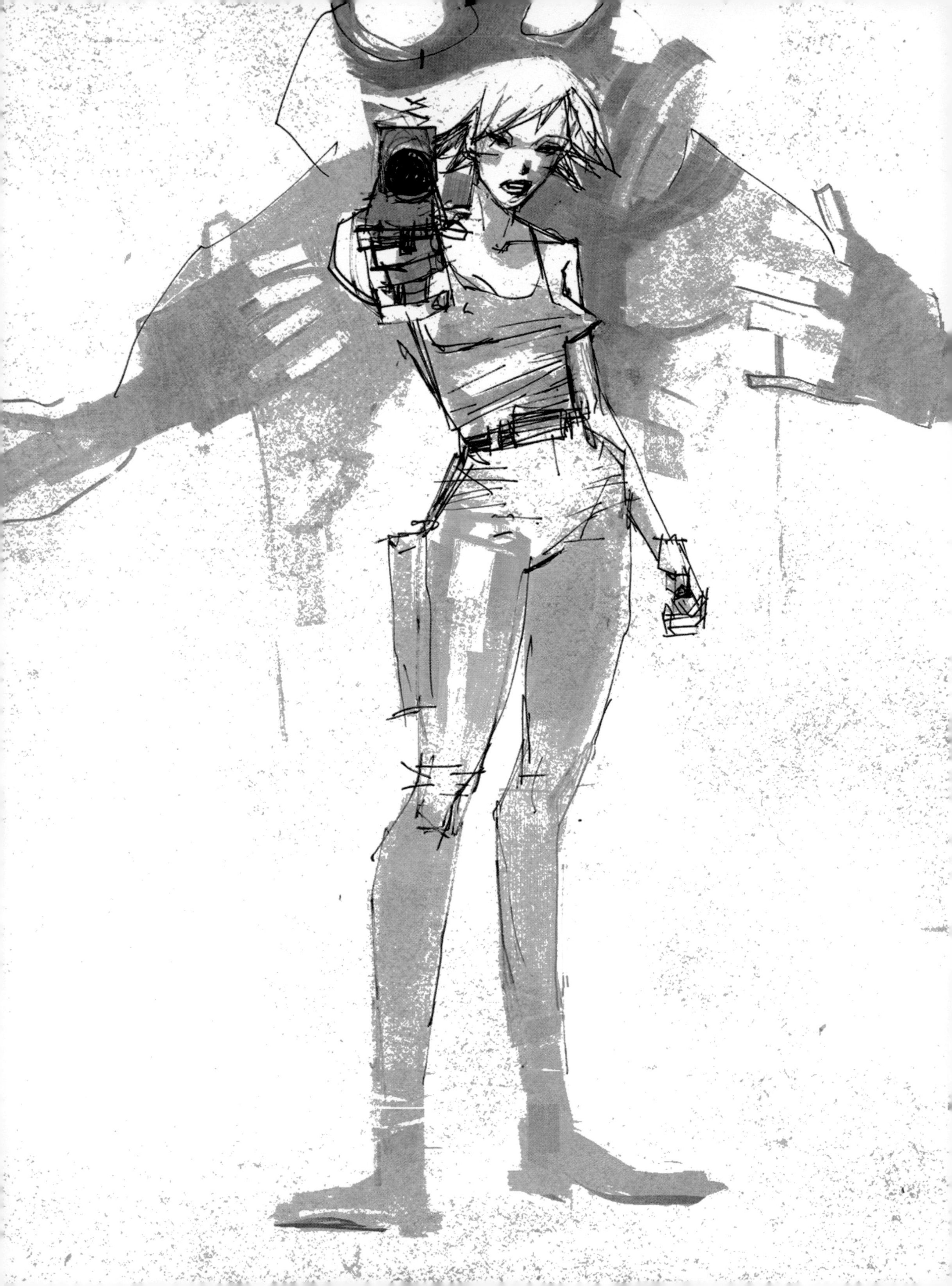

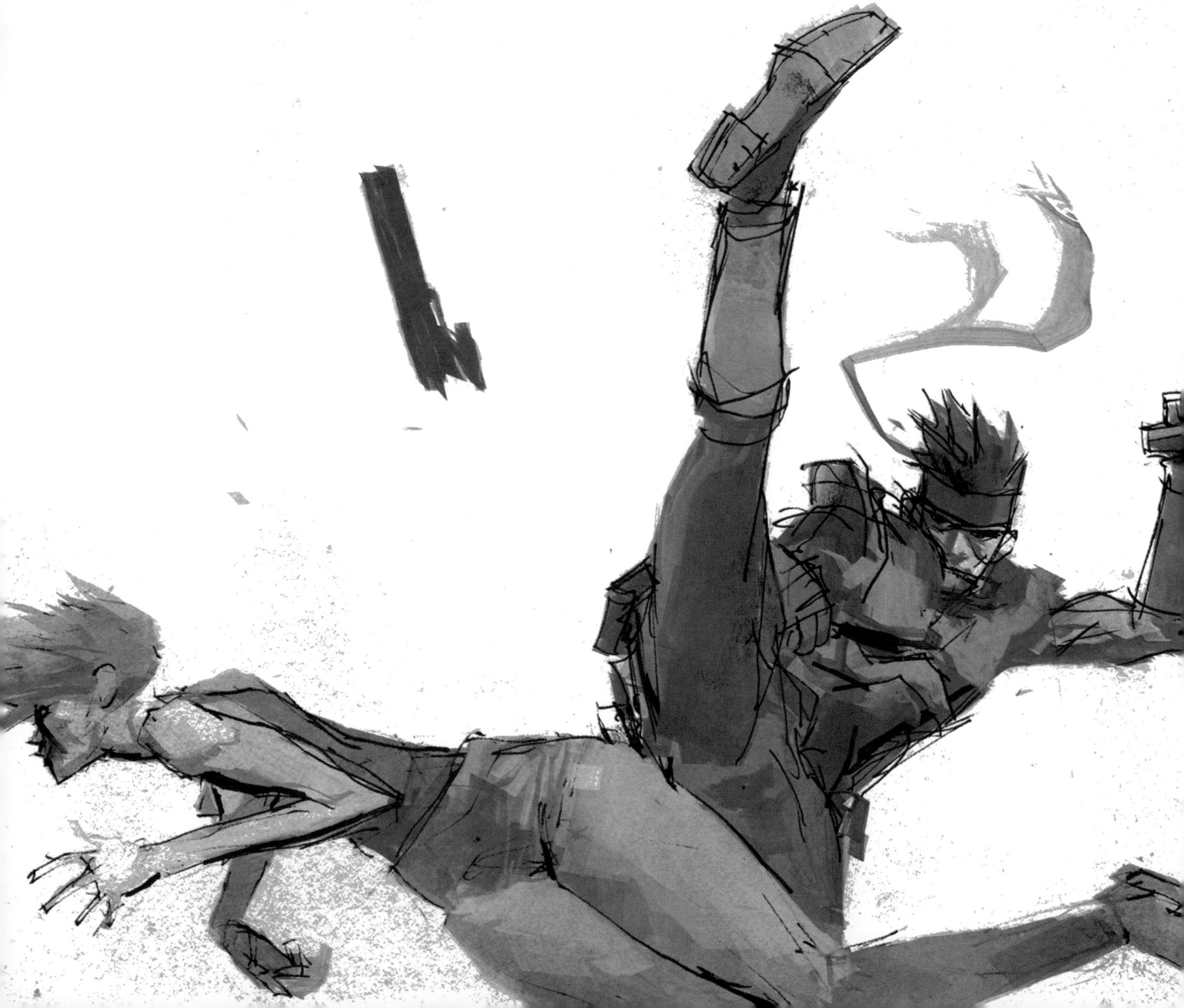

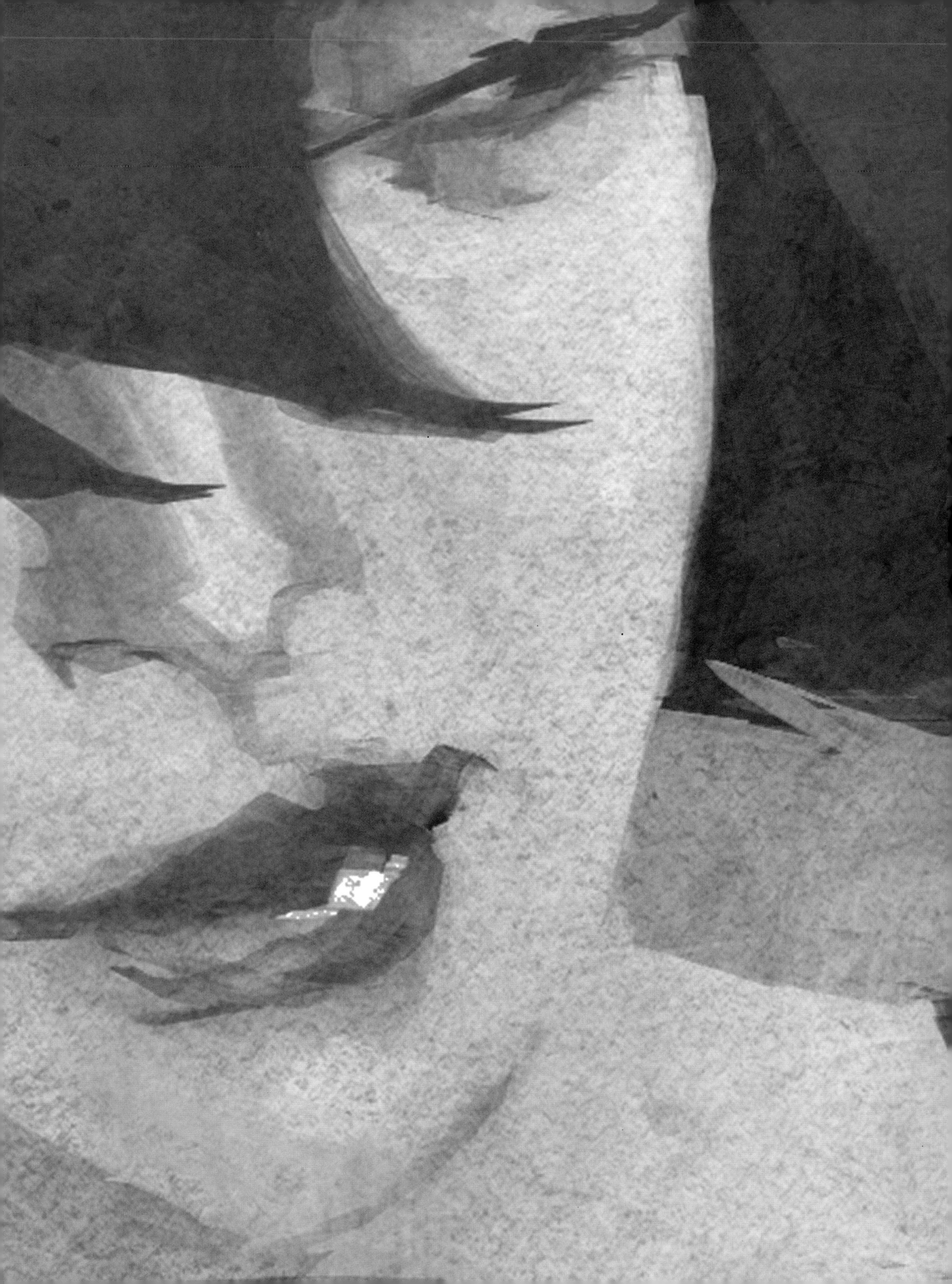

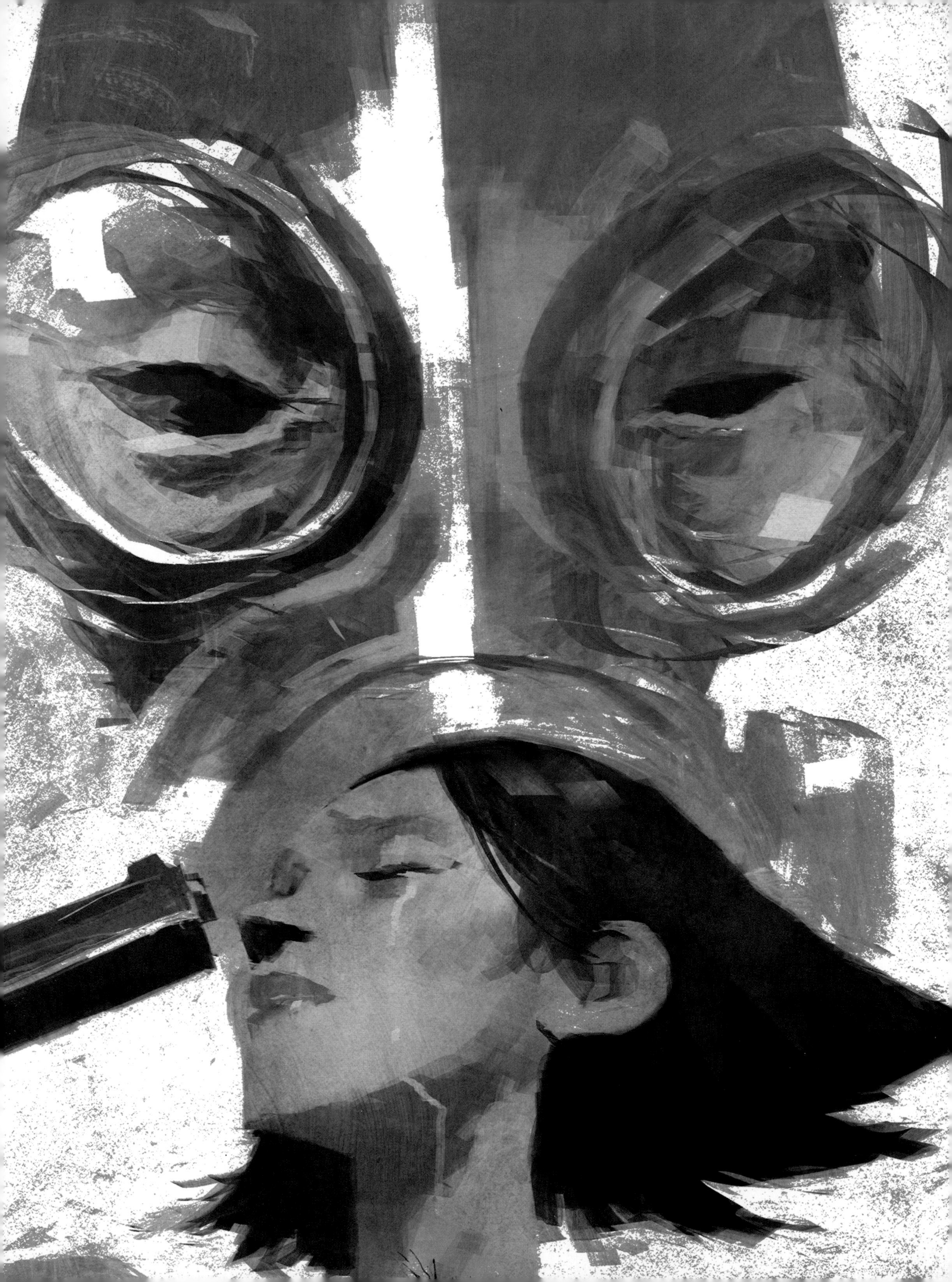

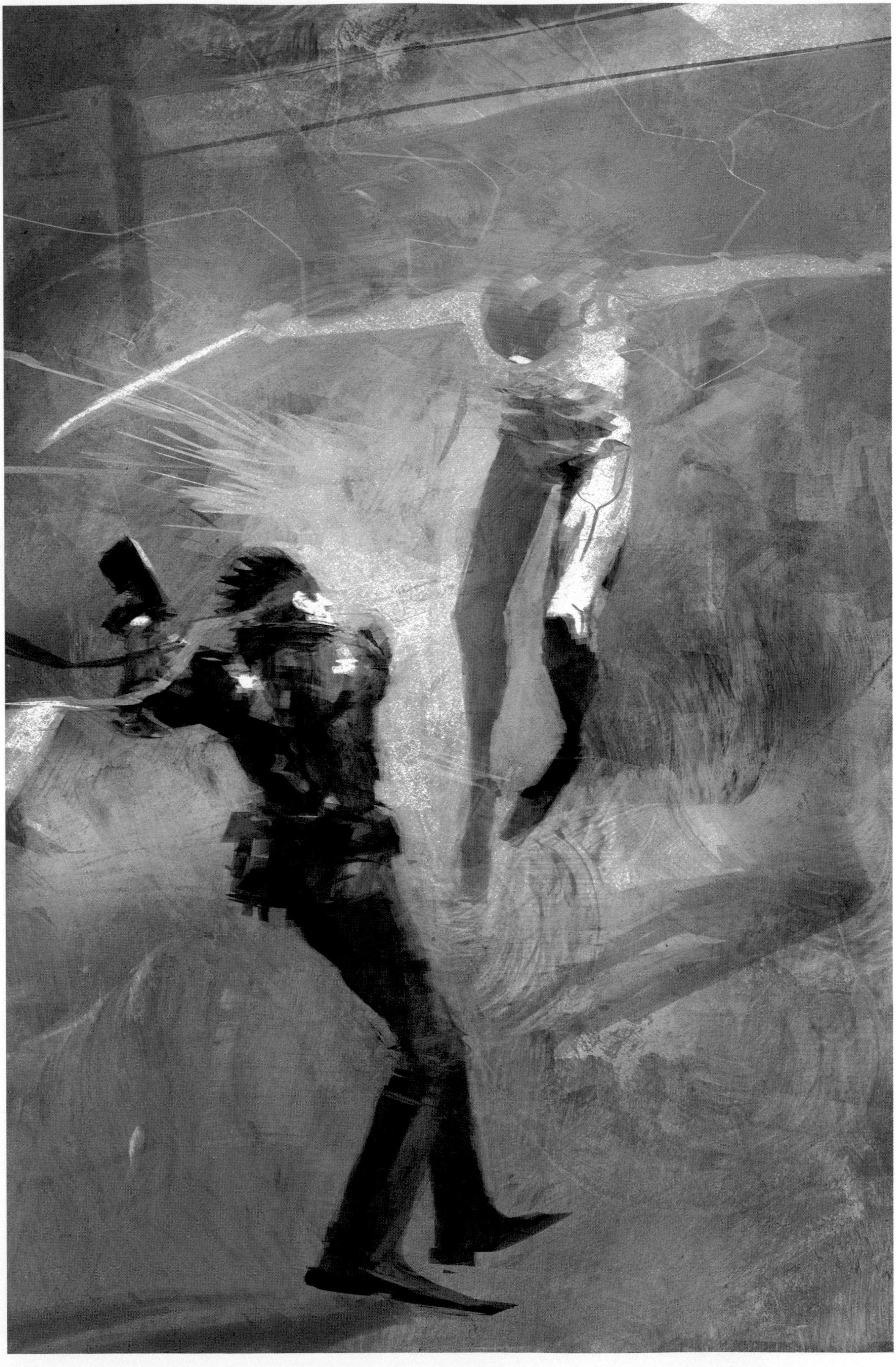

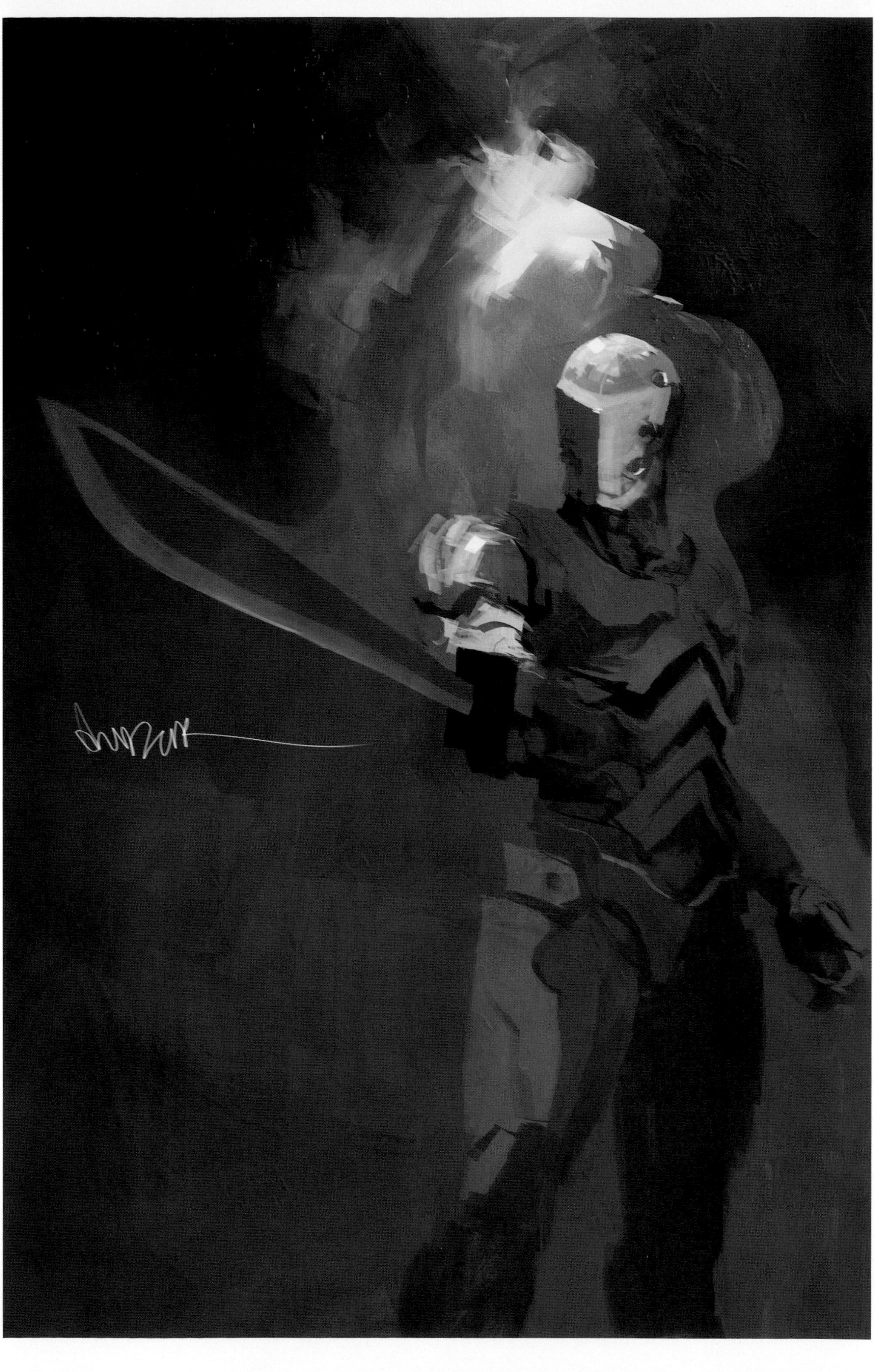

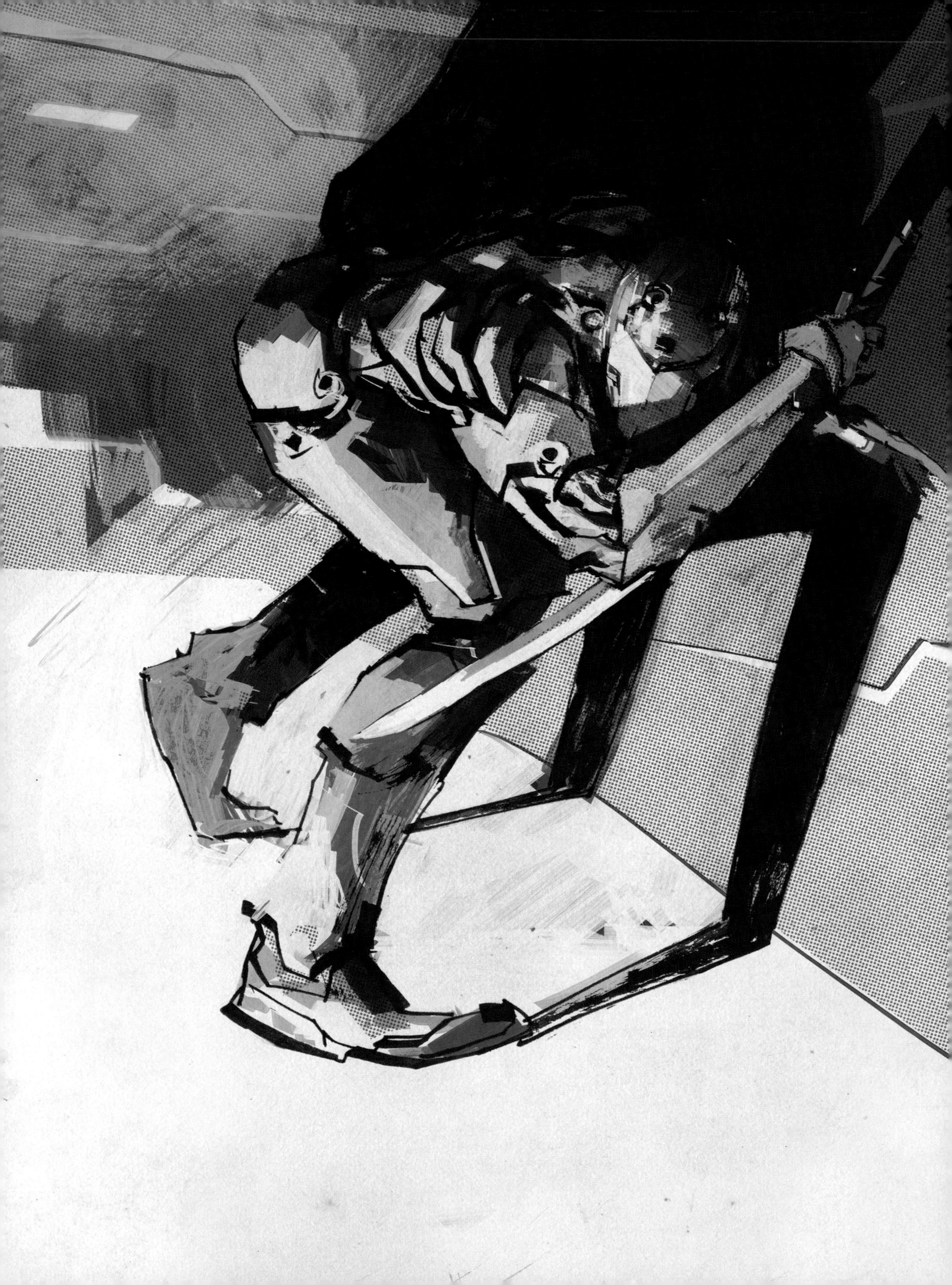

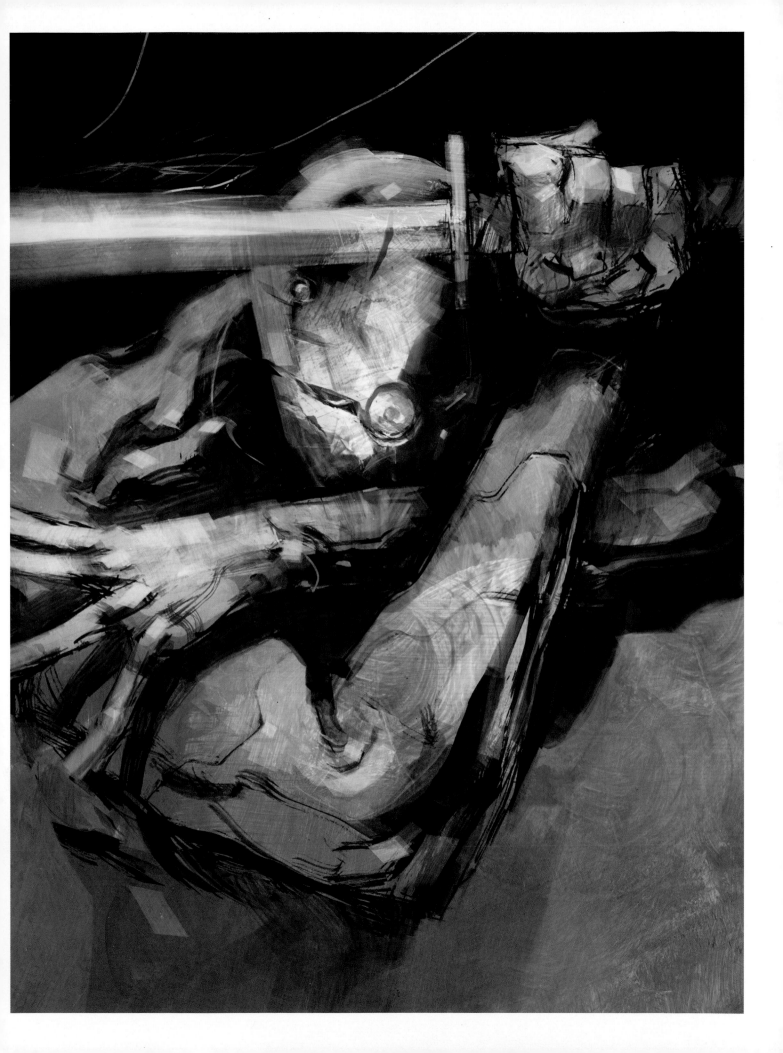

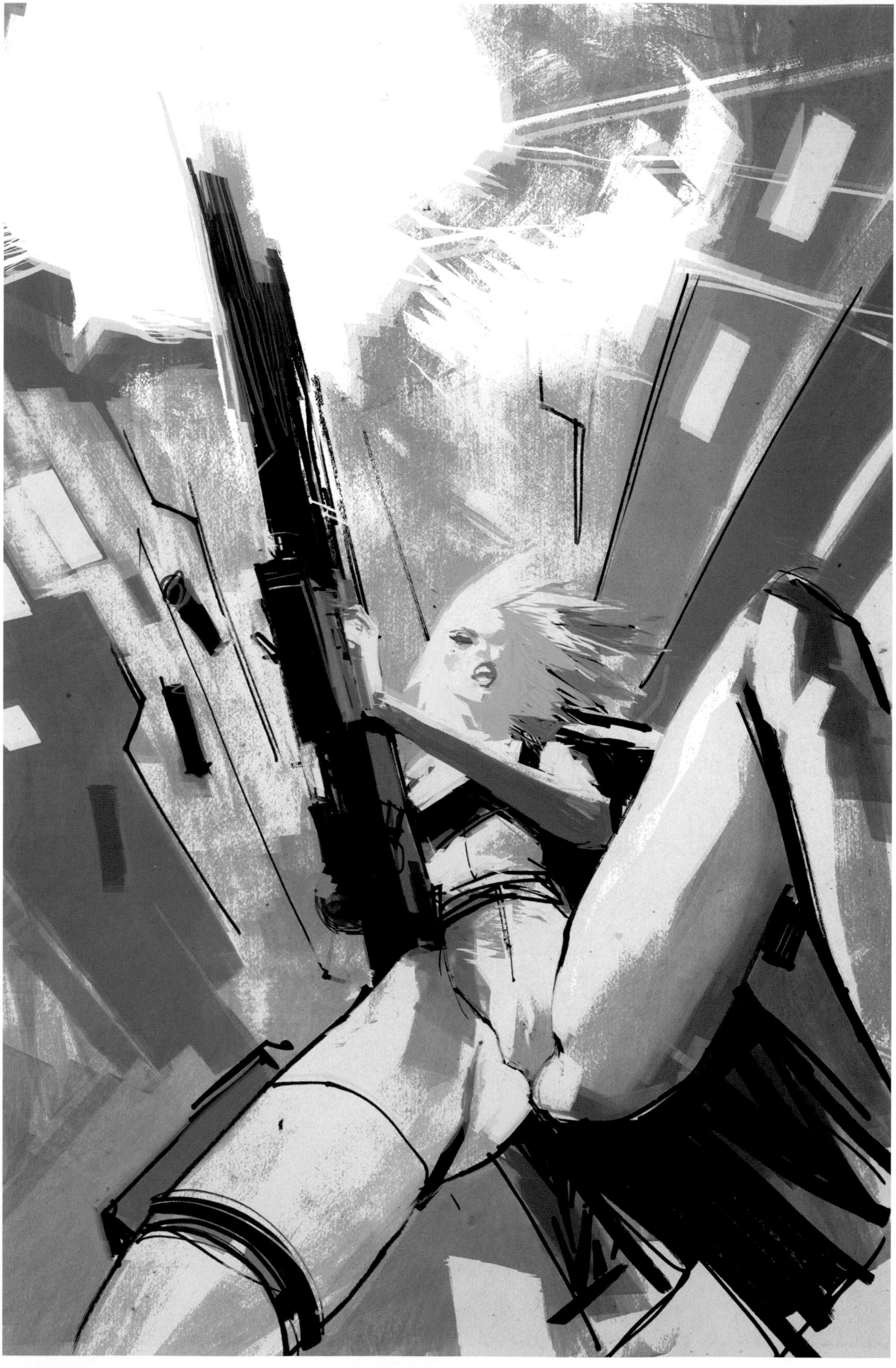

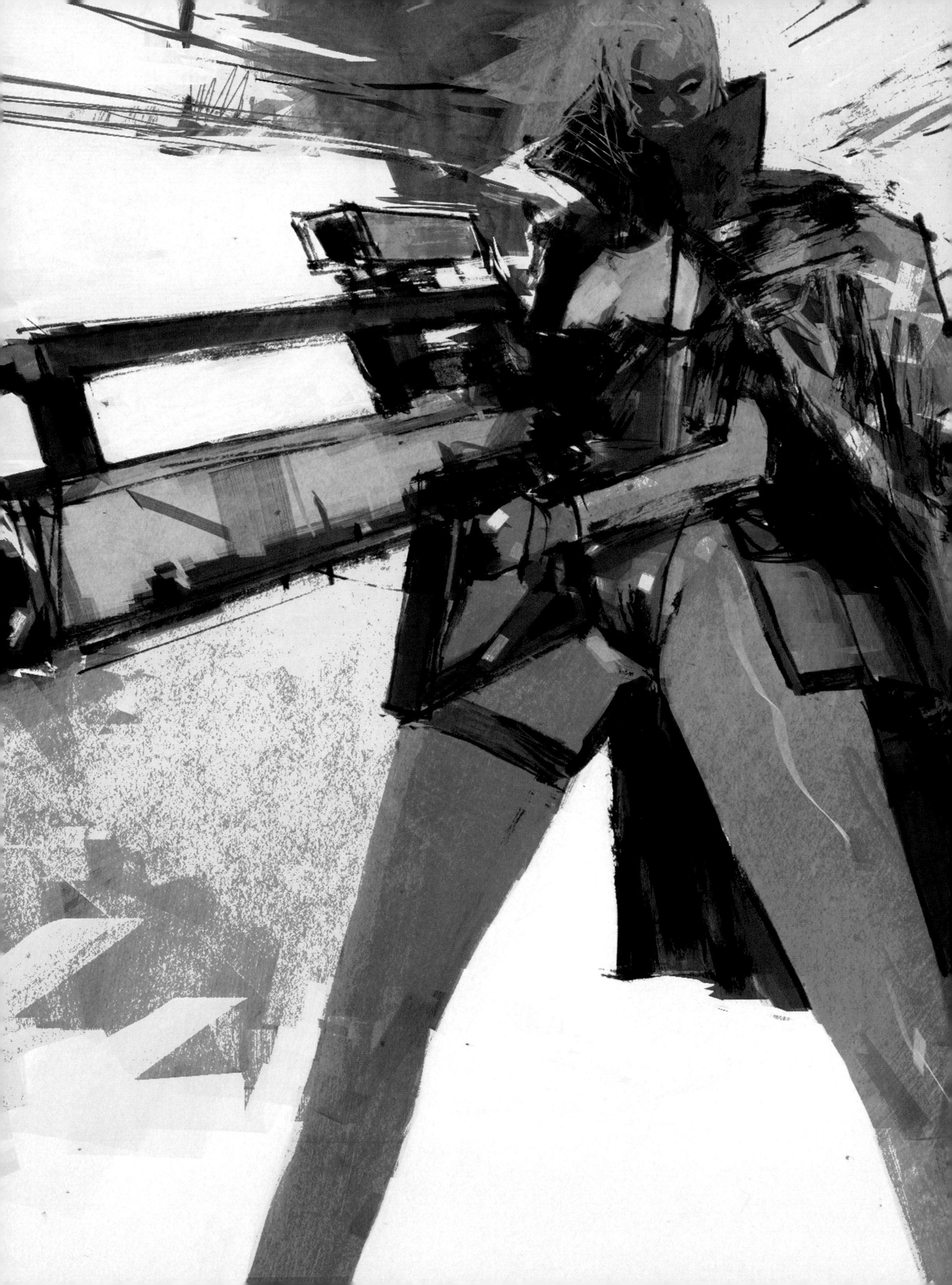

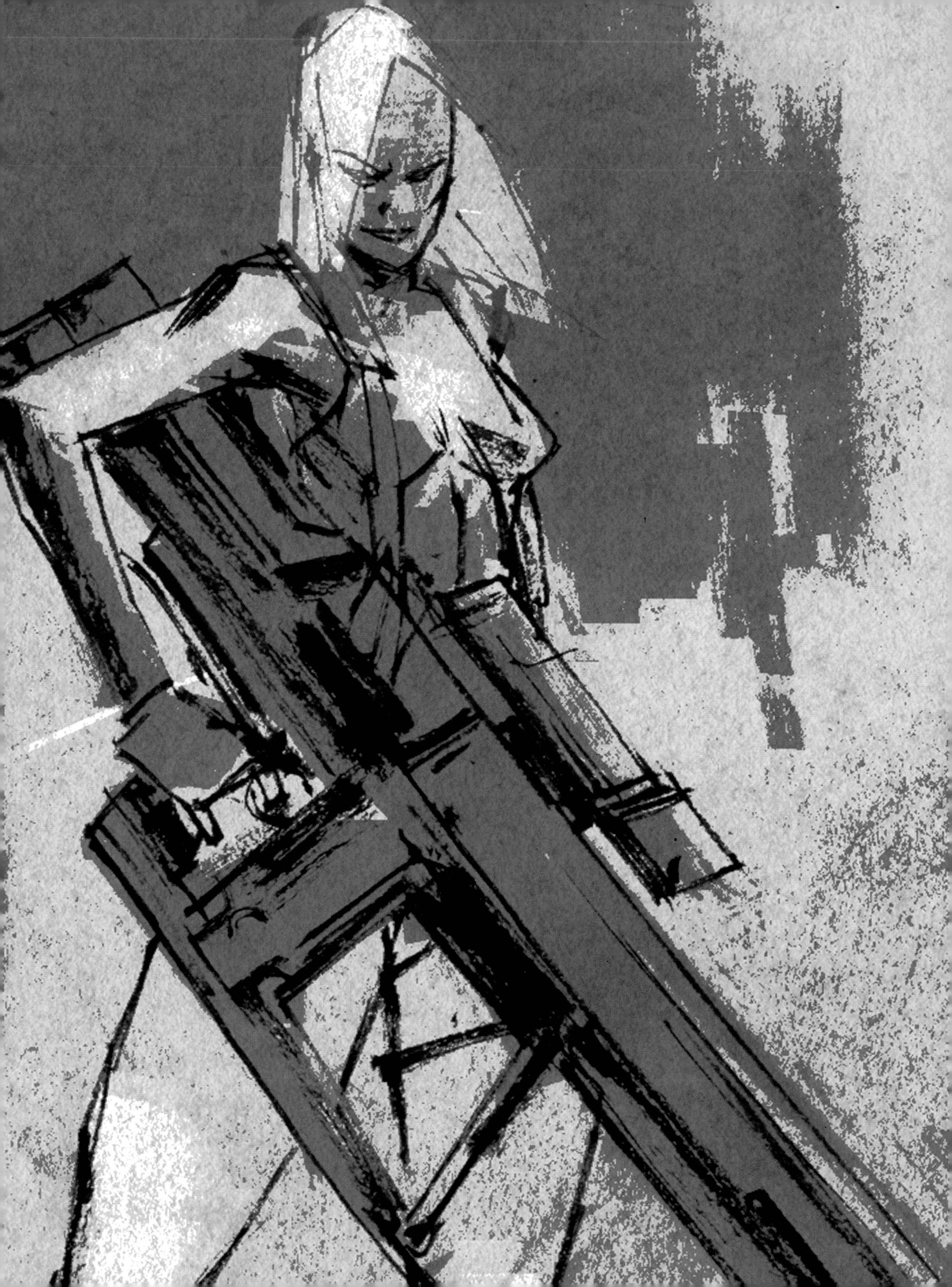

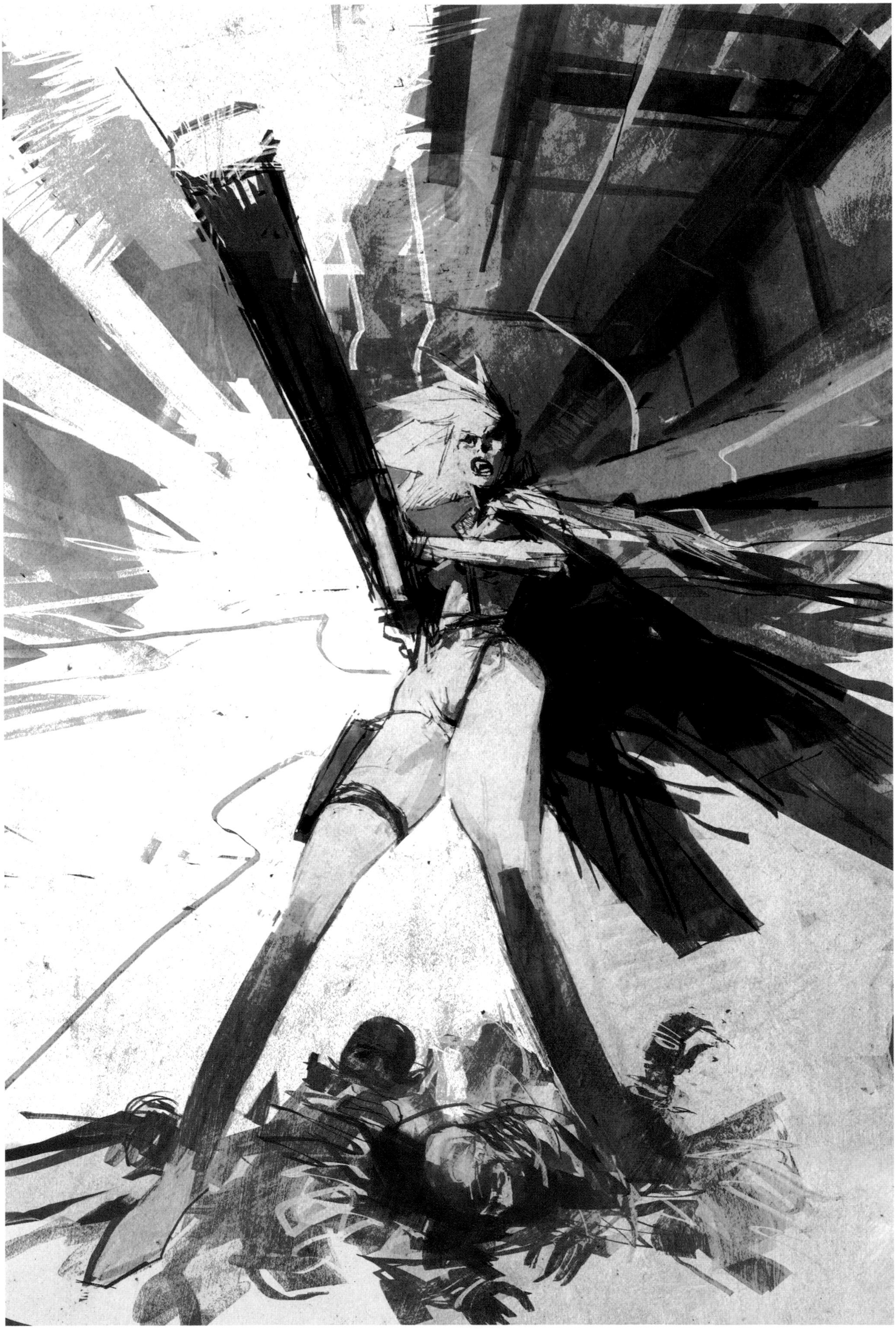

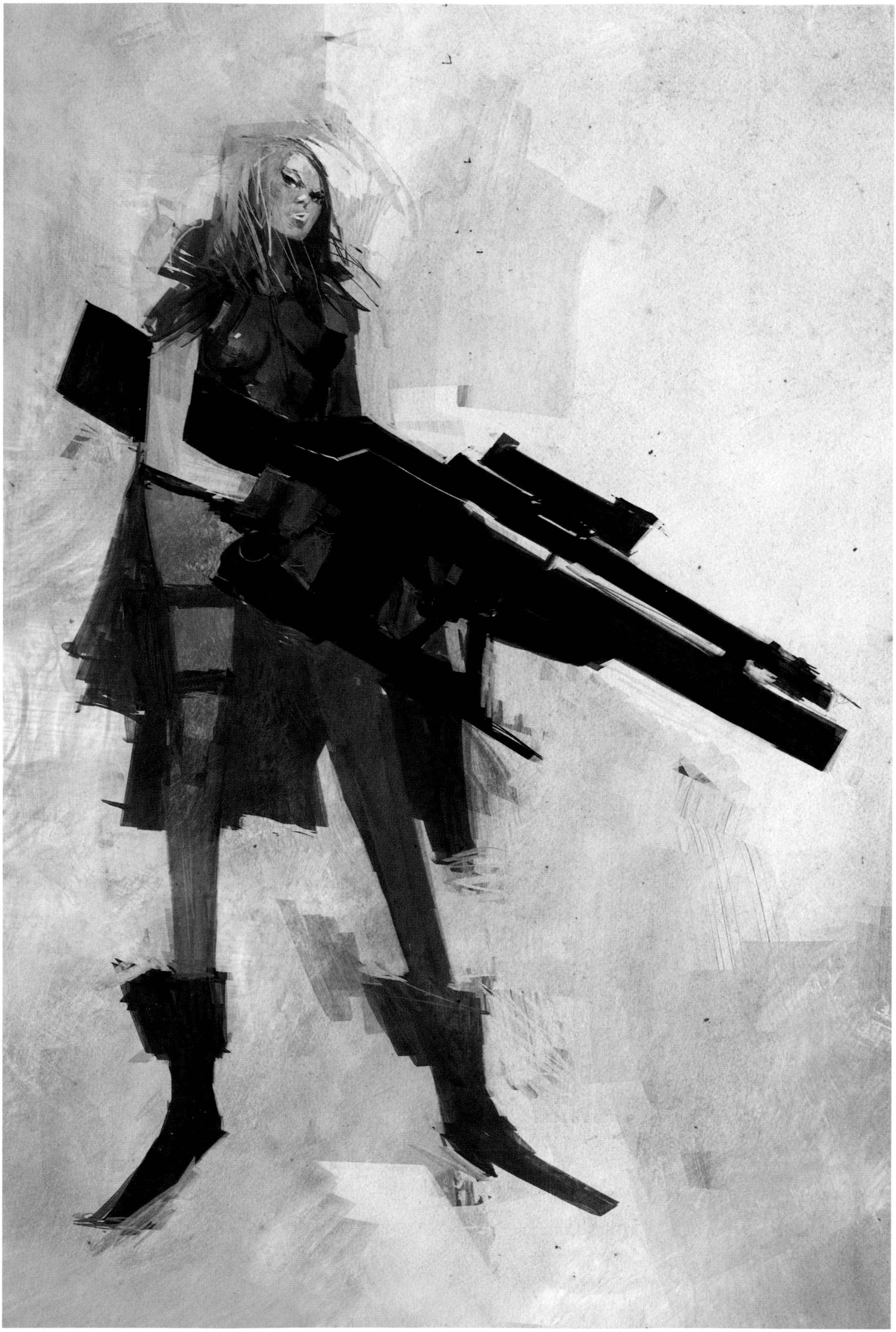

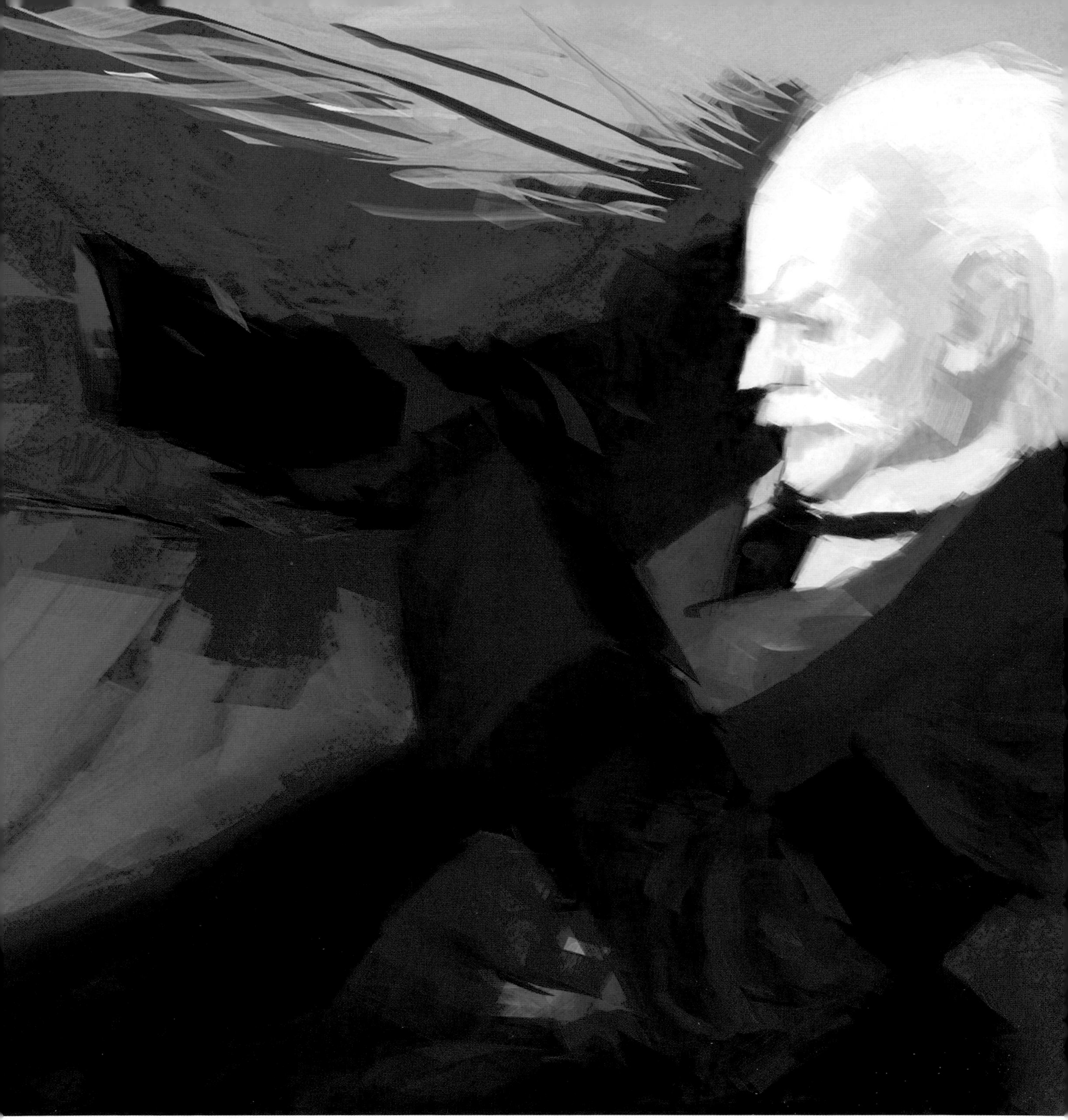

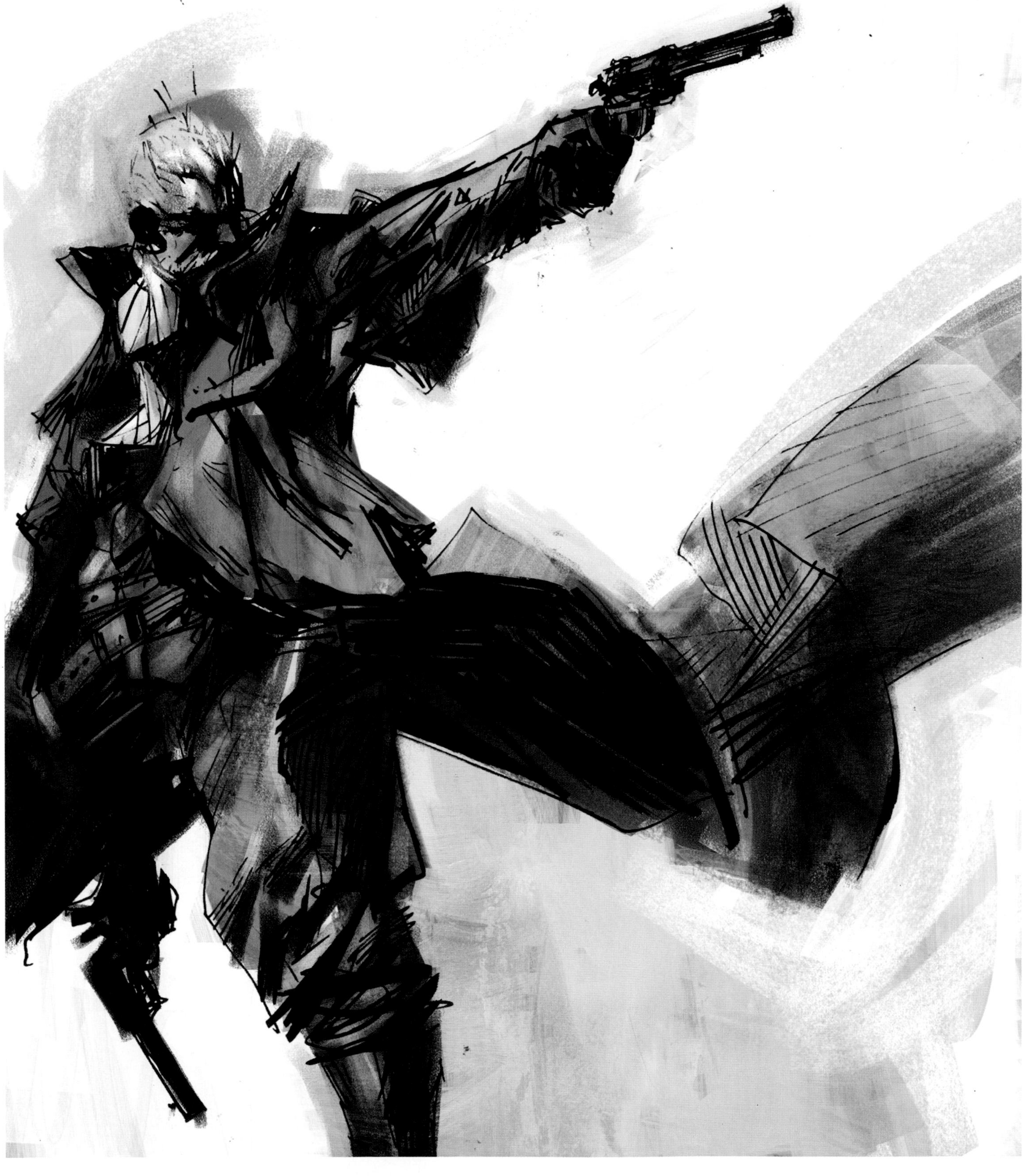

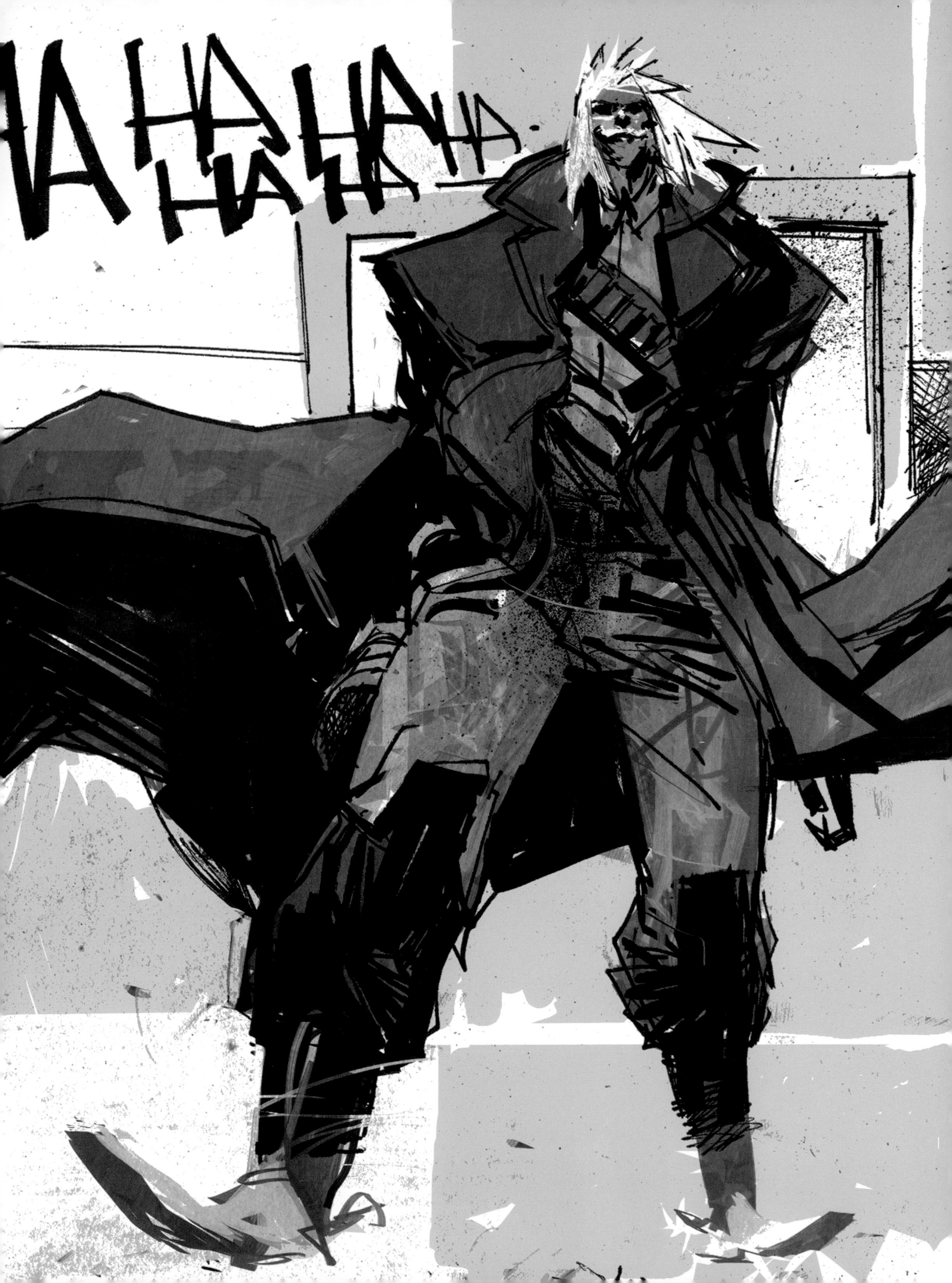
HA HA HA HA HA
HA HA HA

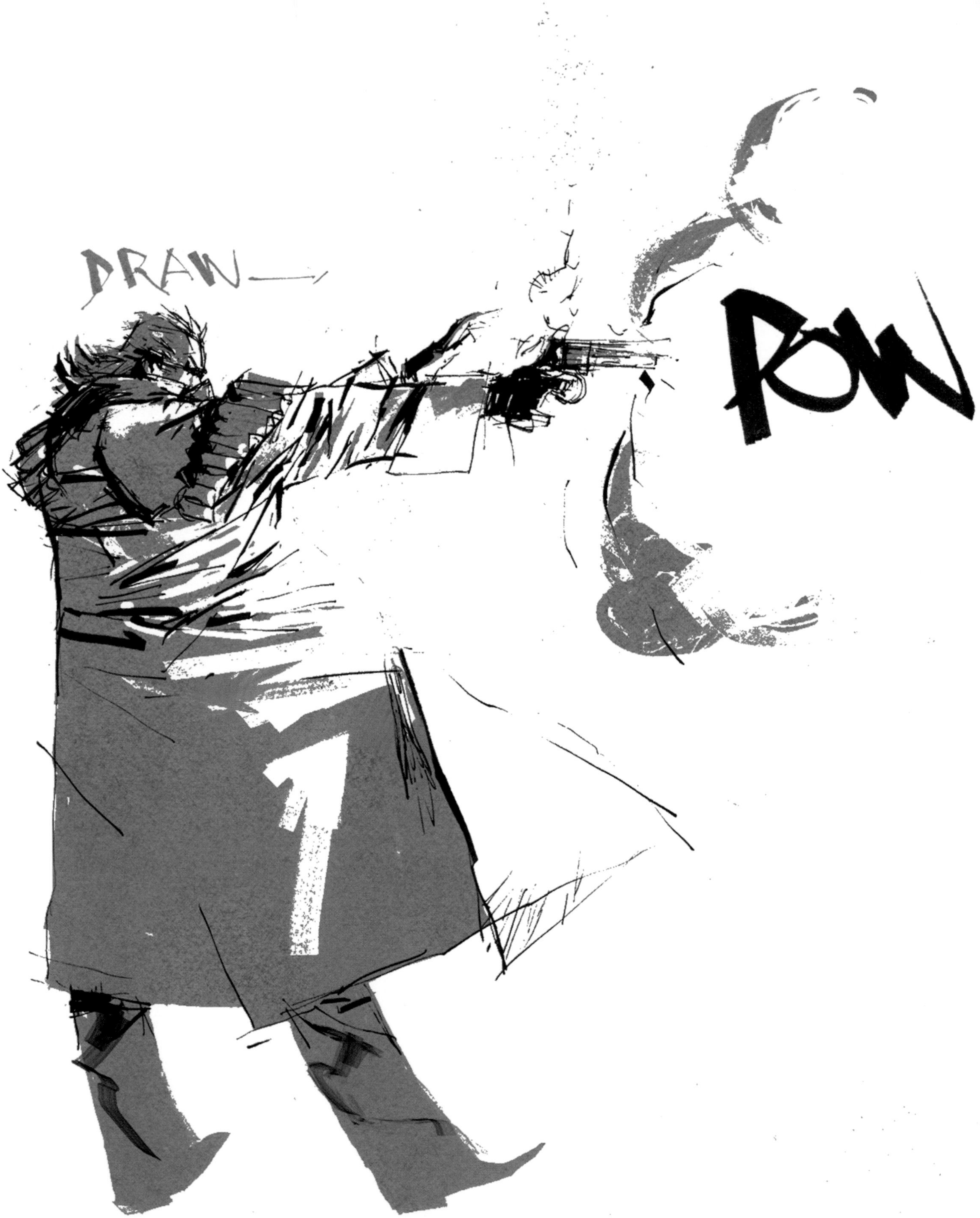

DRAW
POW

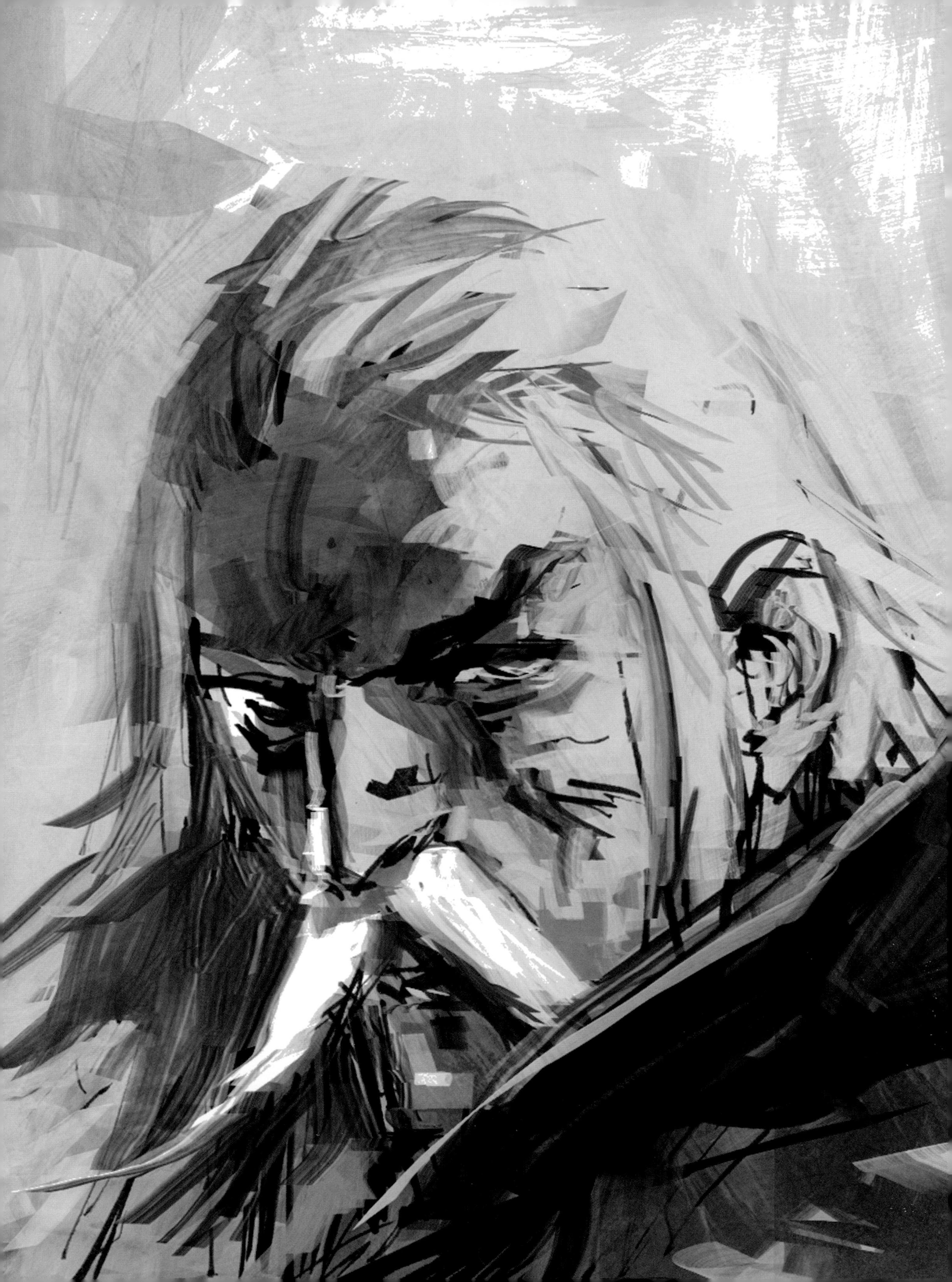

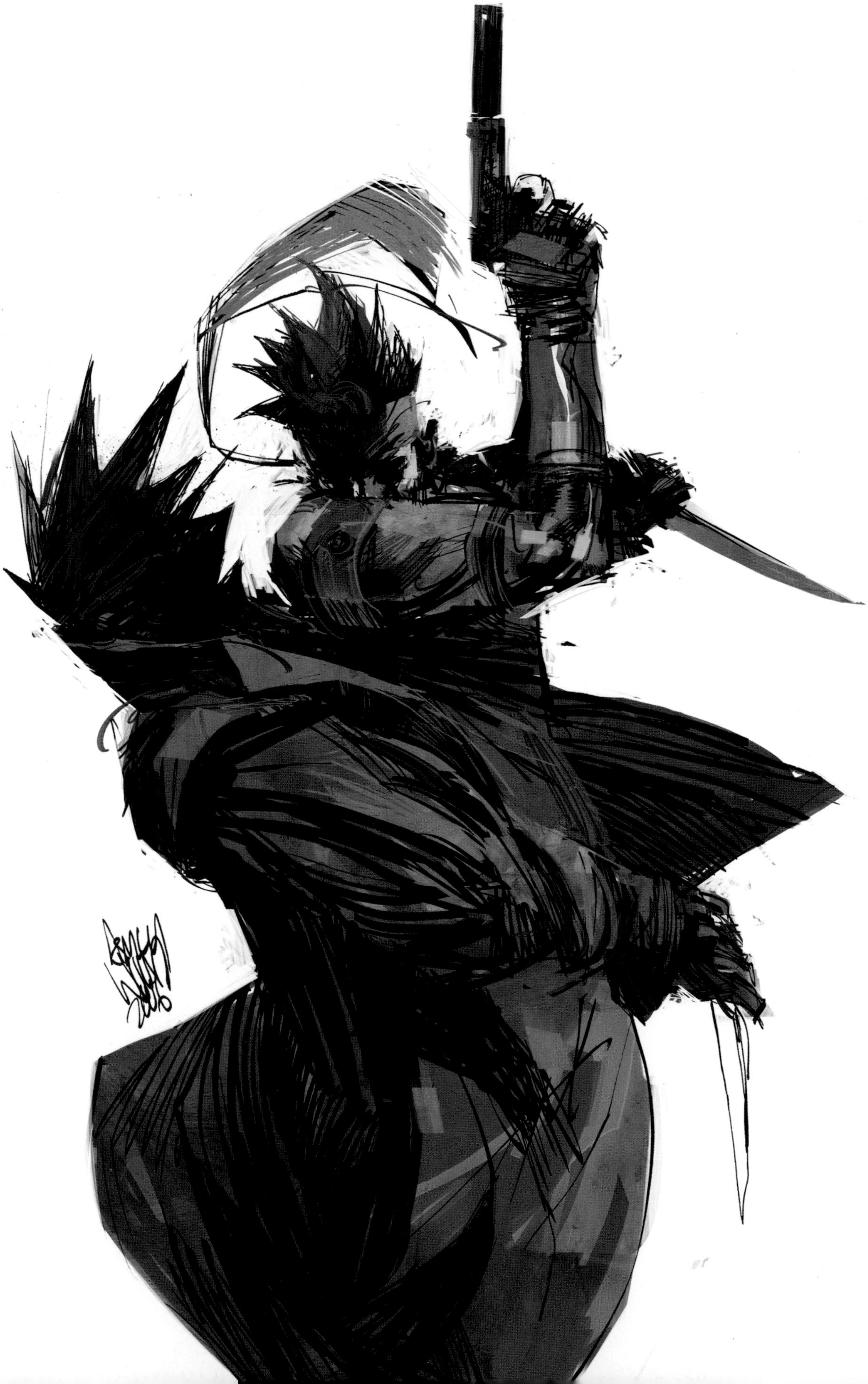

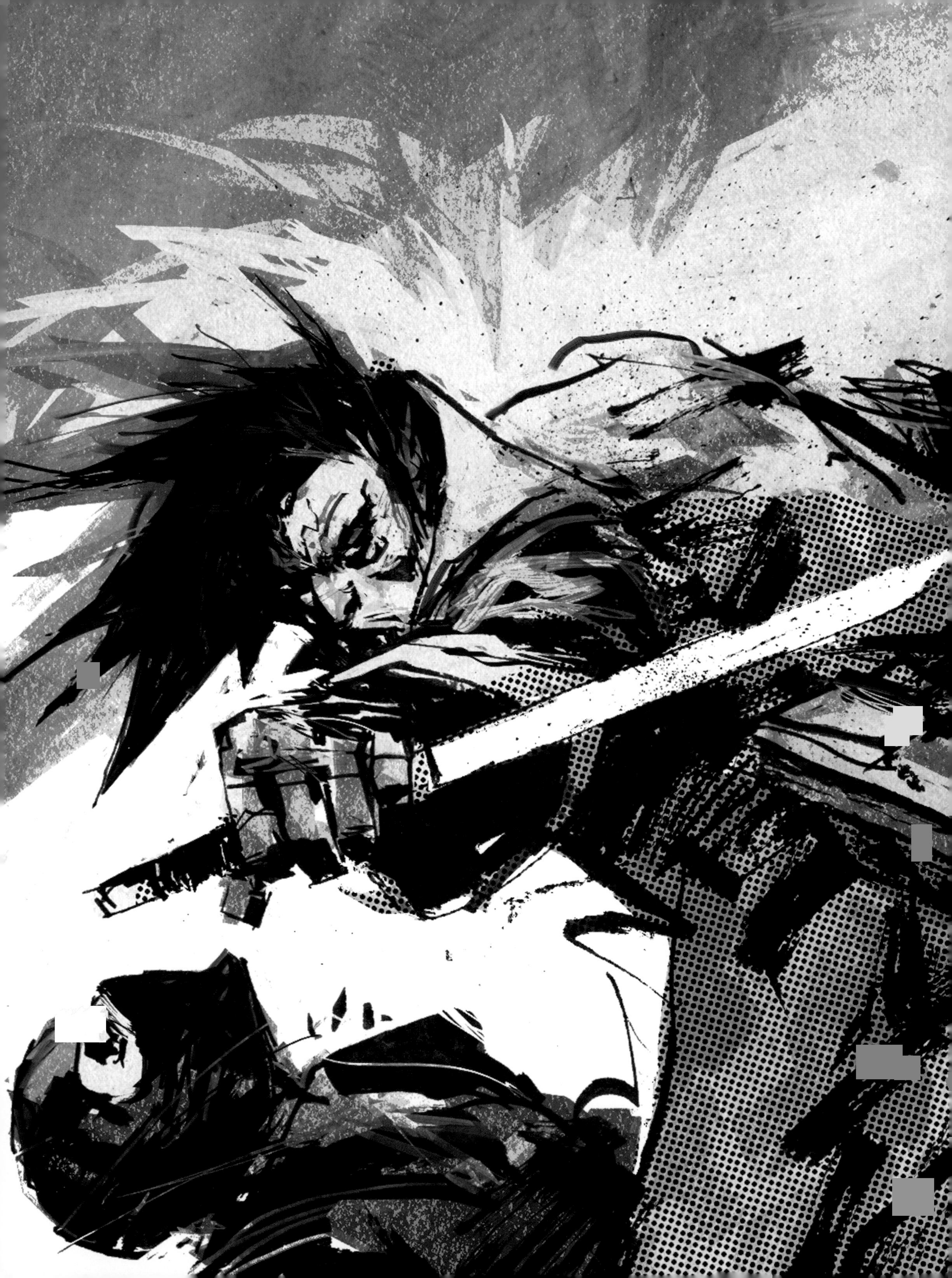

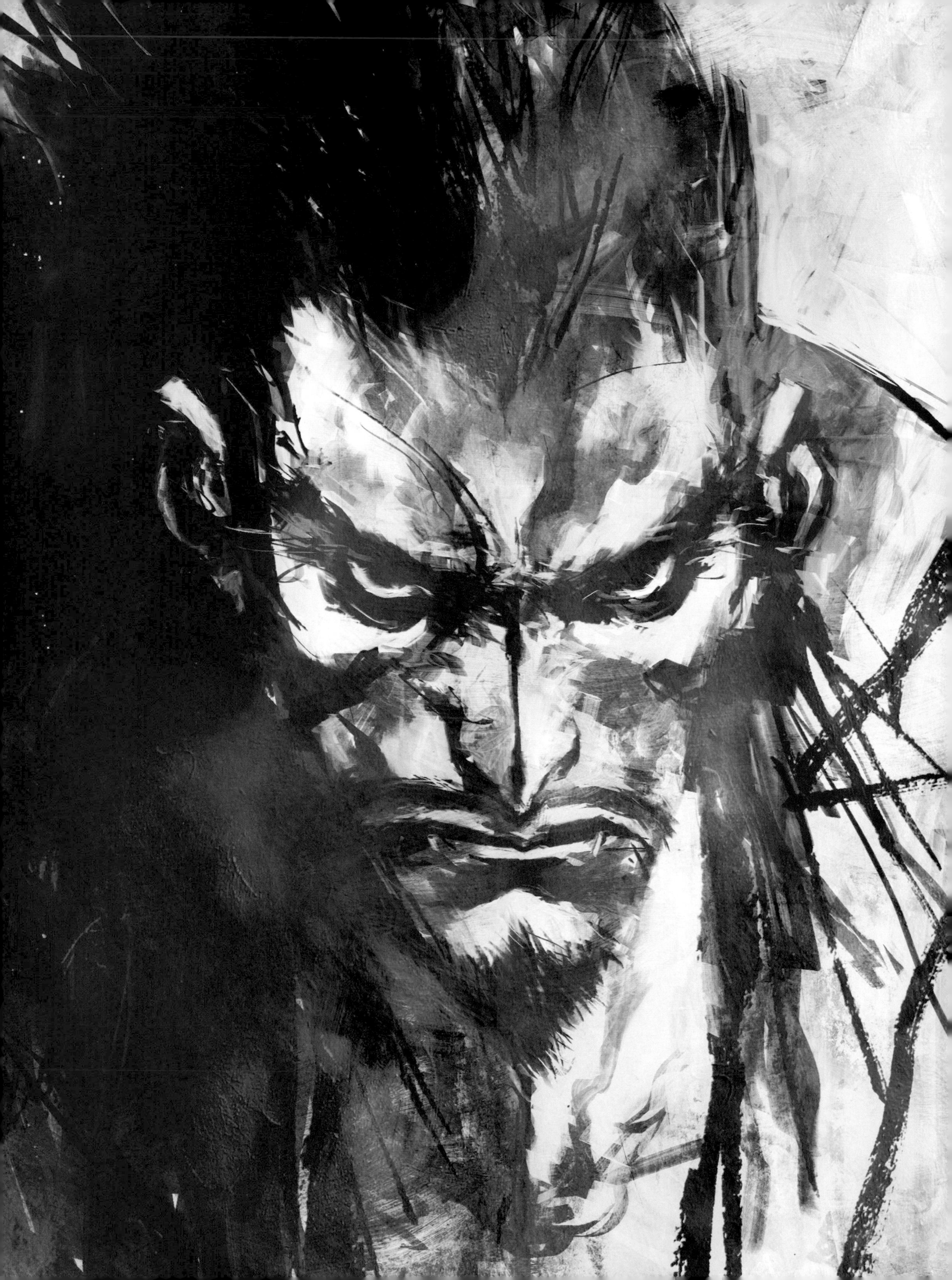

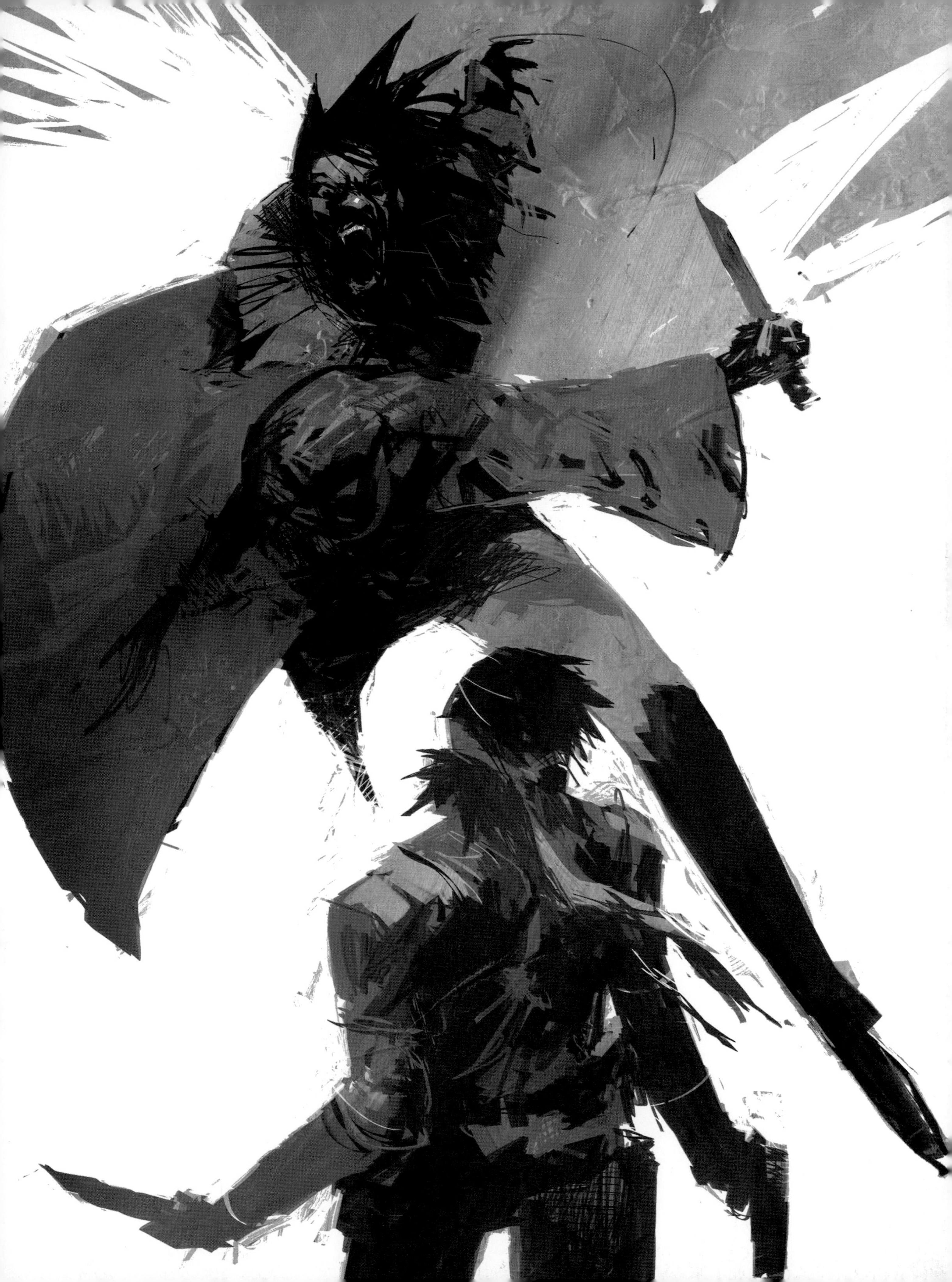

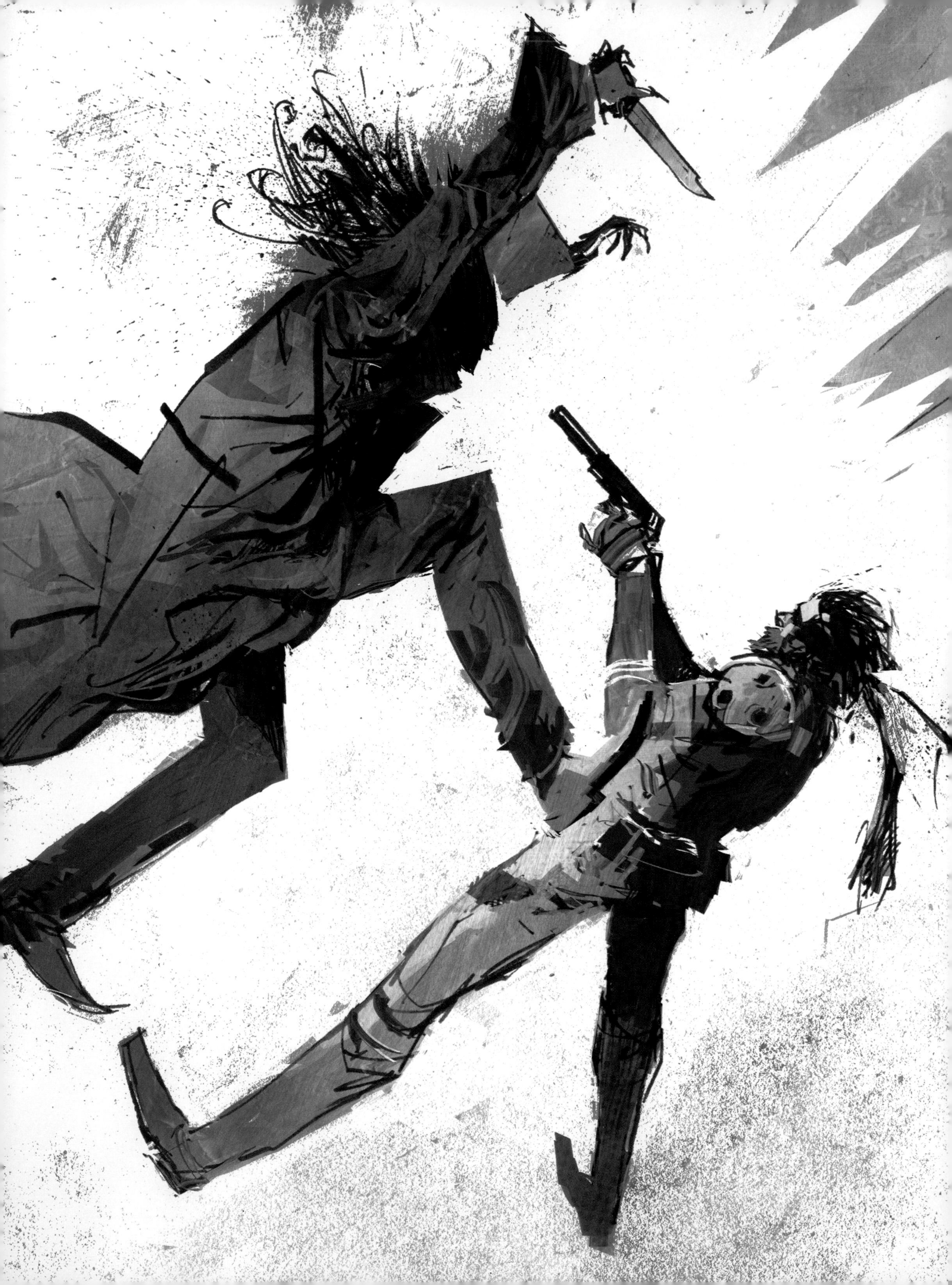

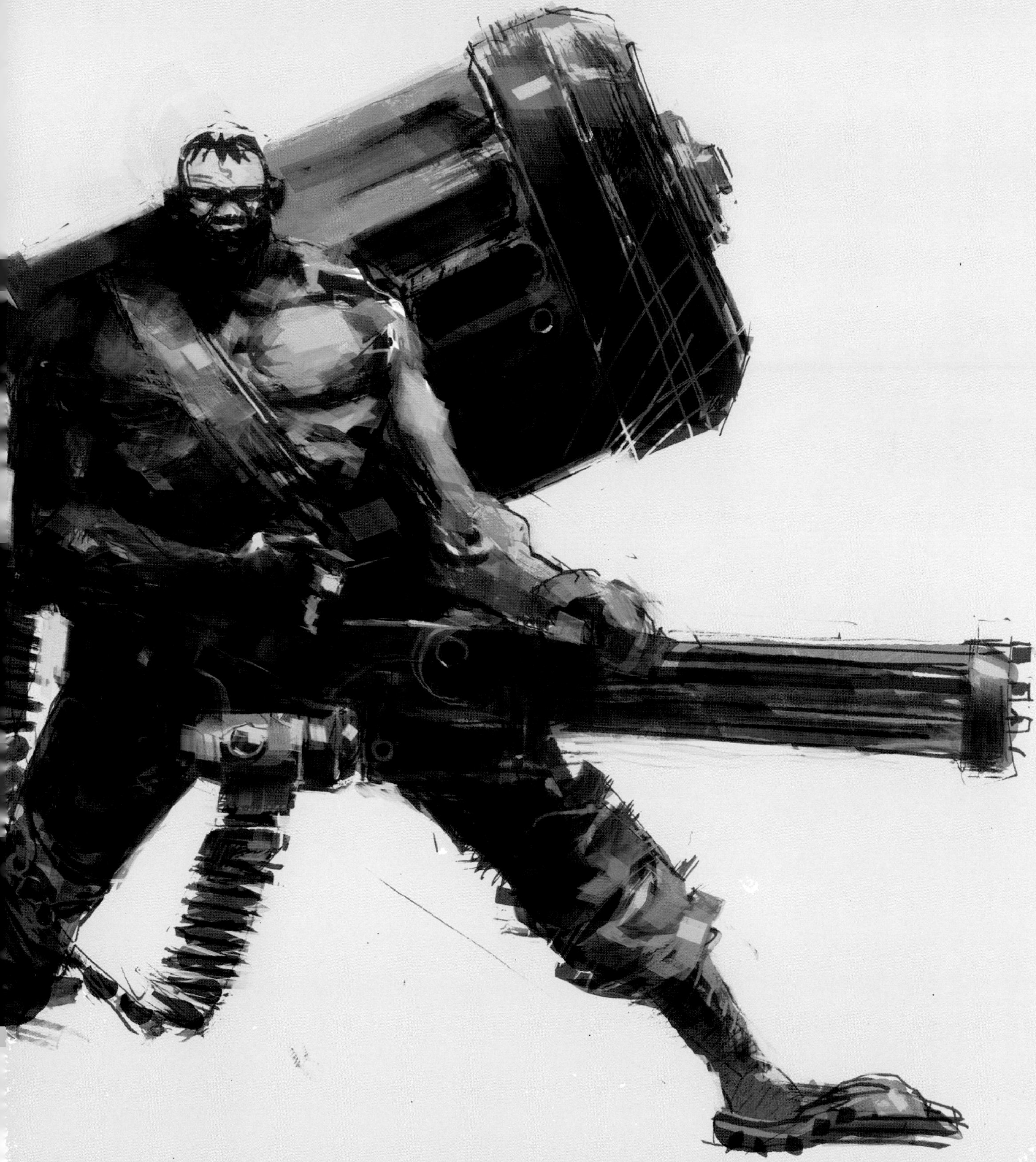

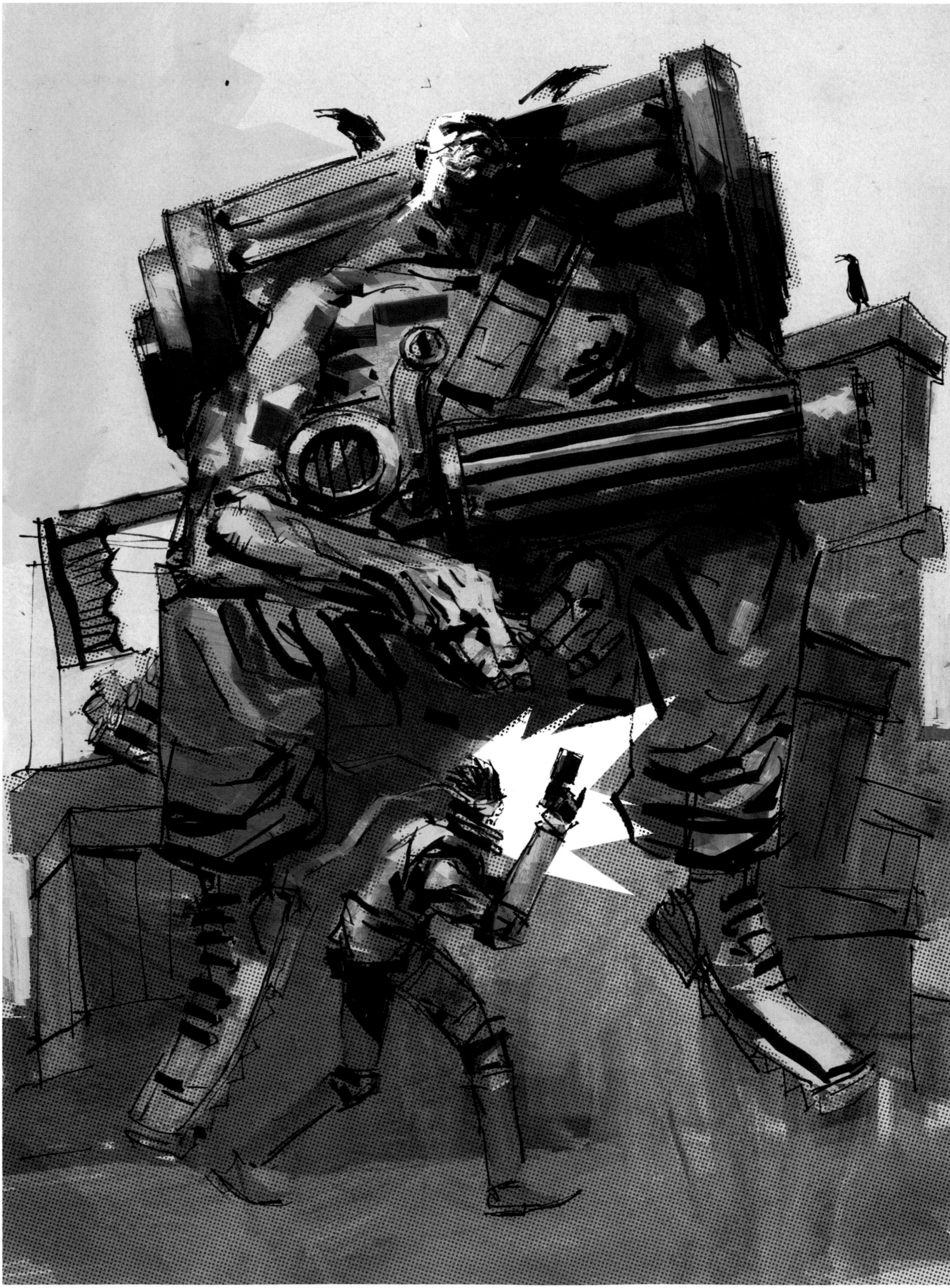

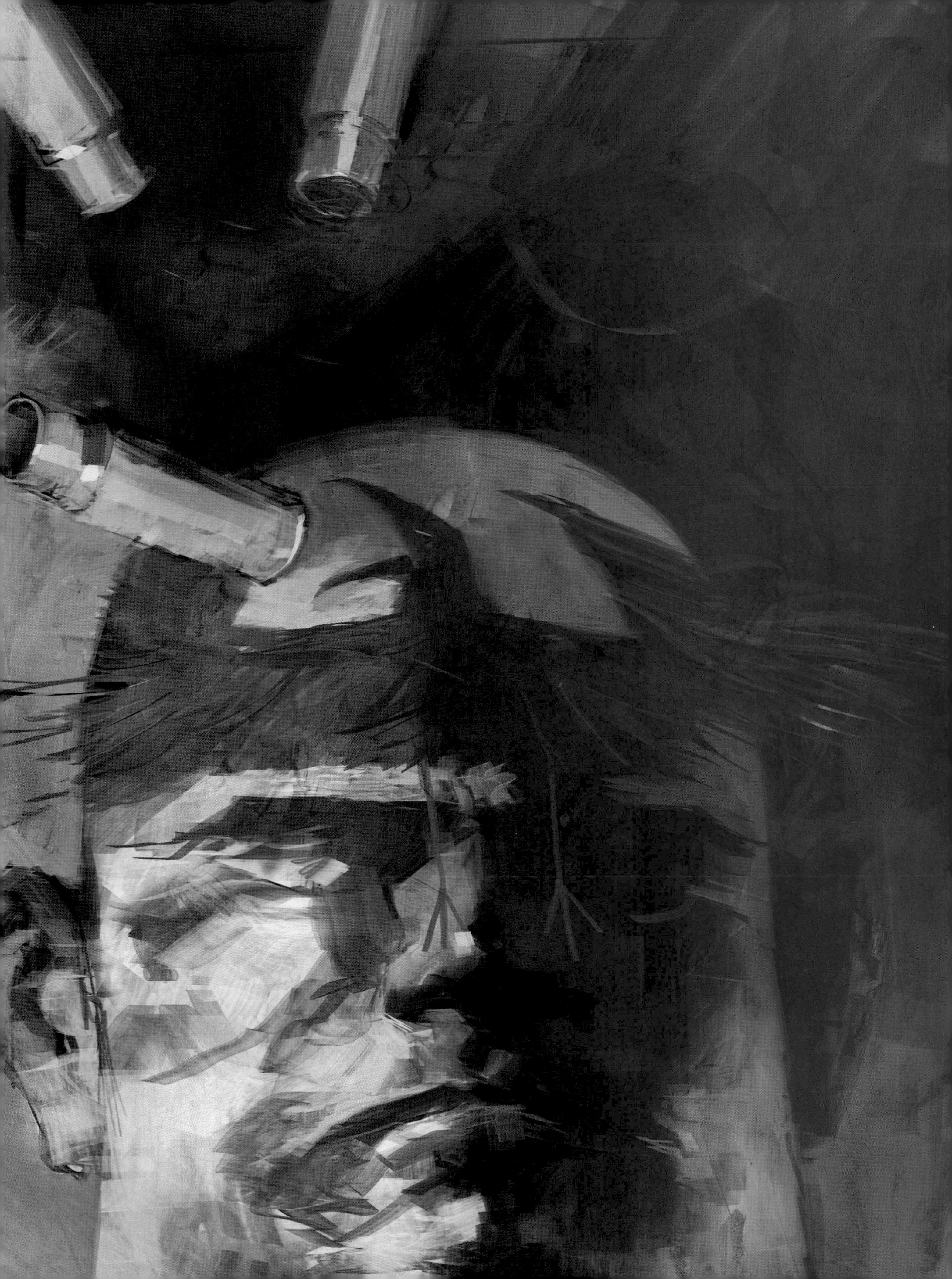

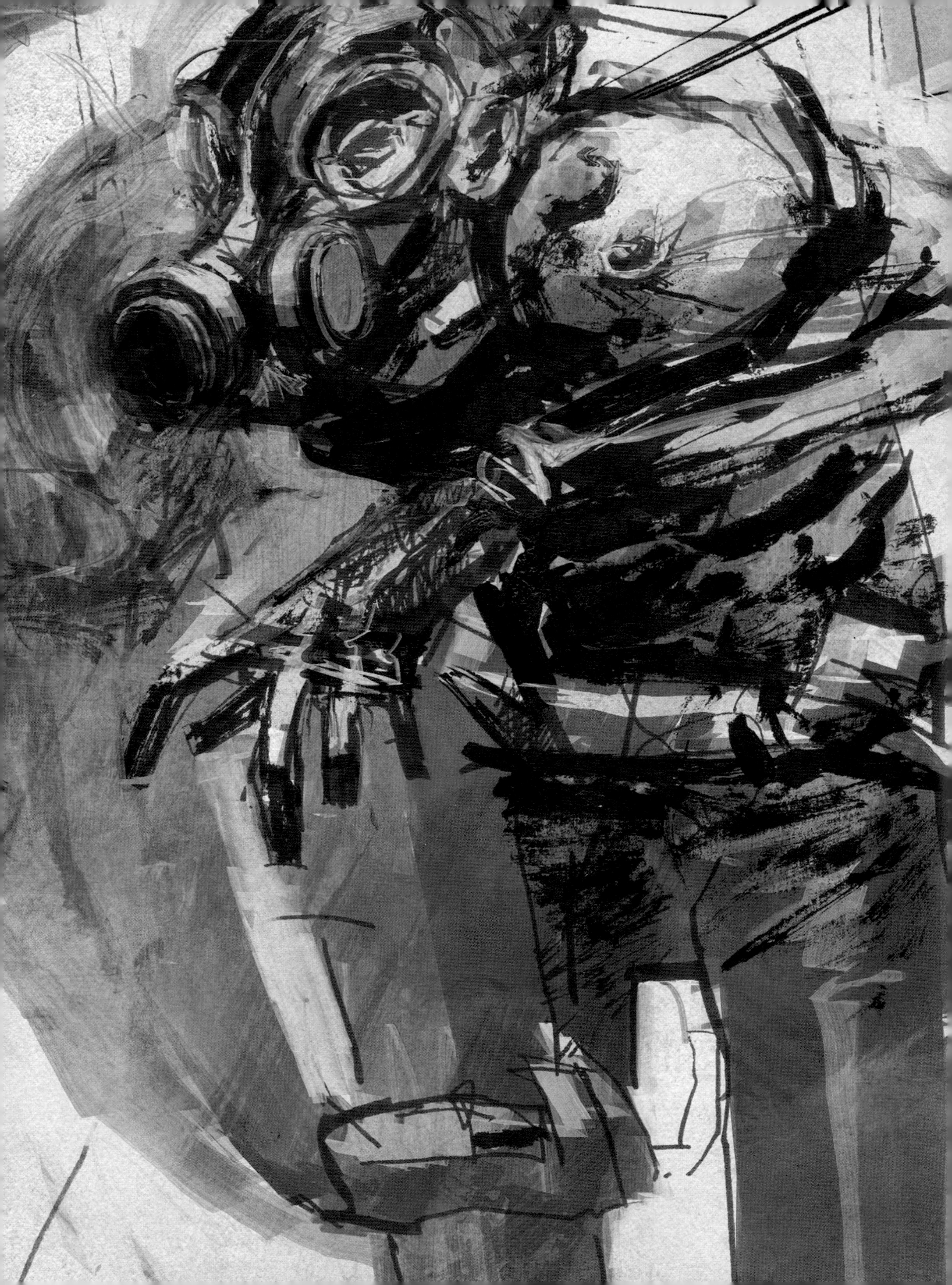

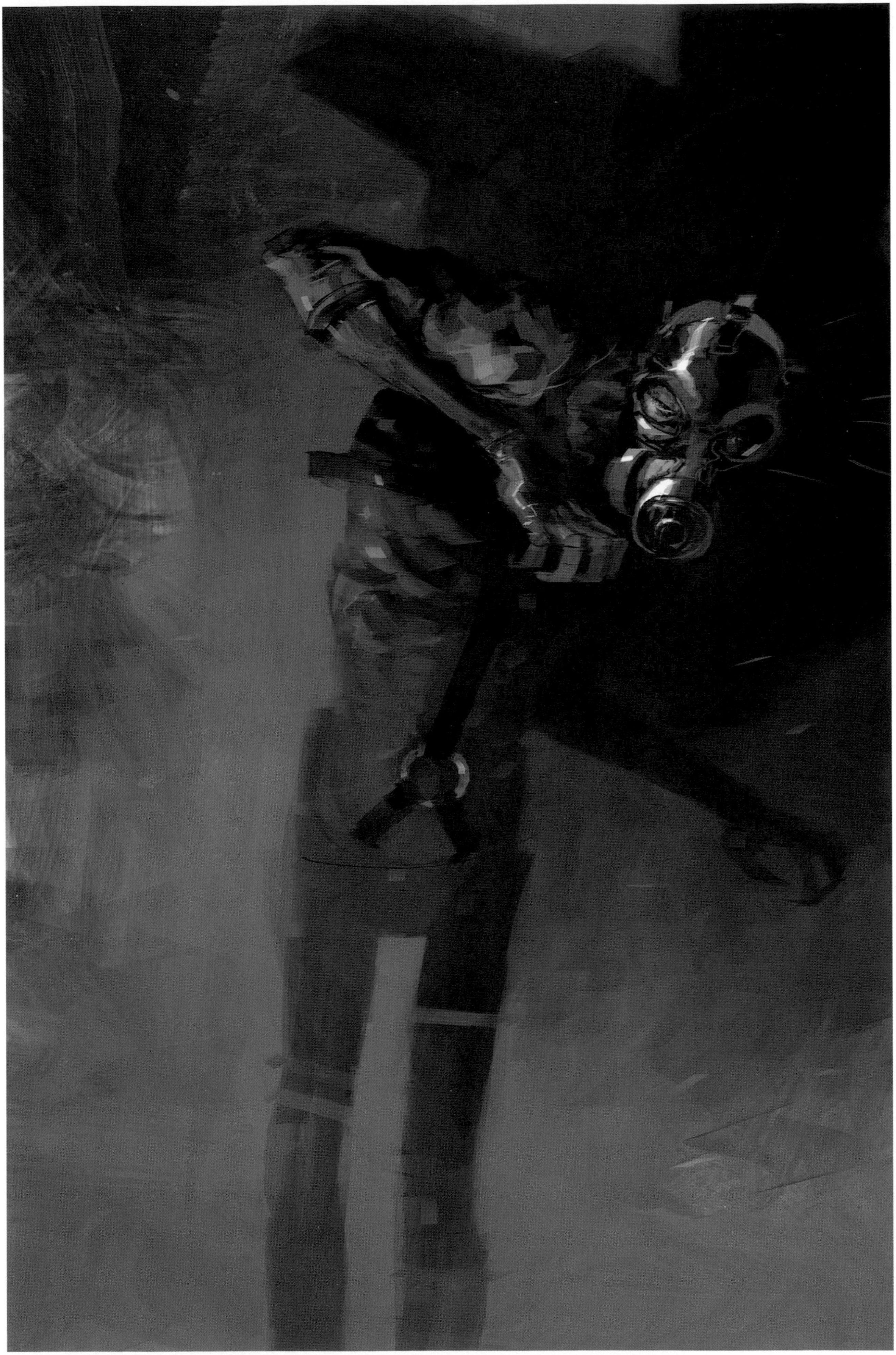

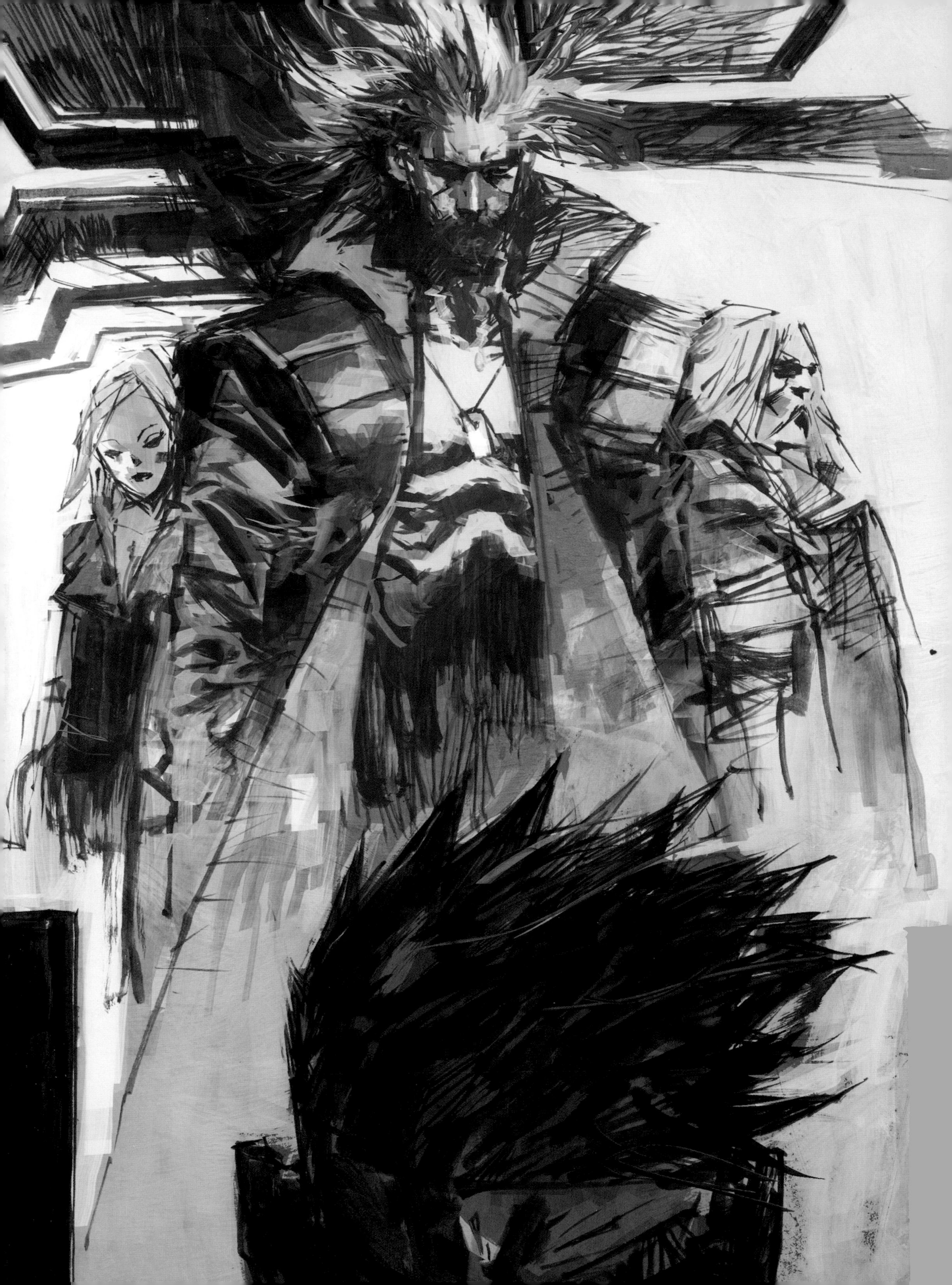

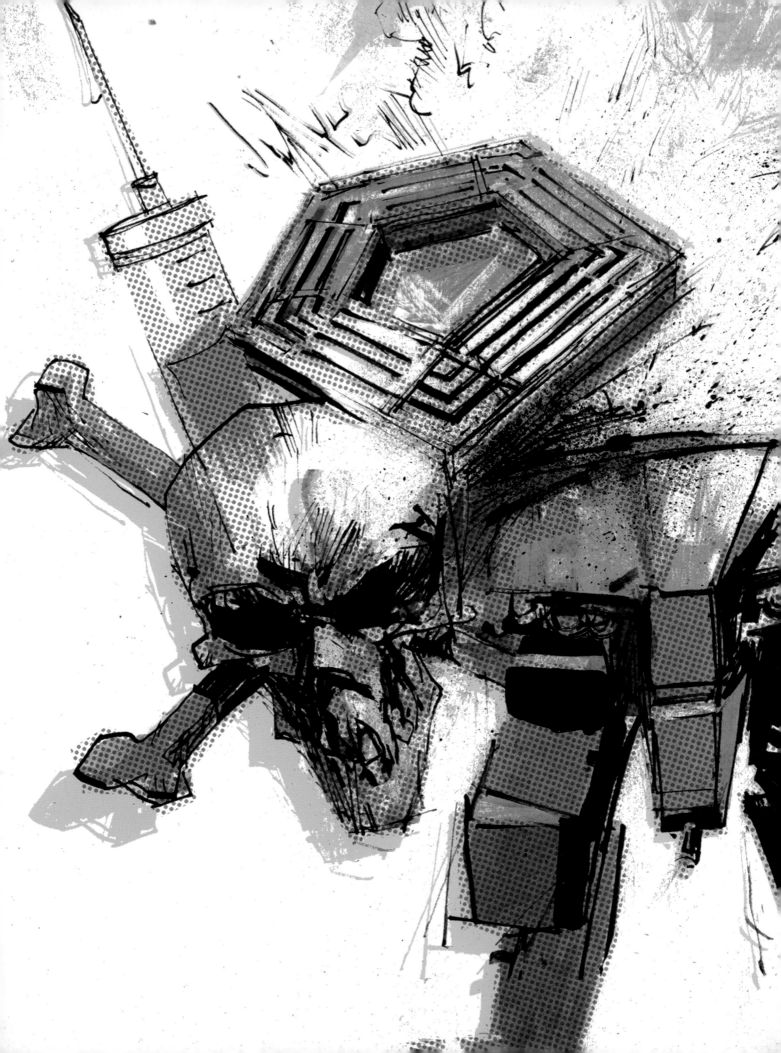

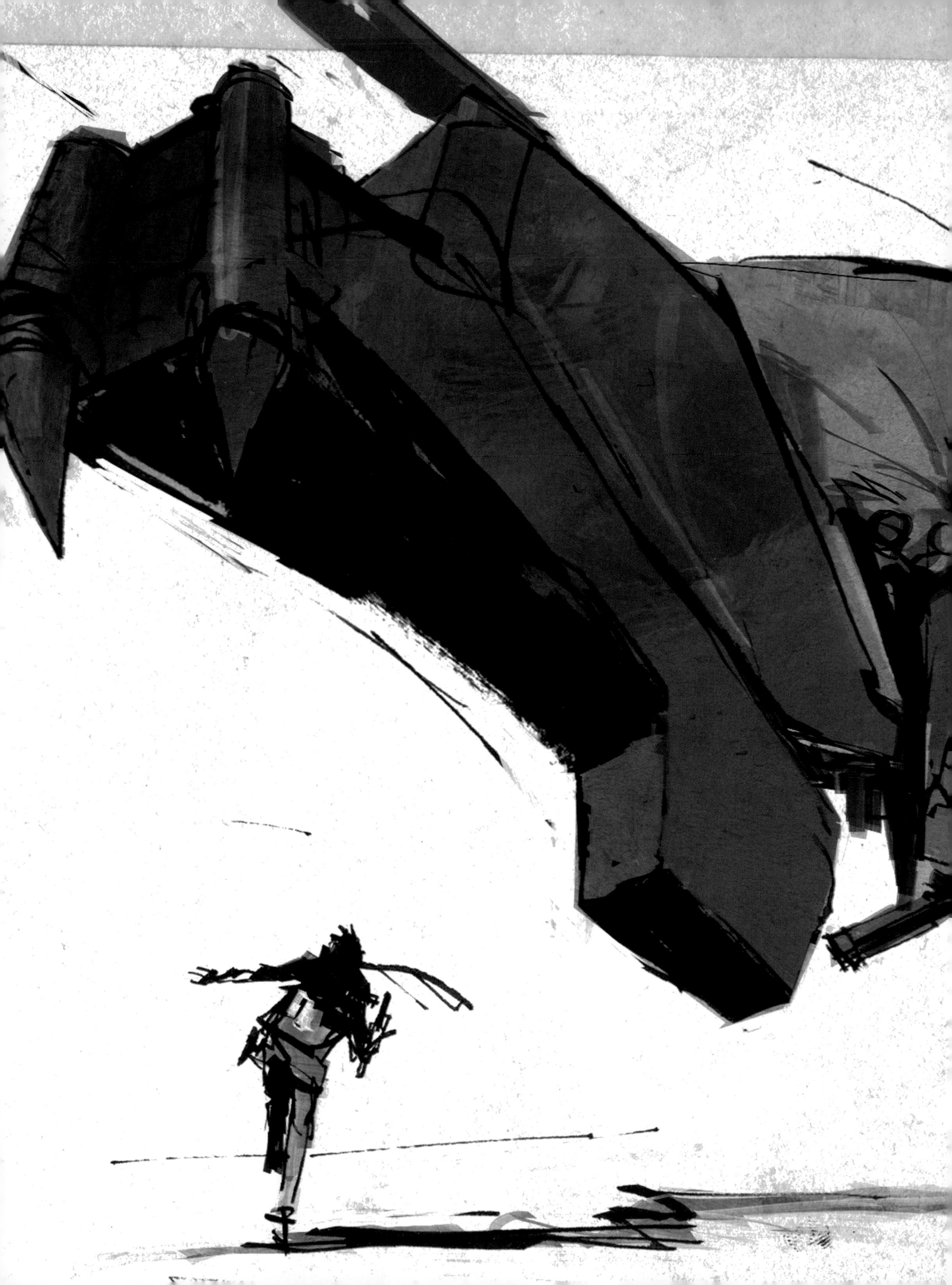

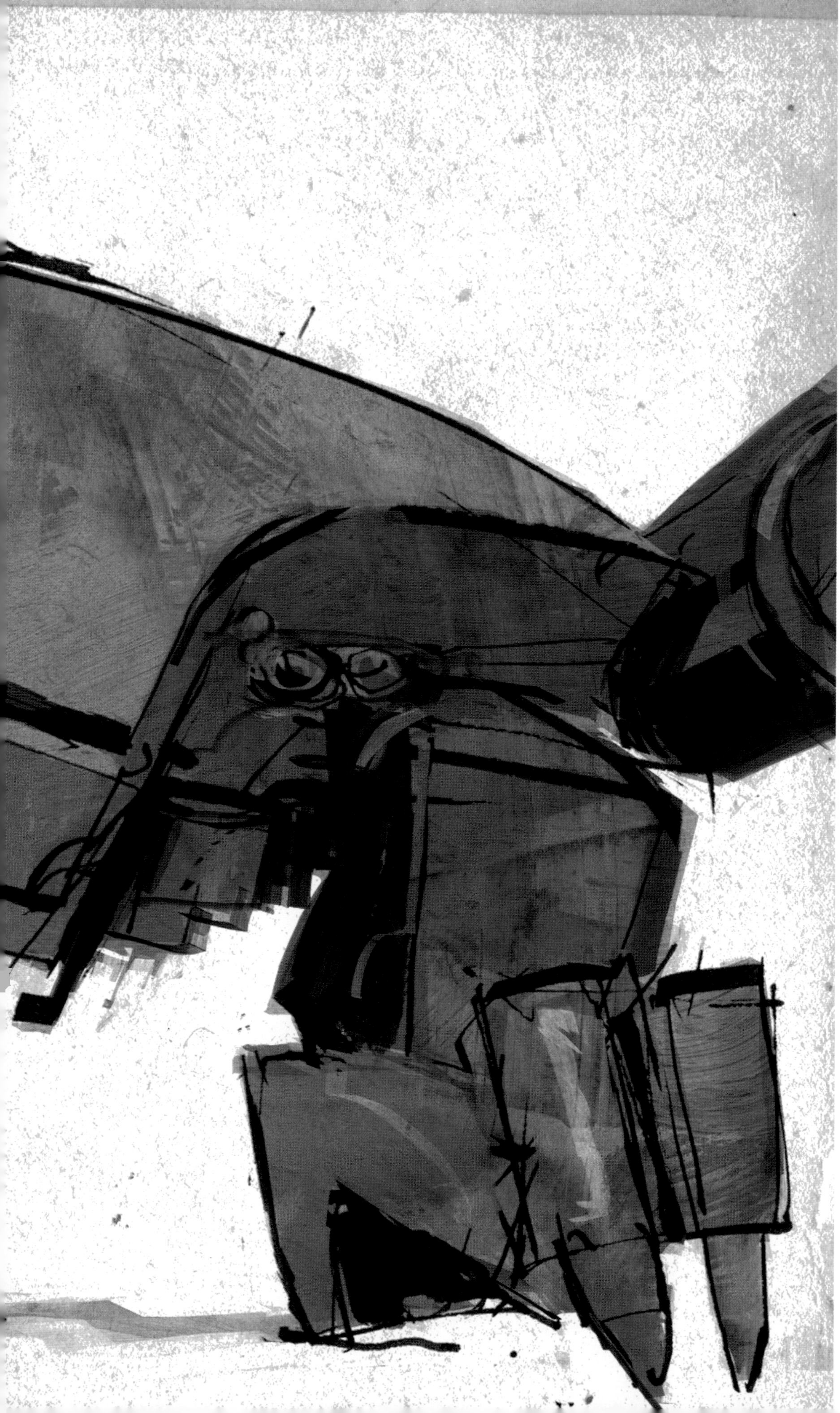

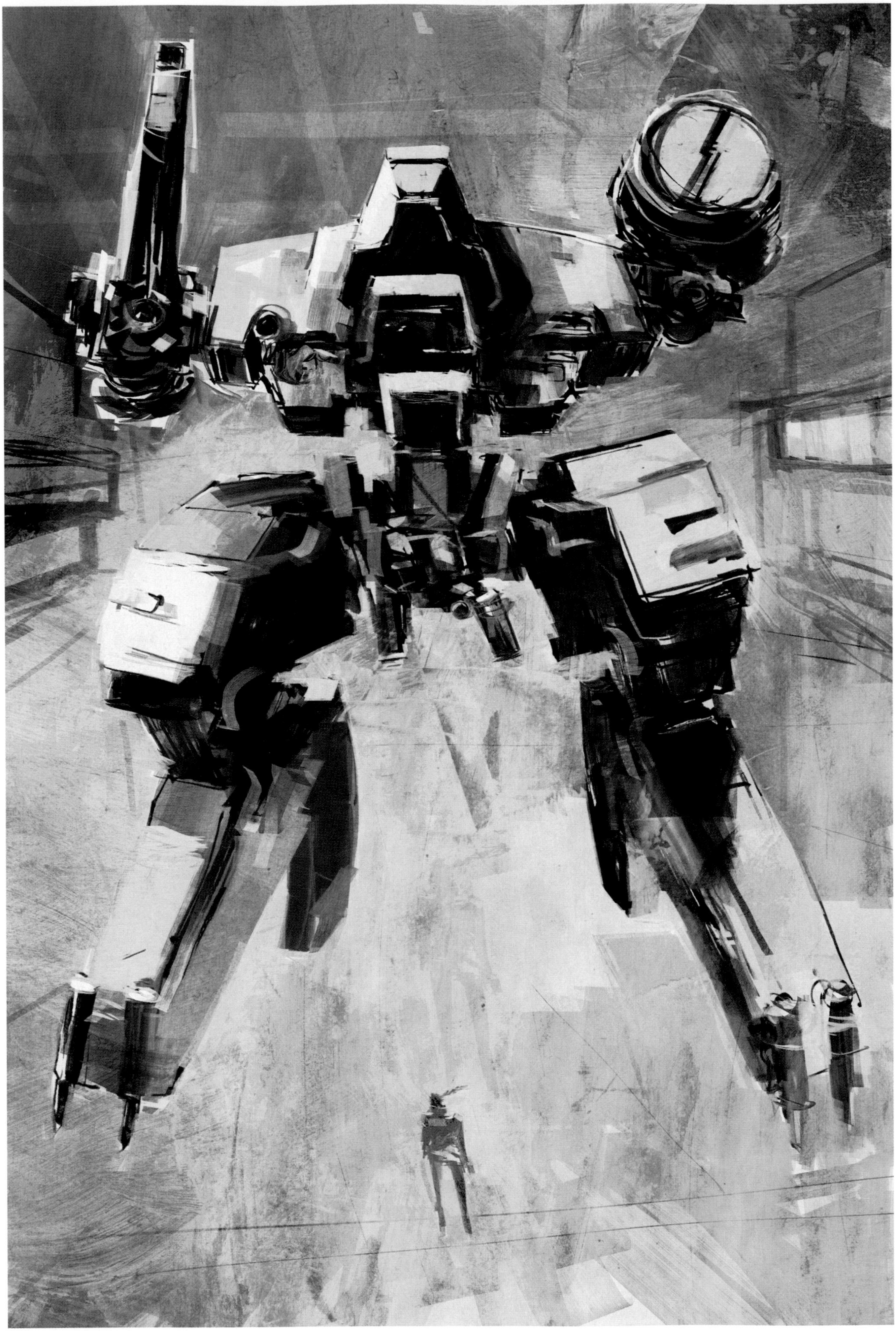

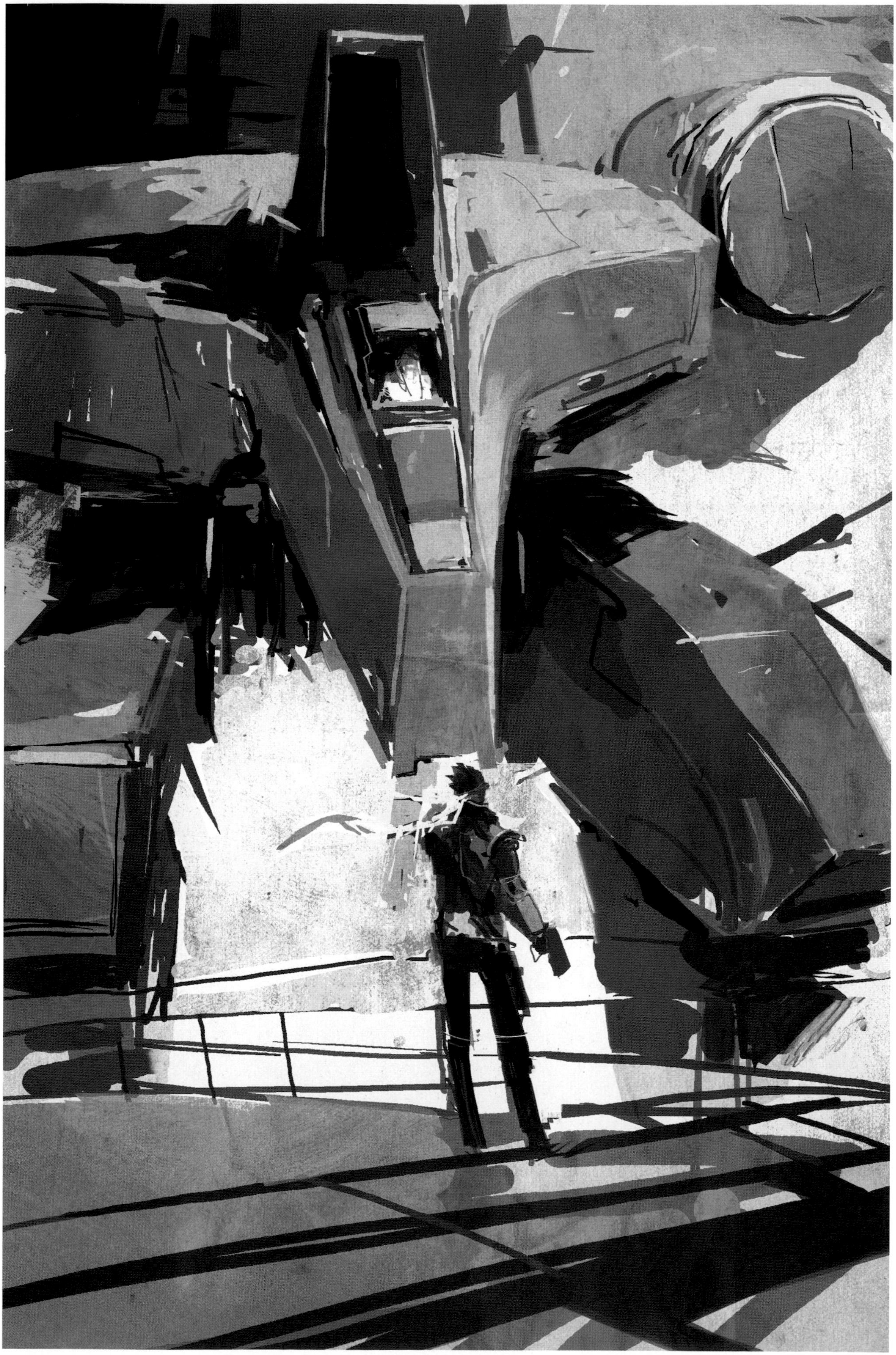

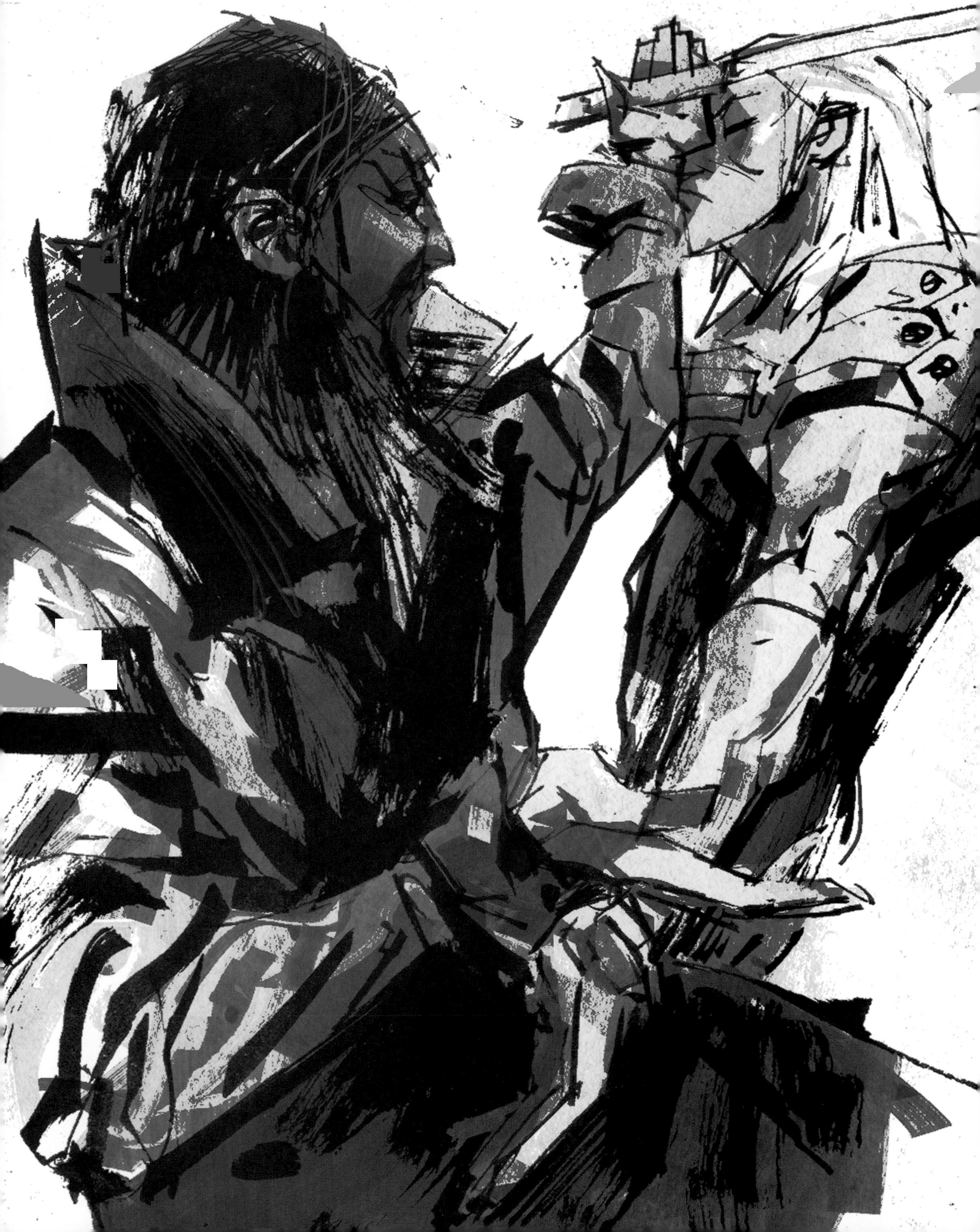

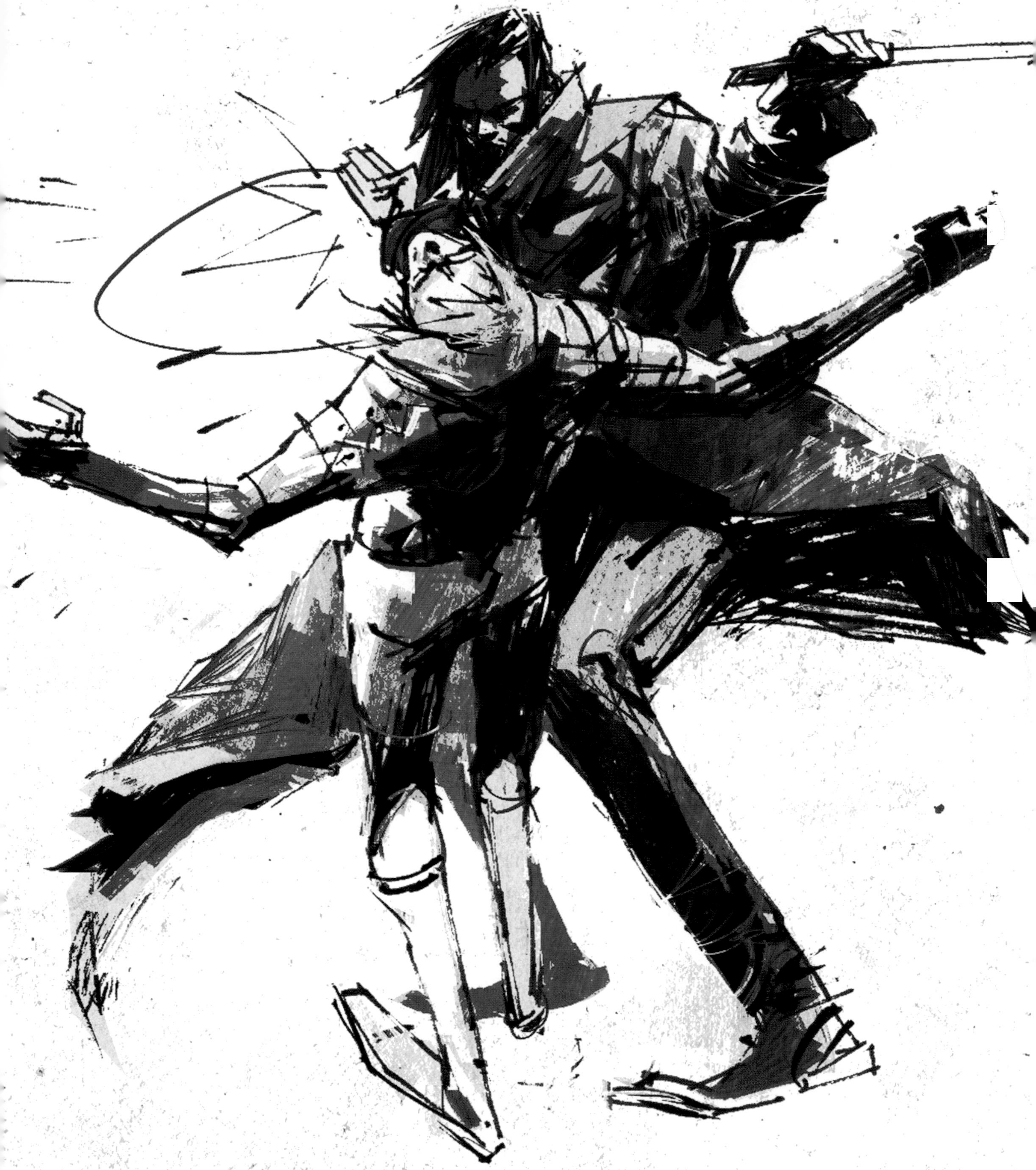

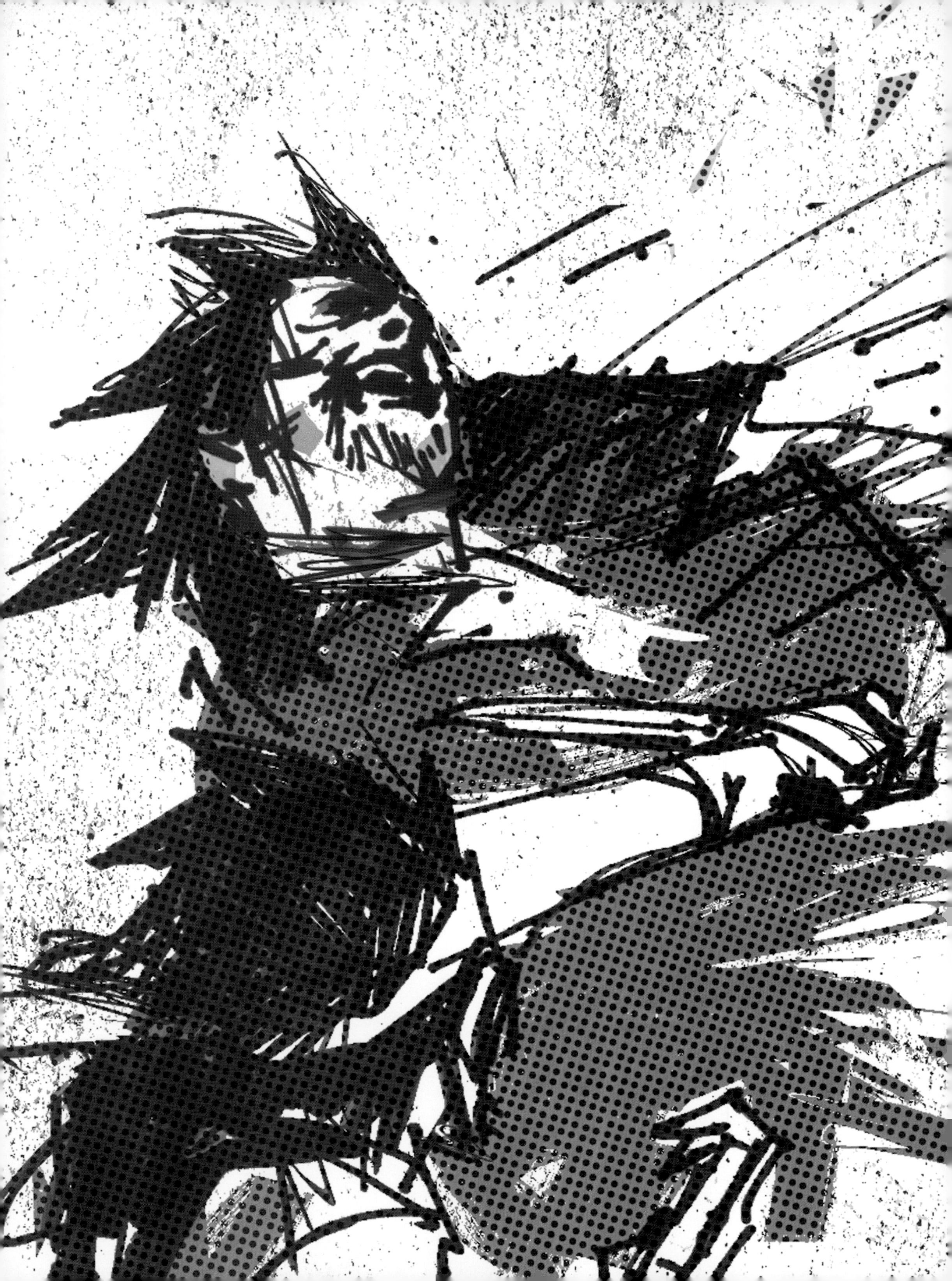

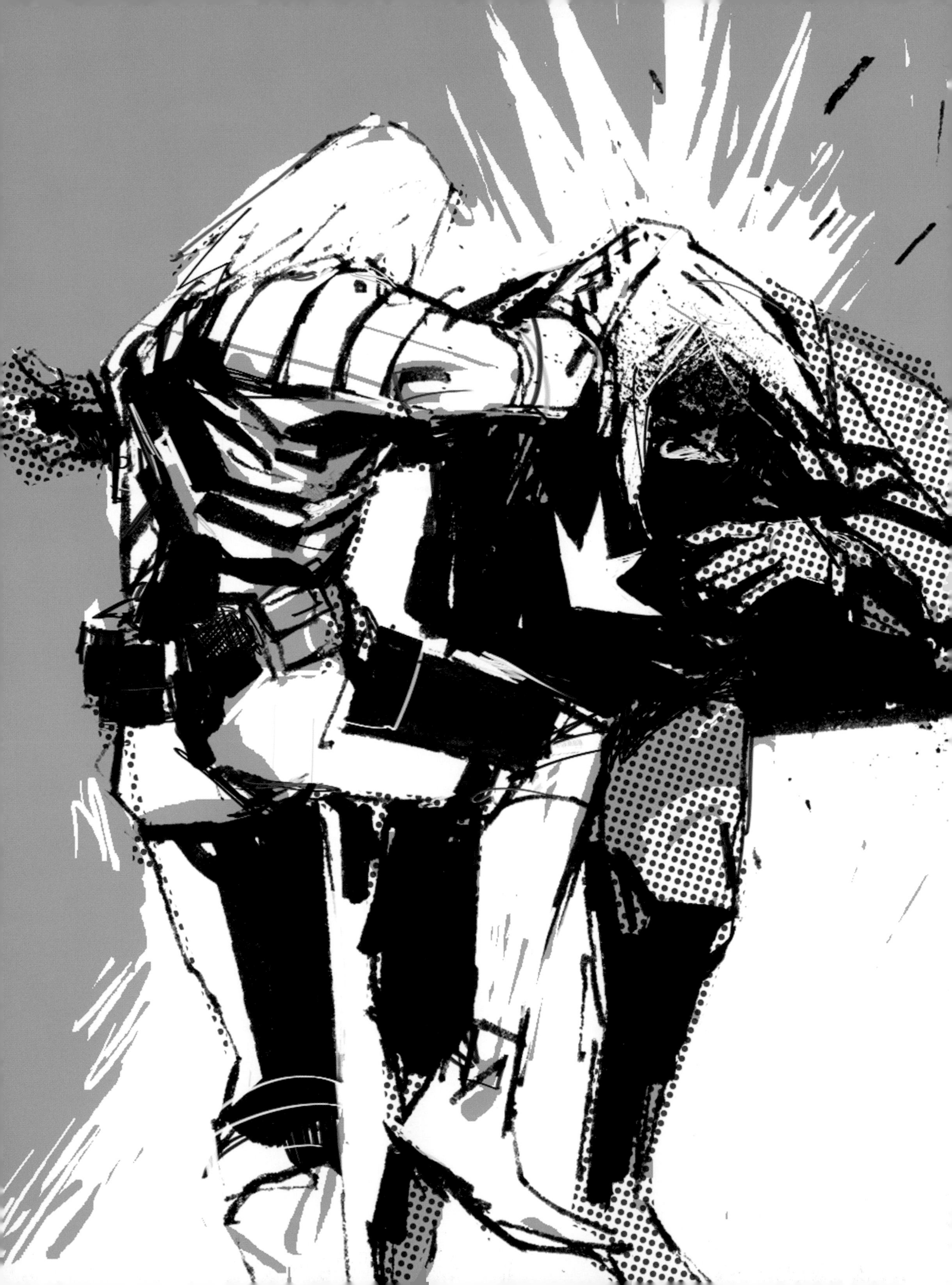

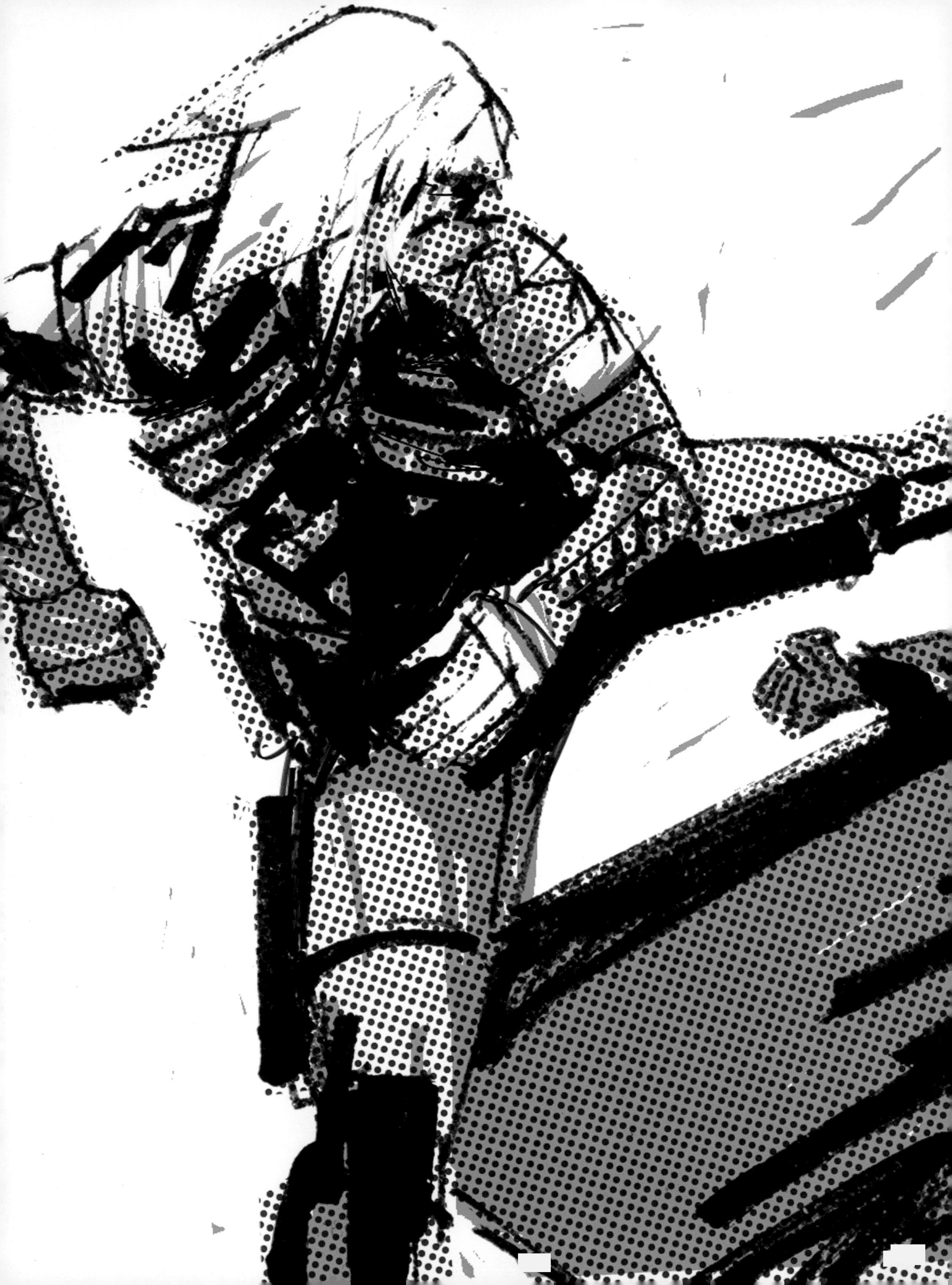

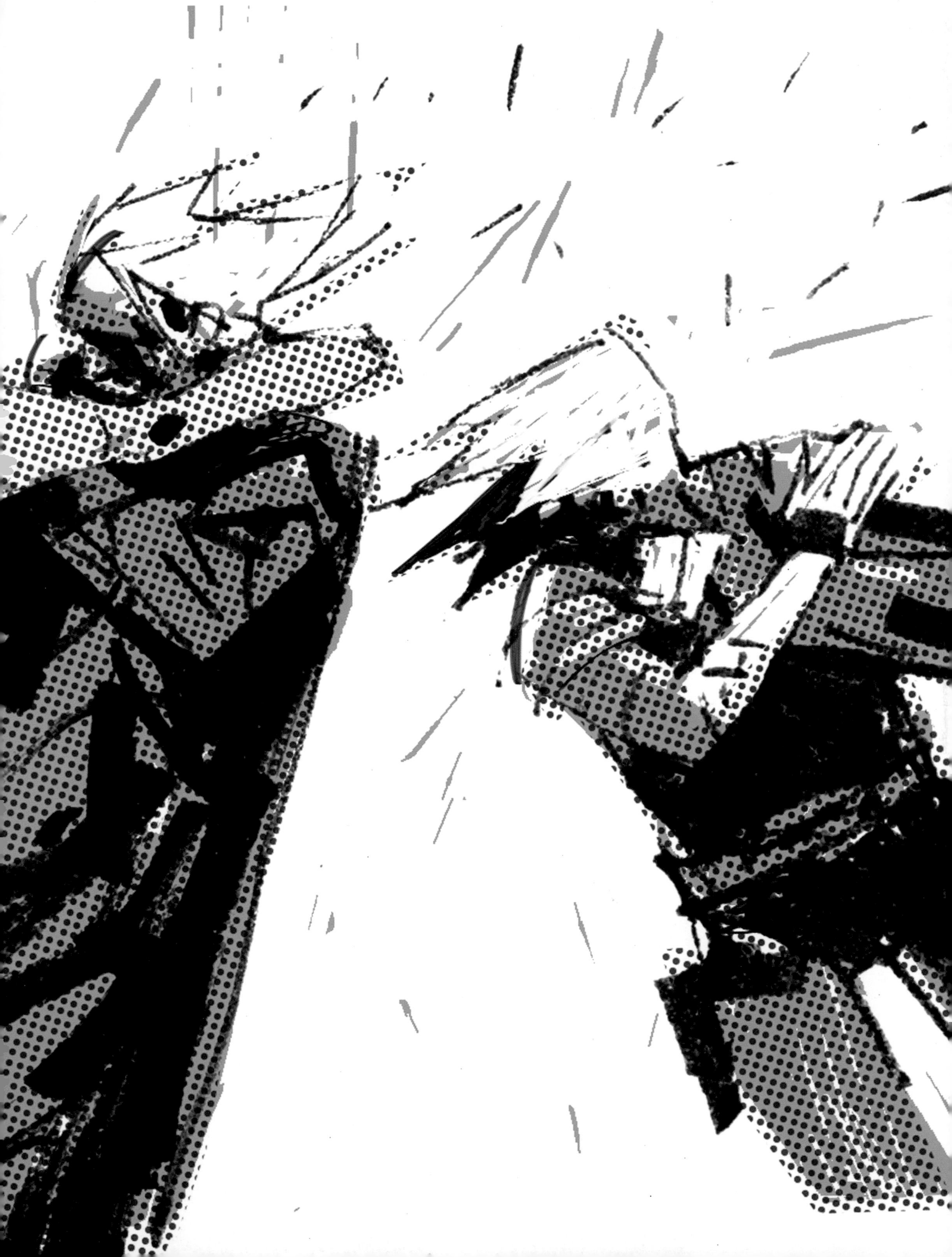

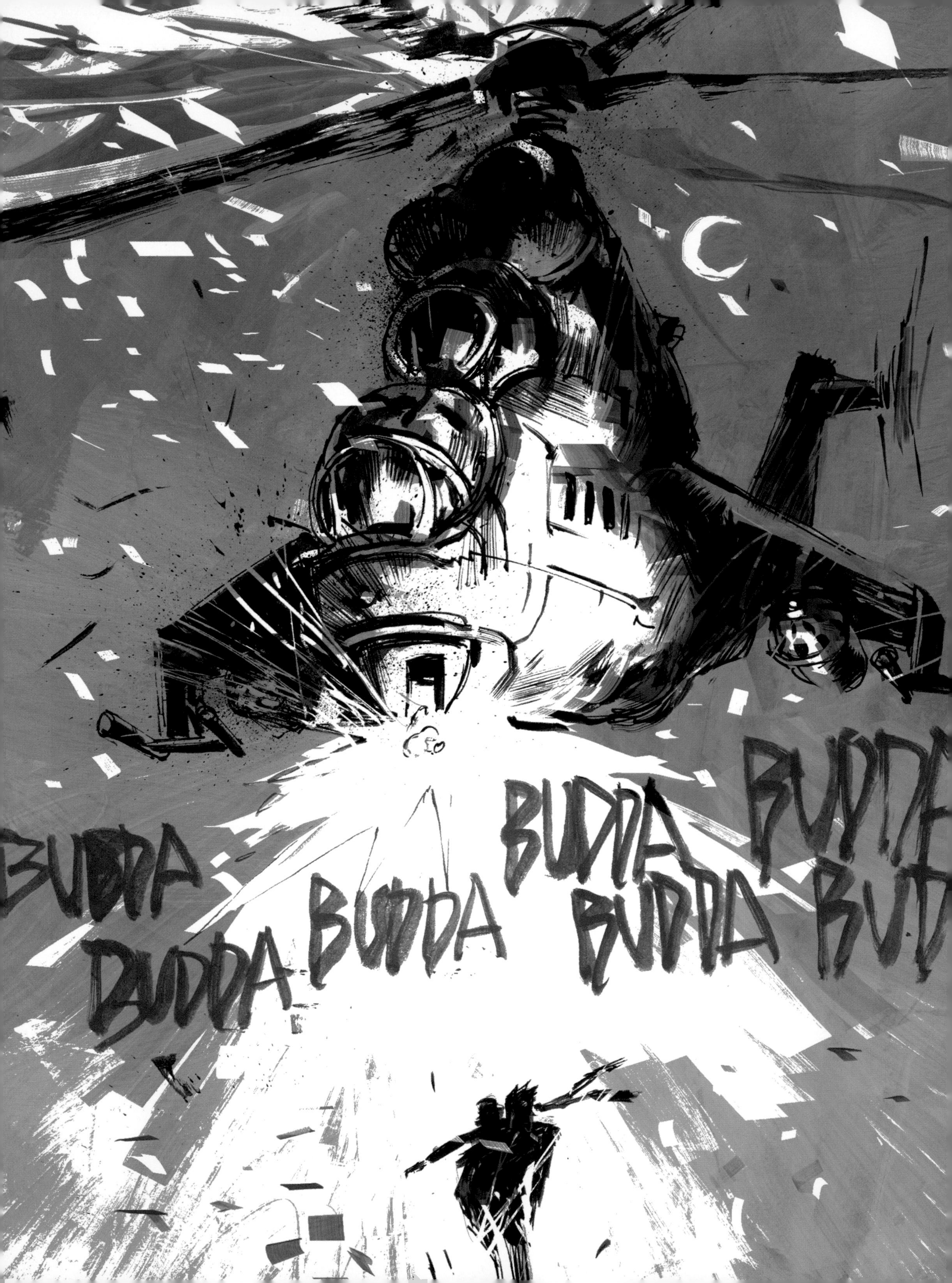
BUDDA
BUDDA
BUDDA
BUDDA
BUDDA

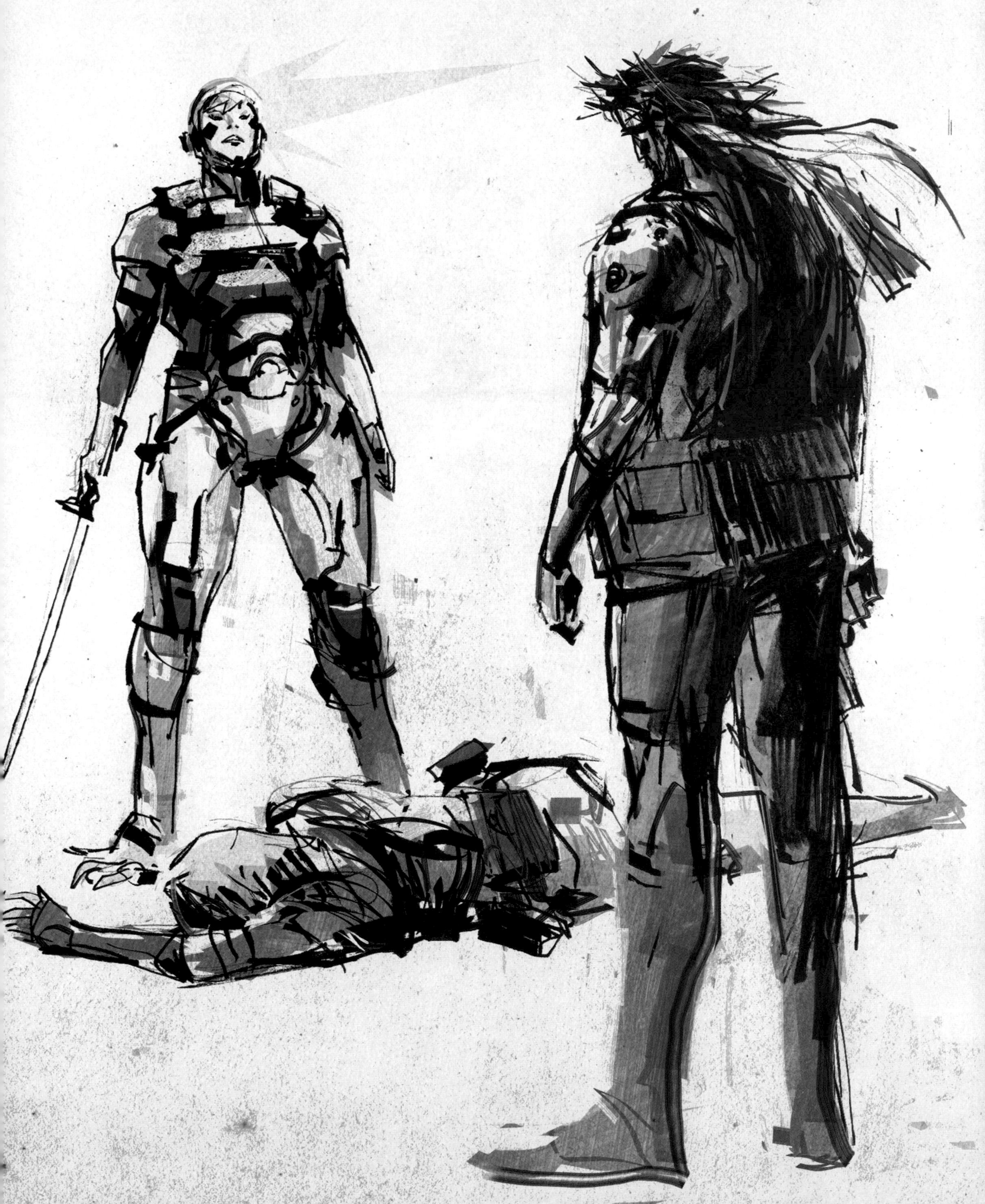

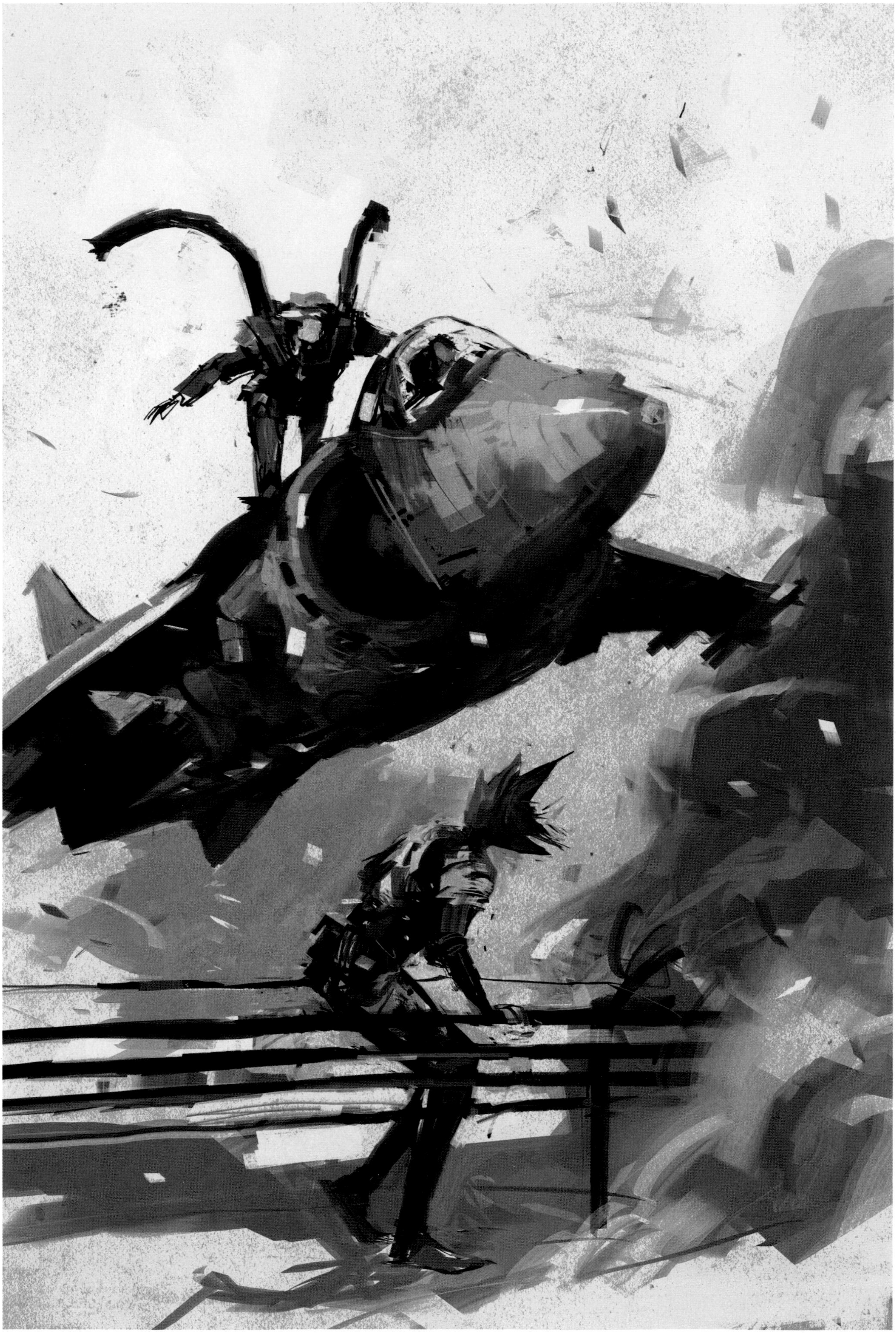

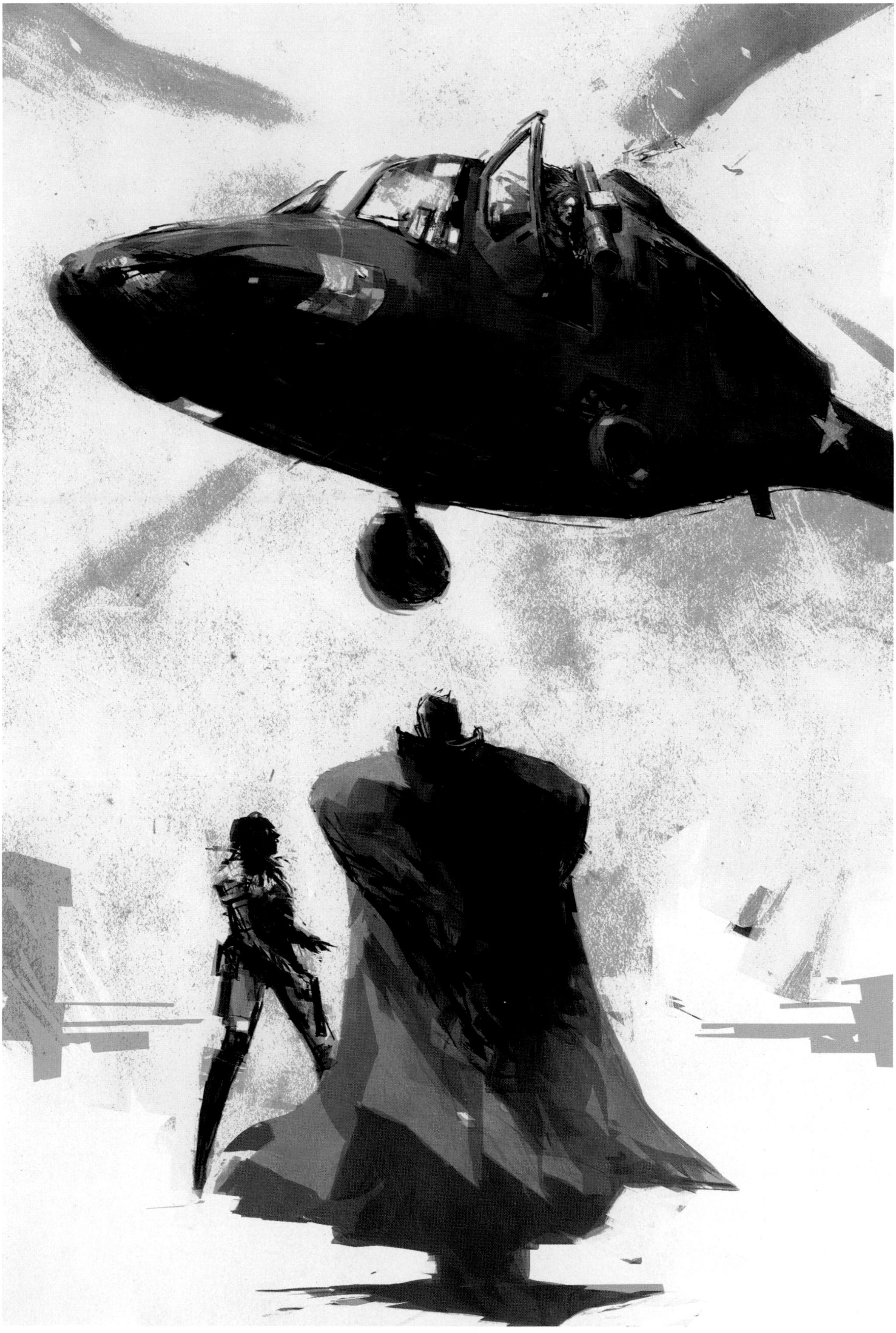

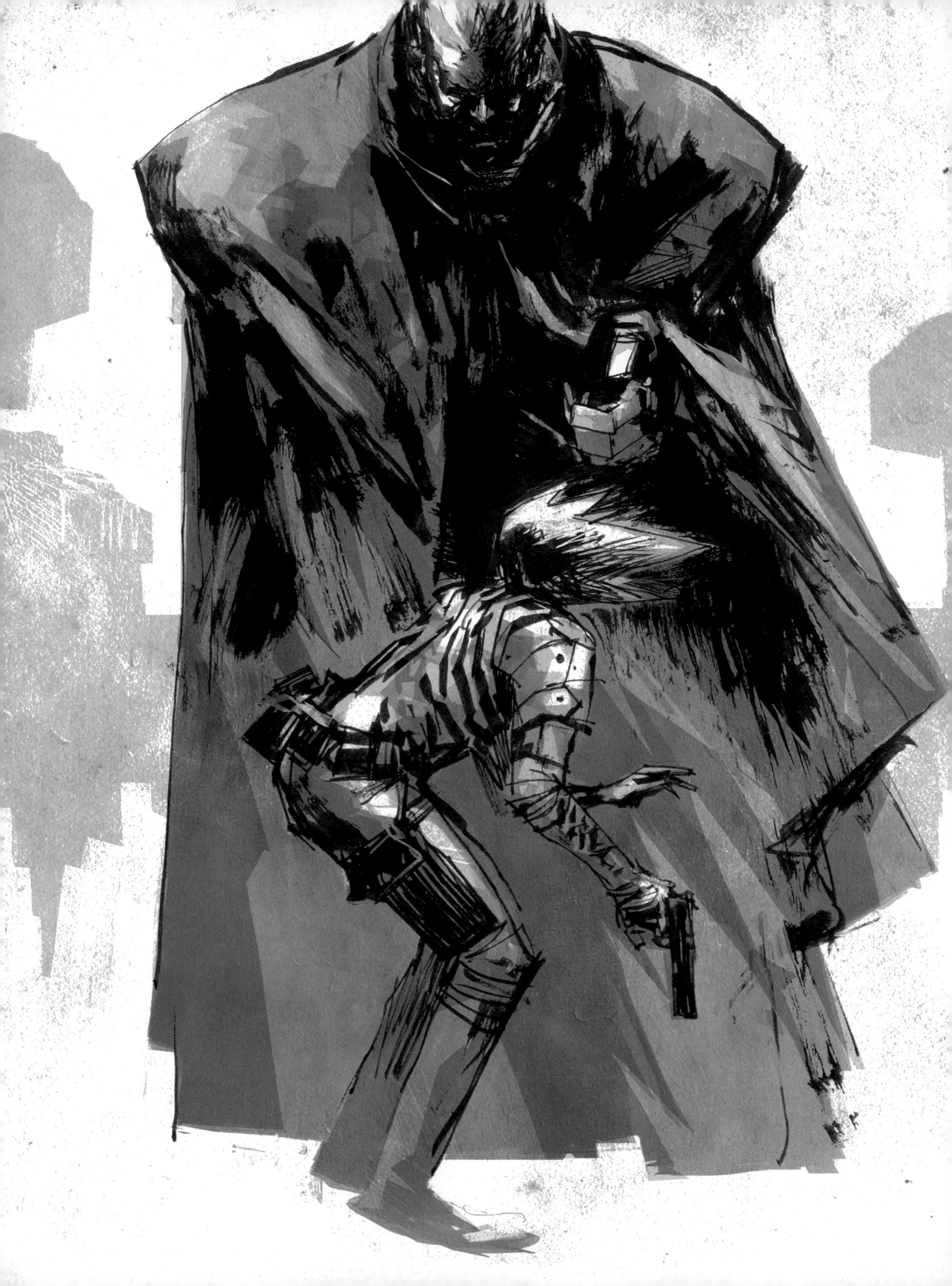

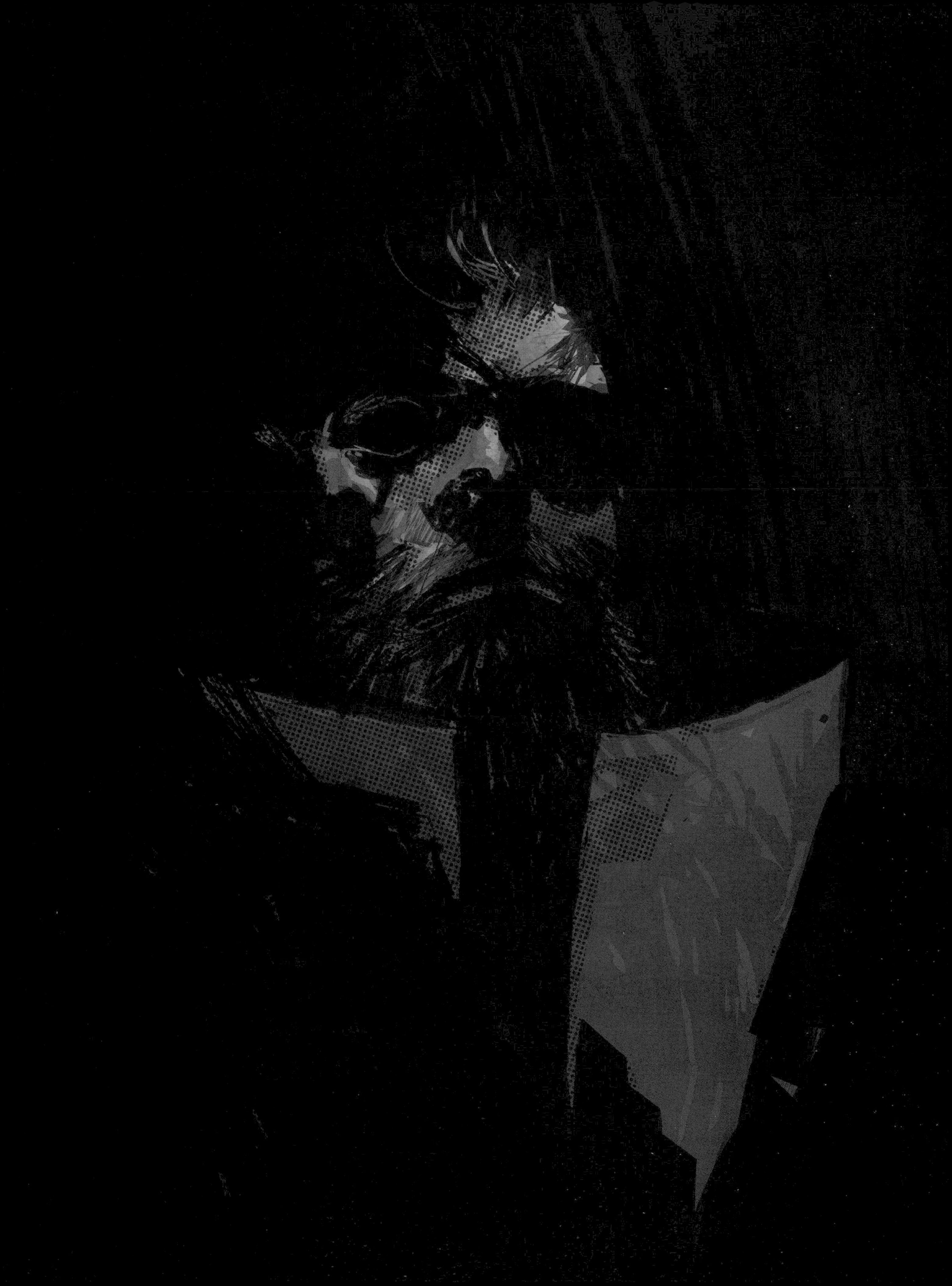

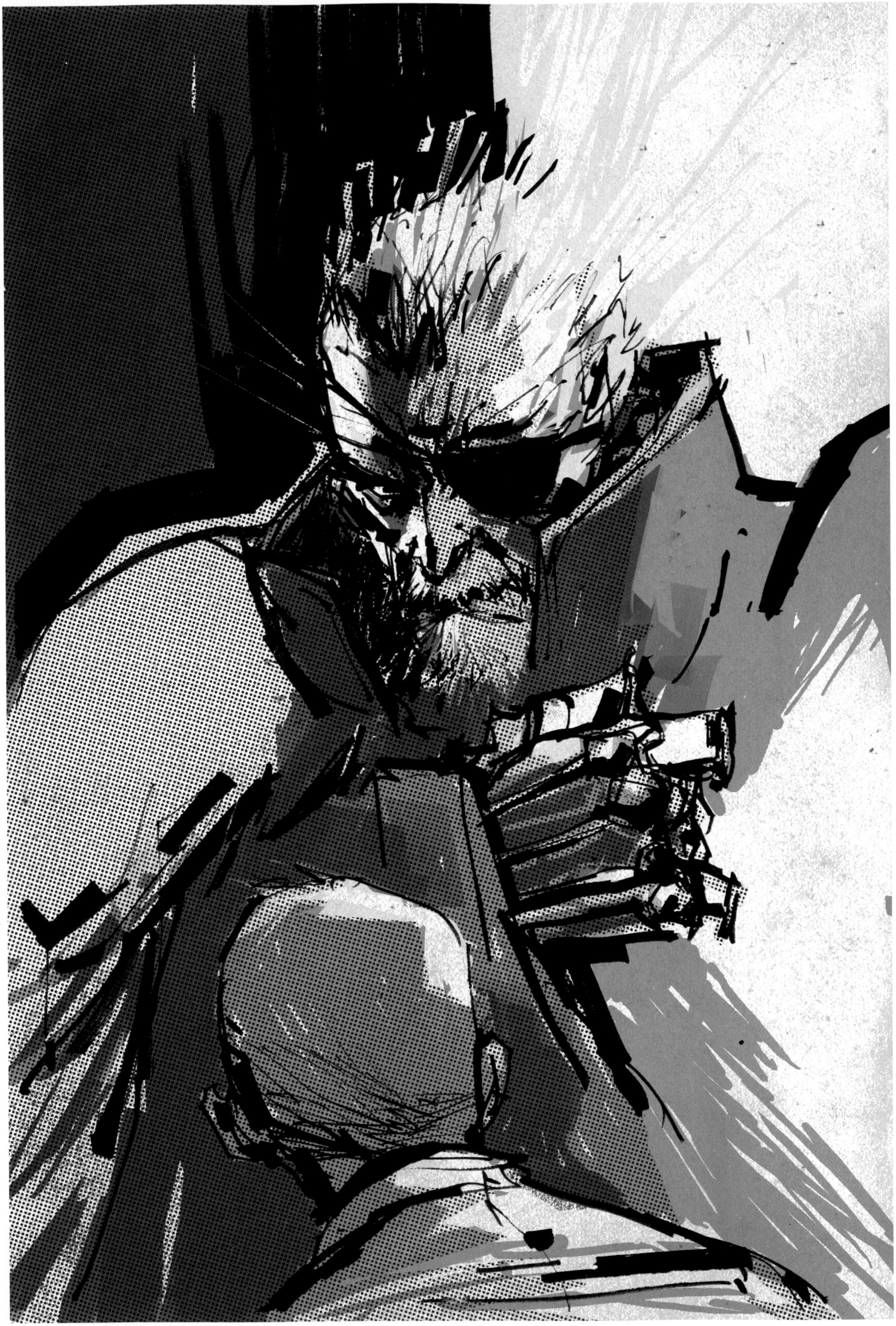

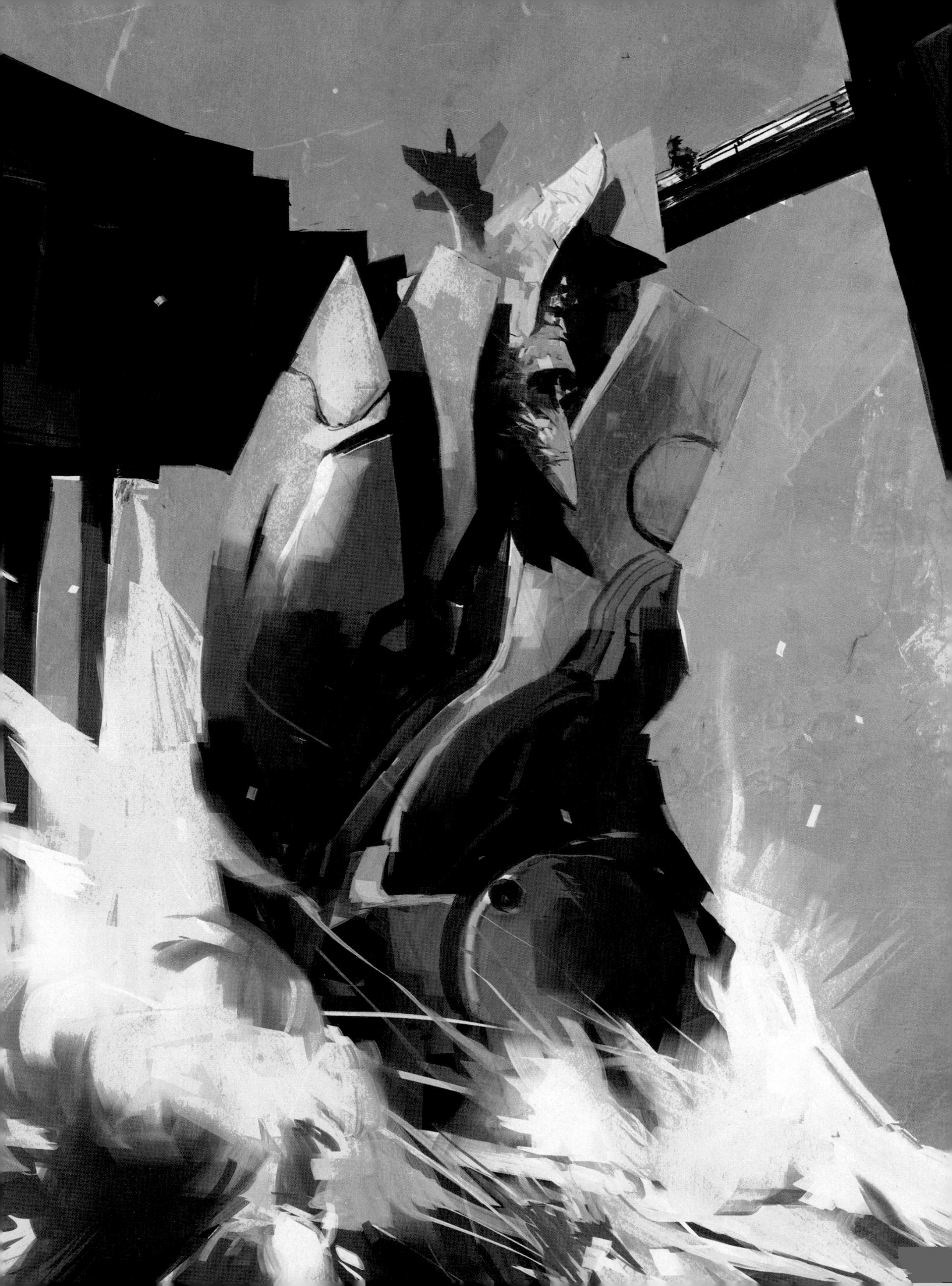

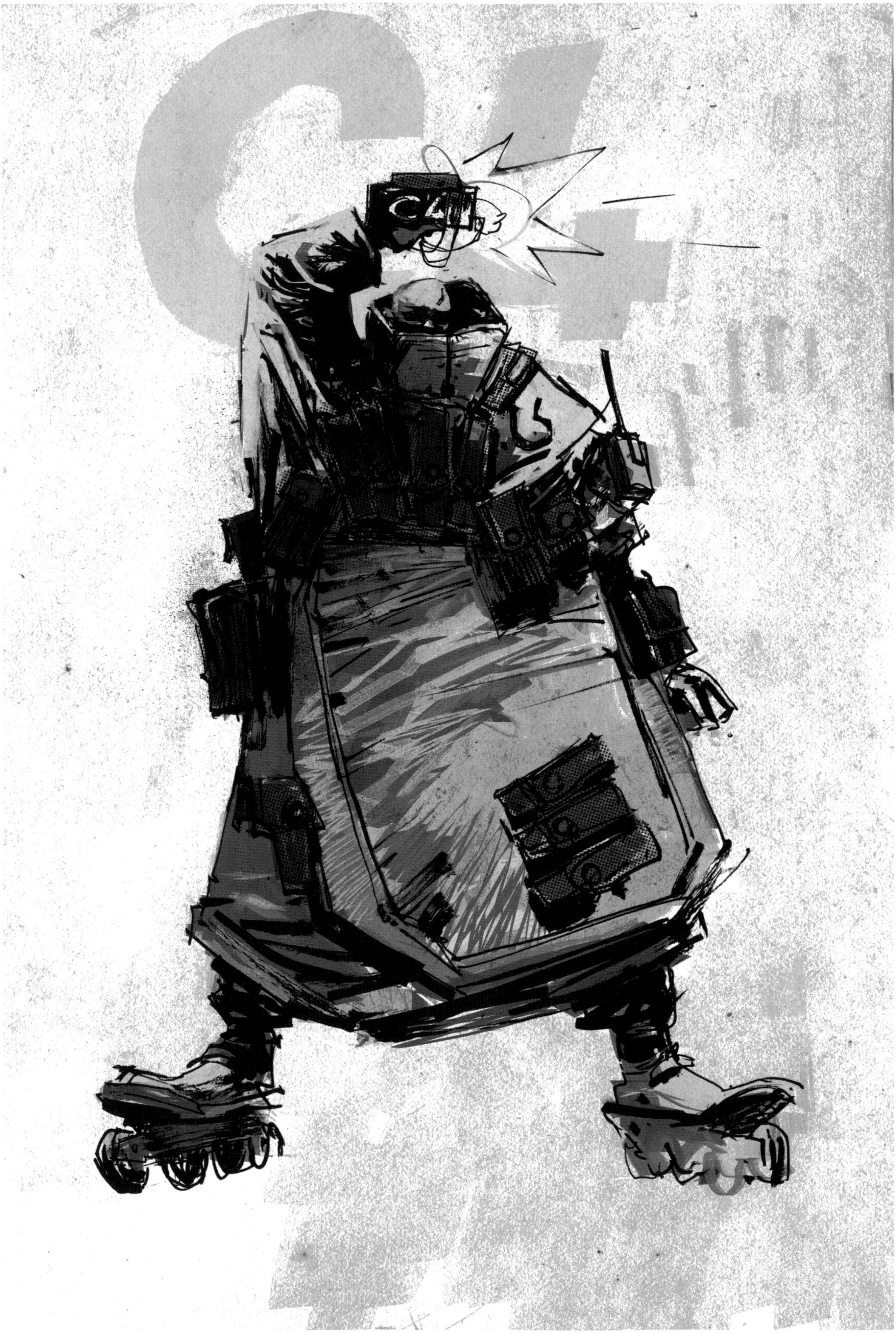
C4

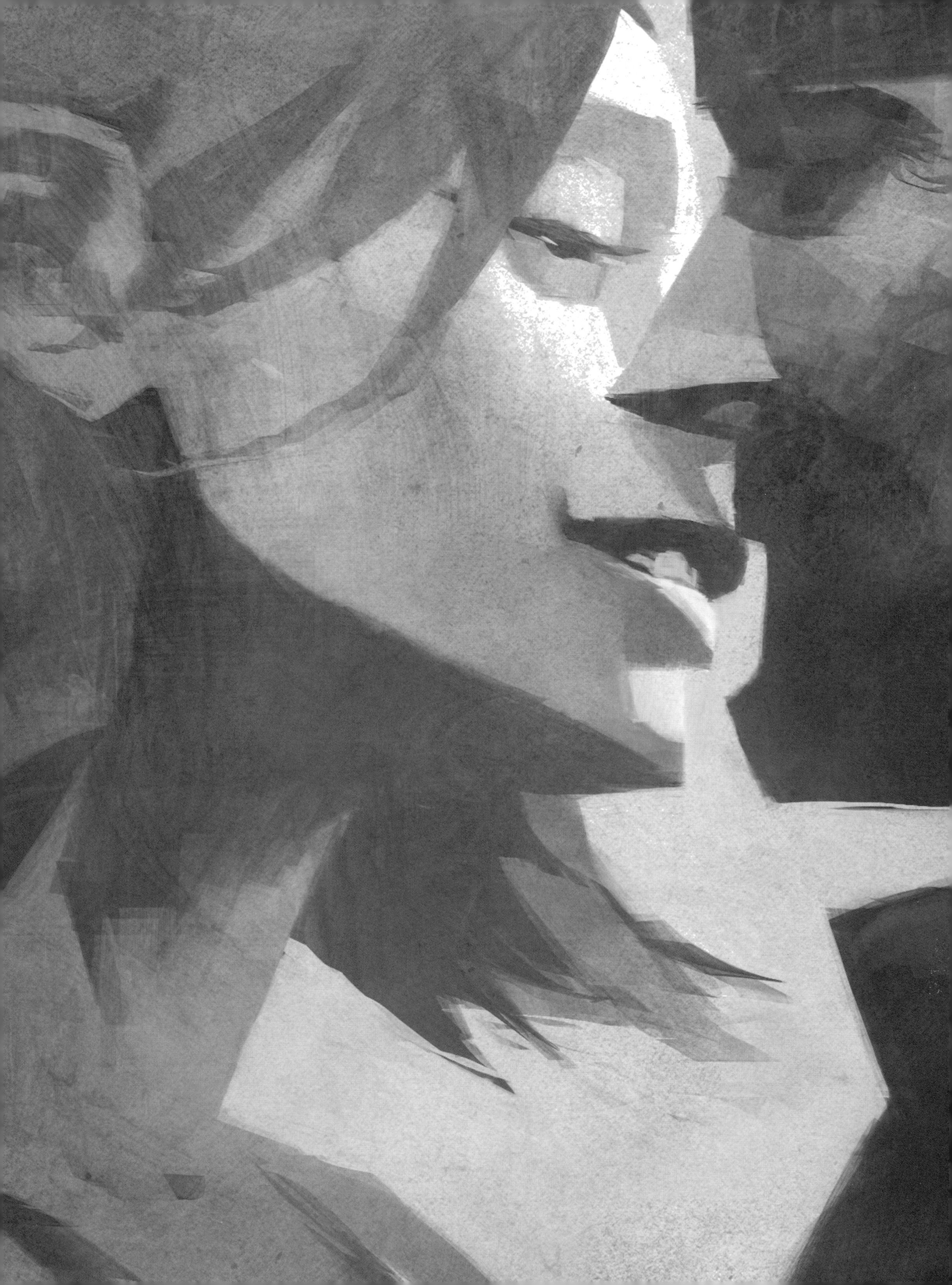

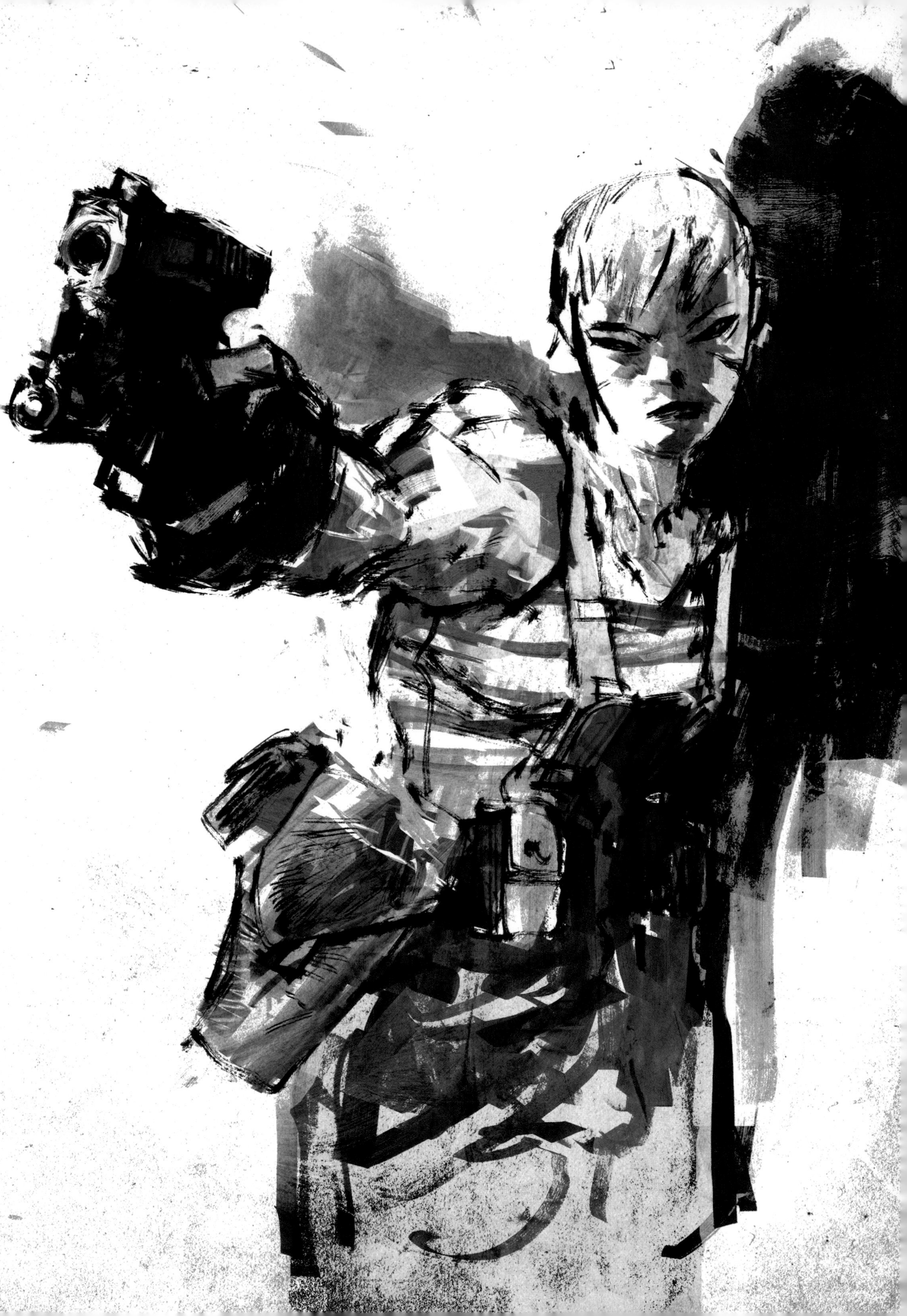

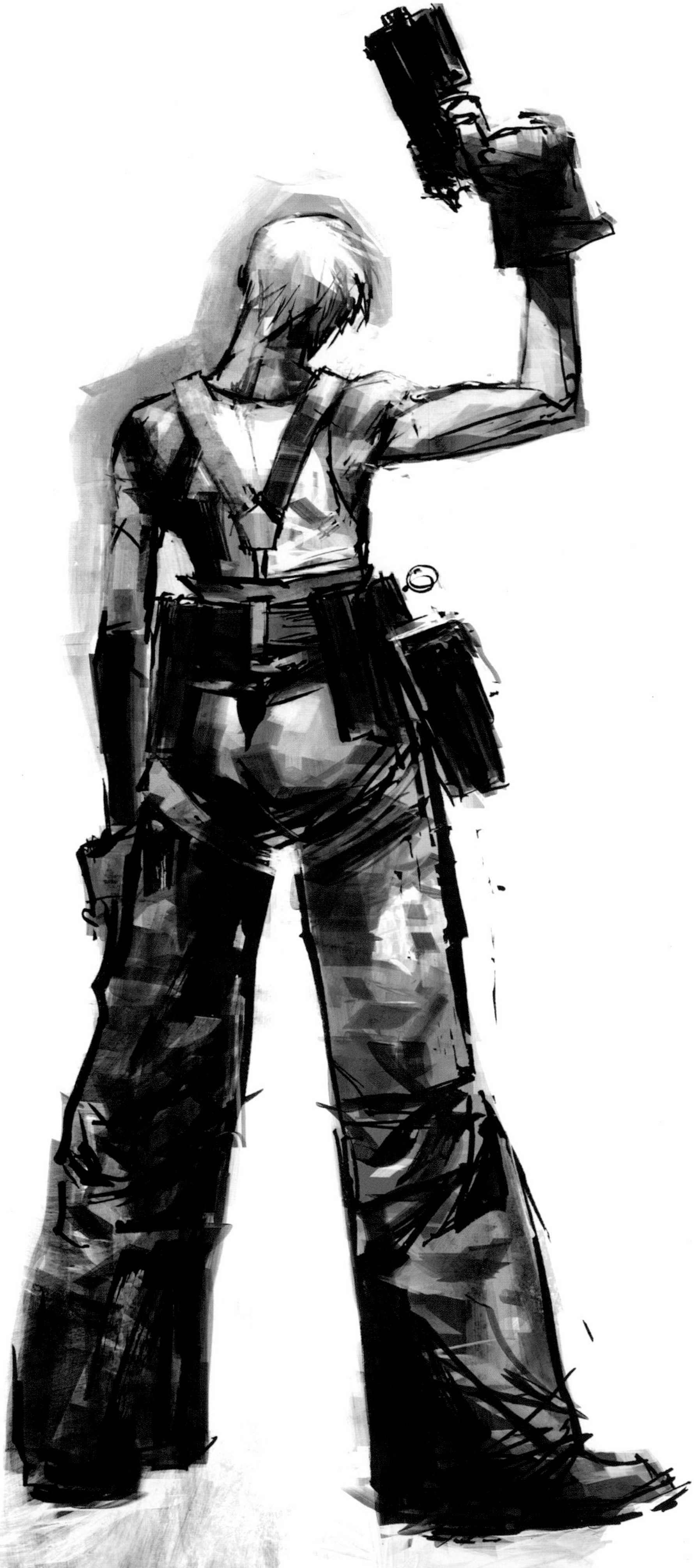

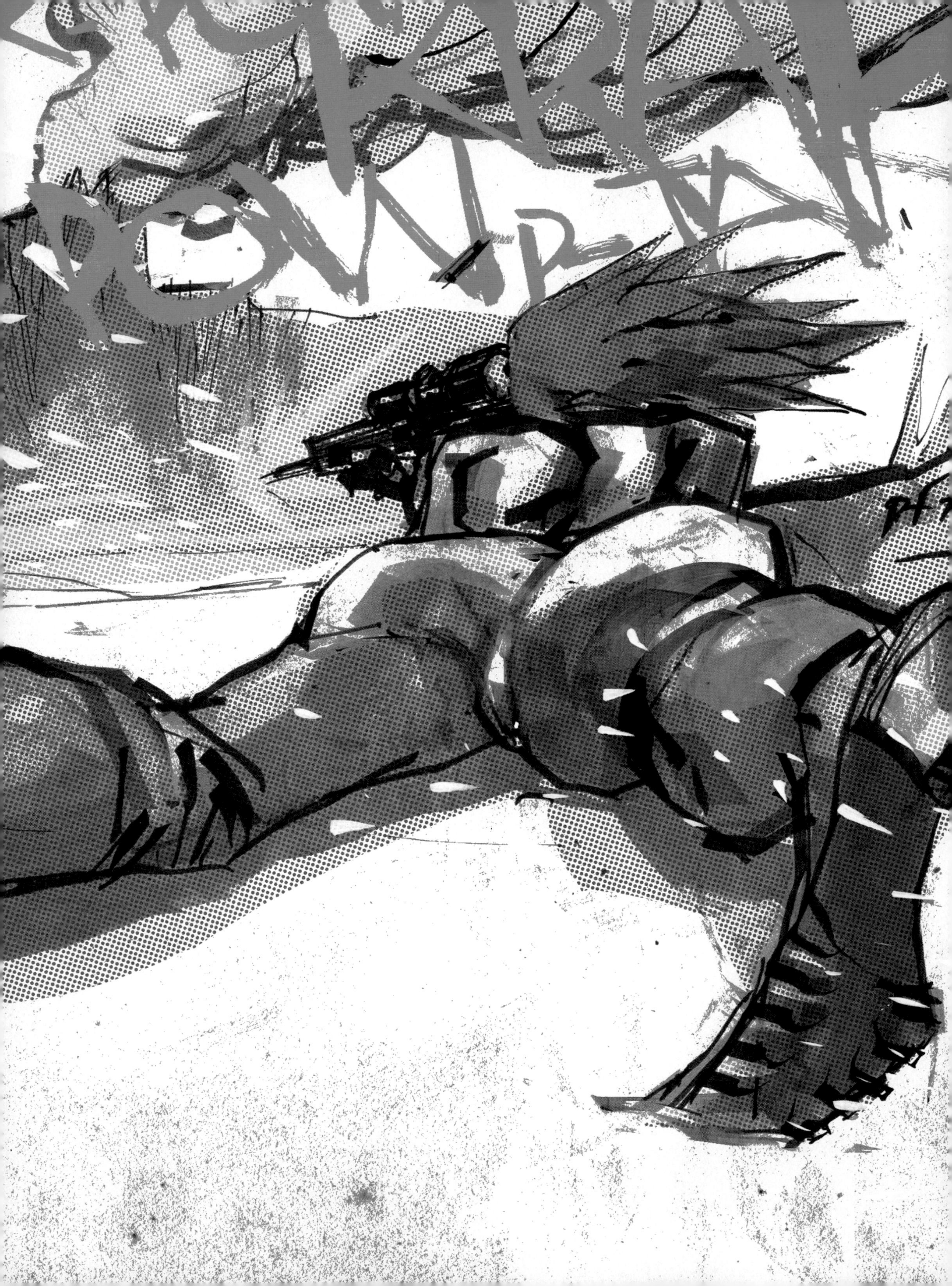

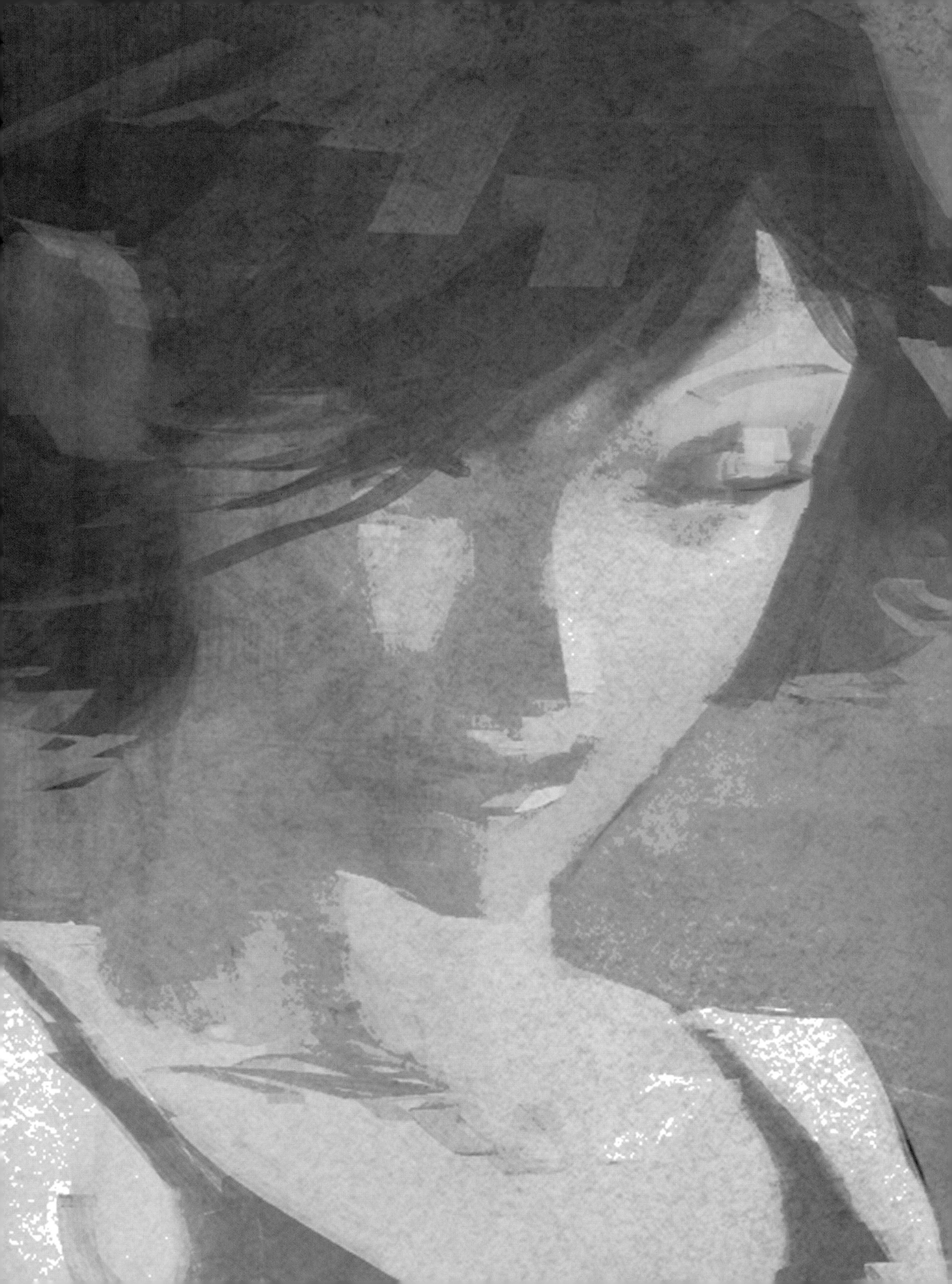

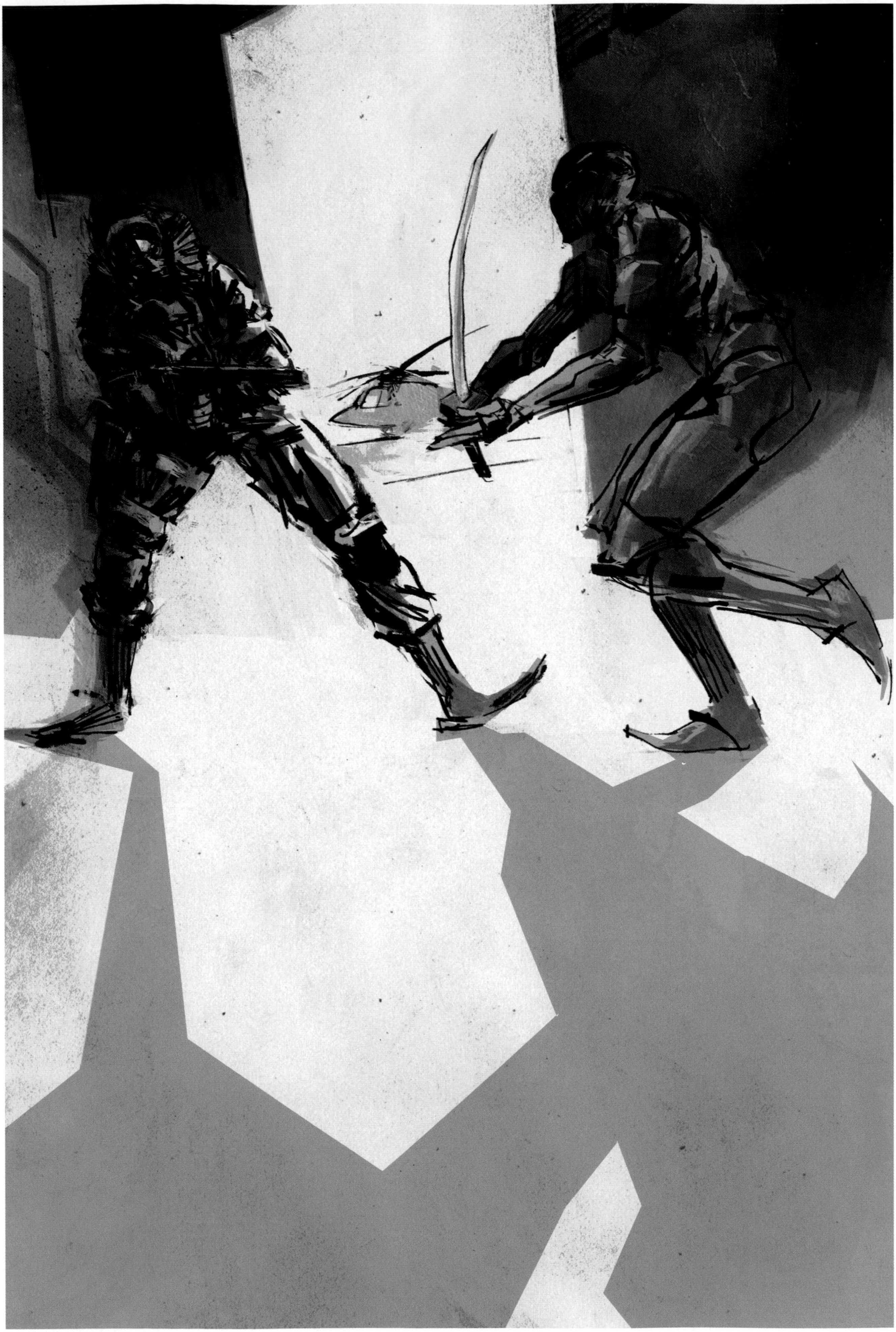

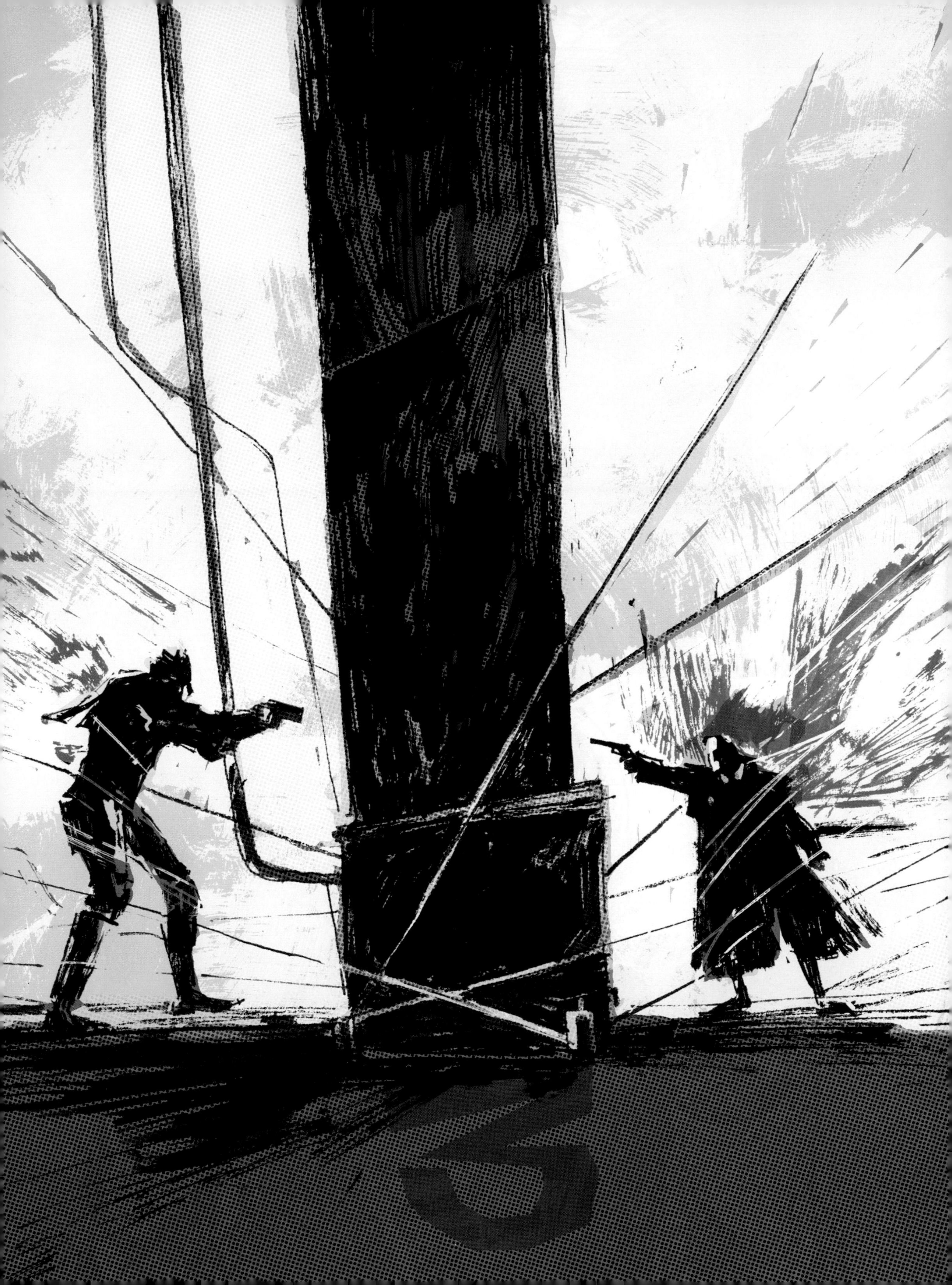

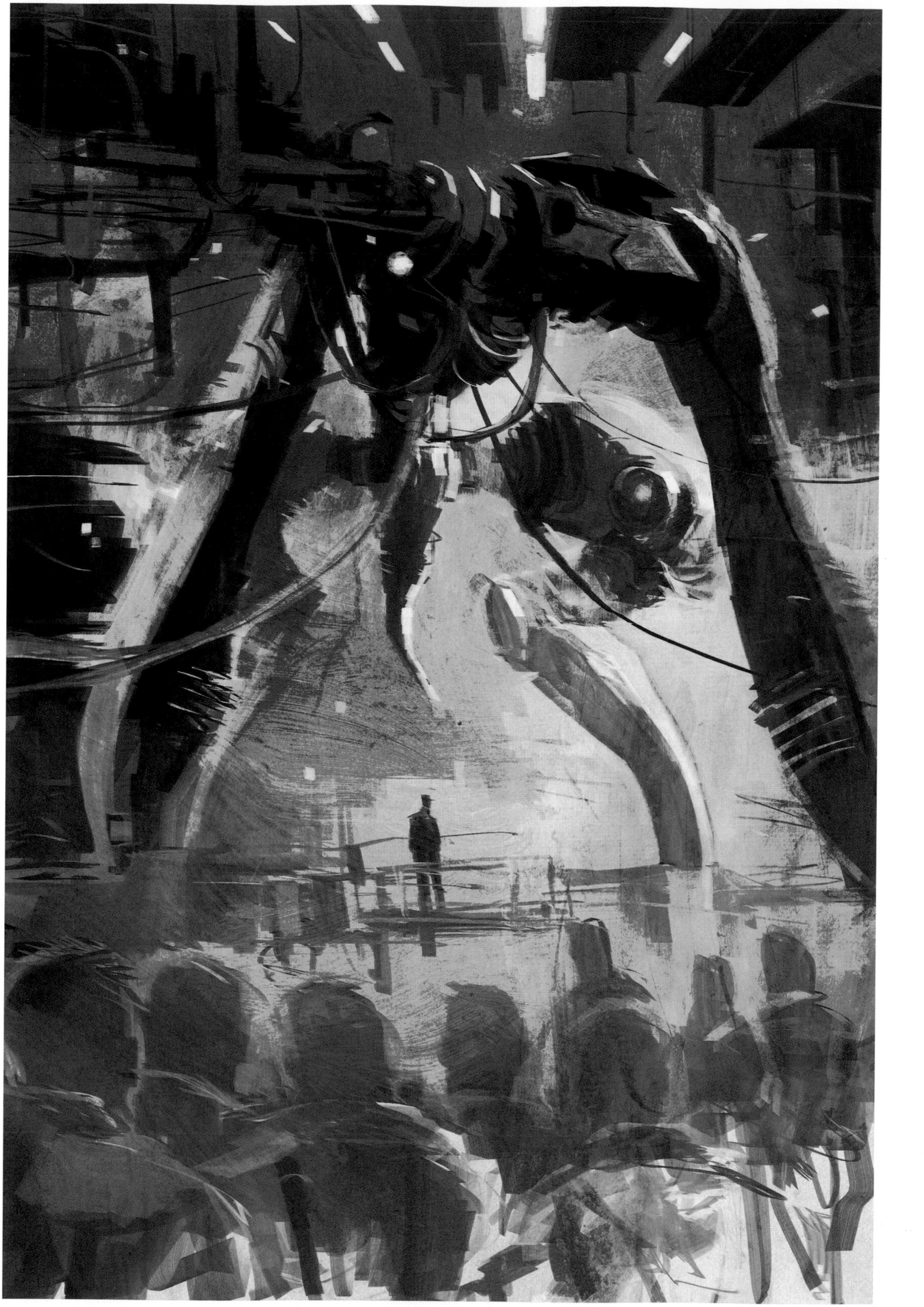

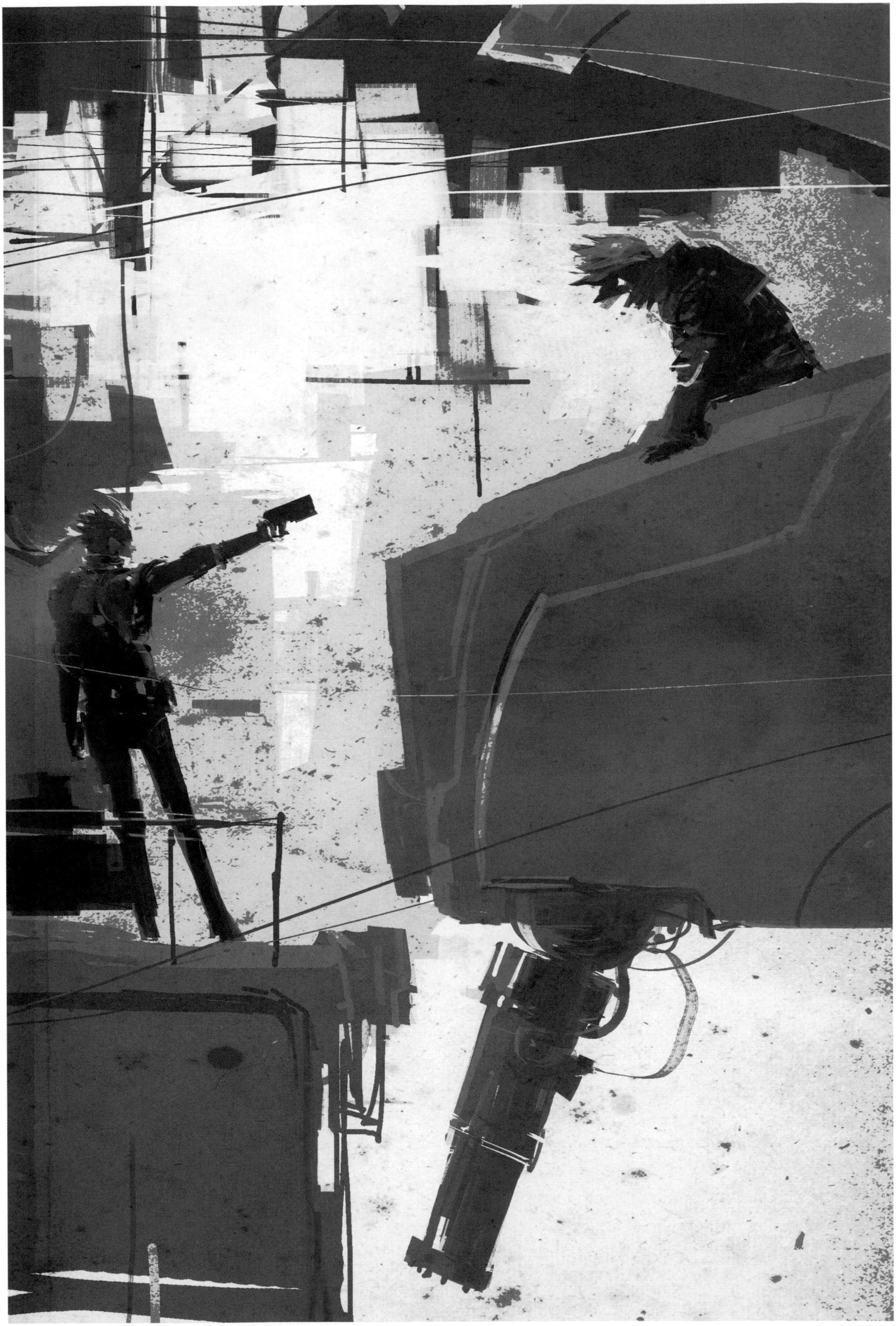

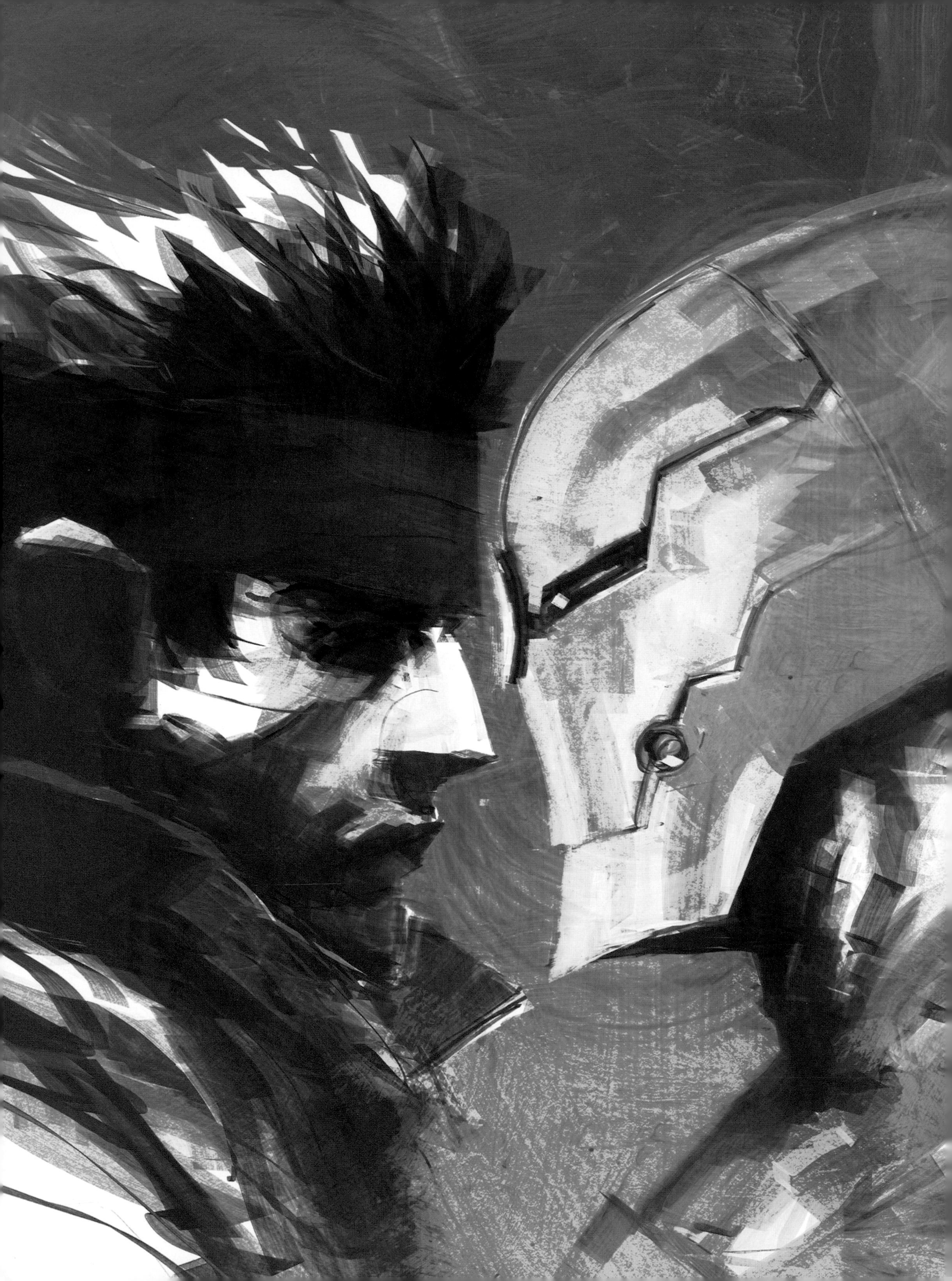

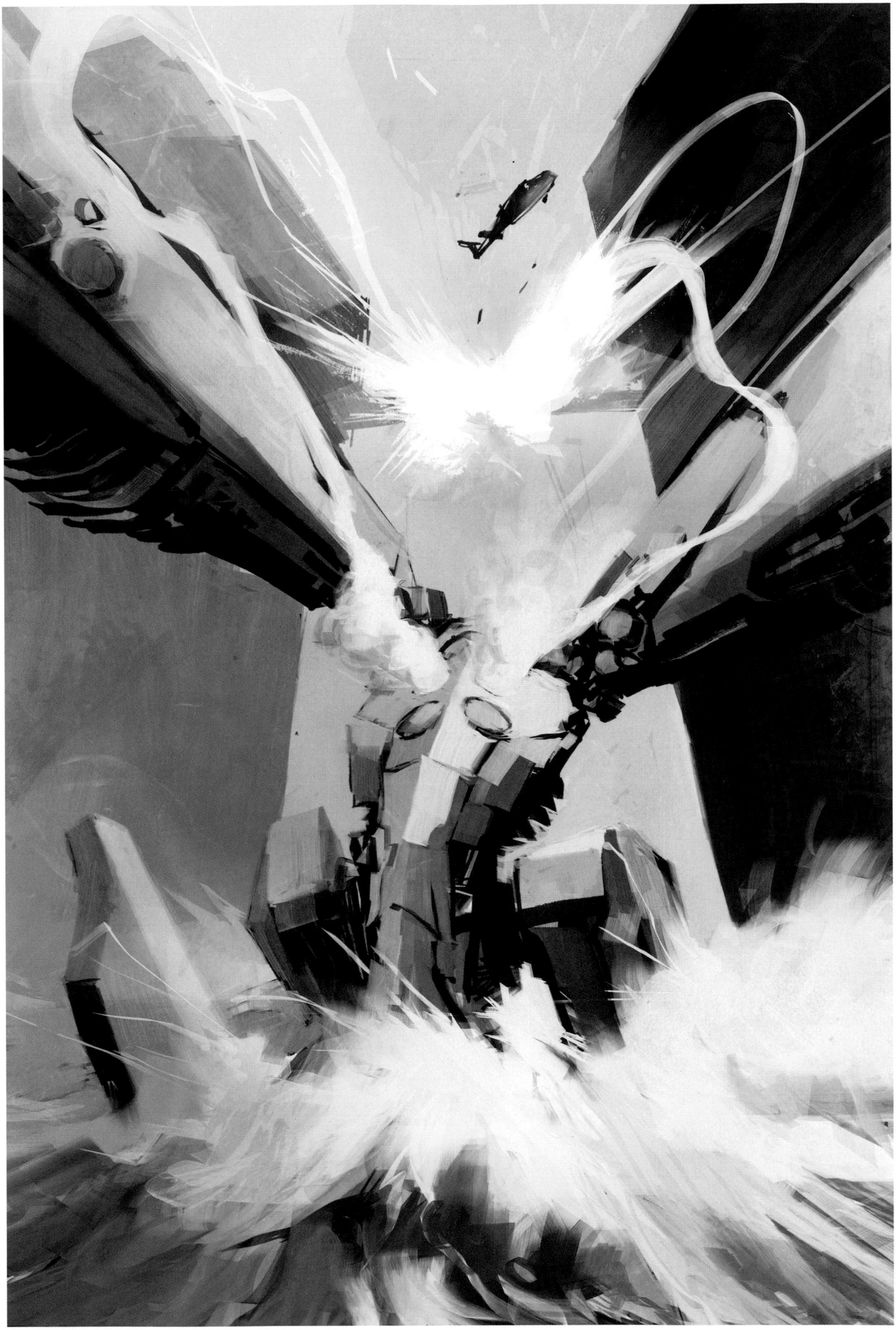

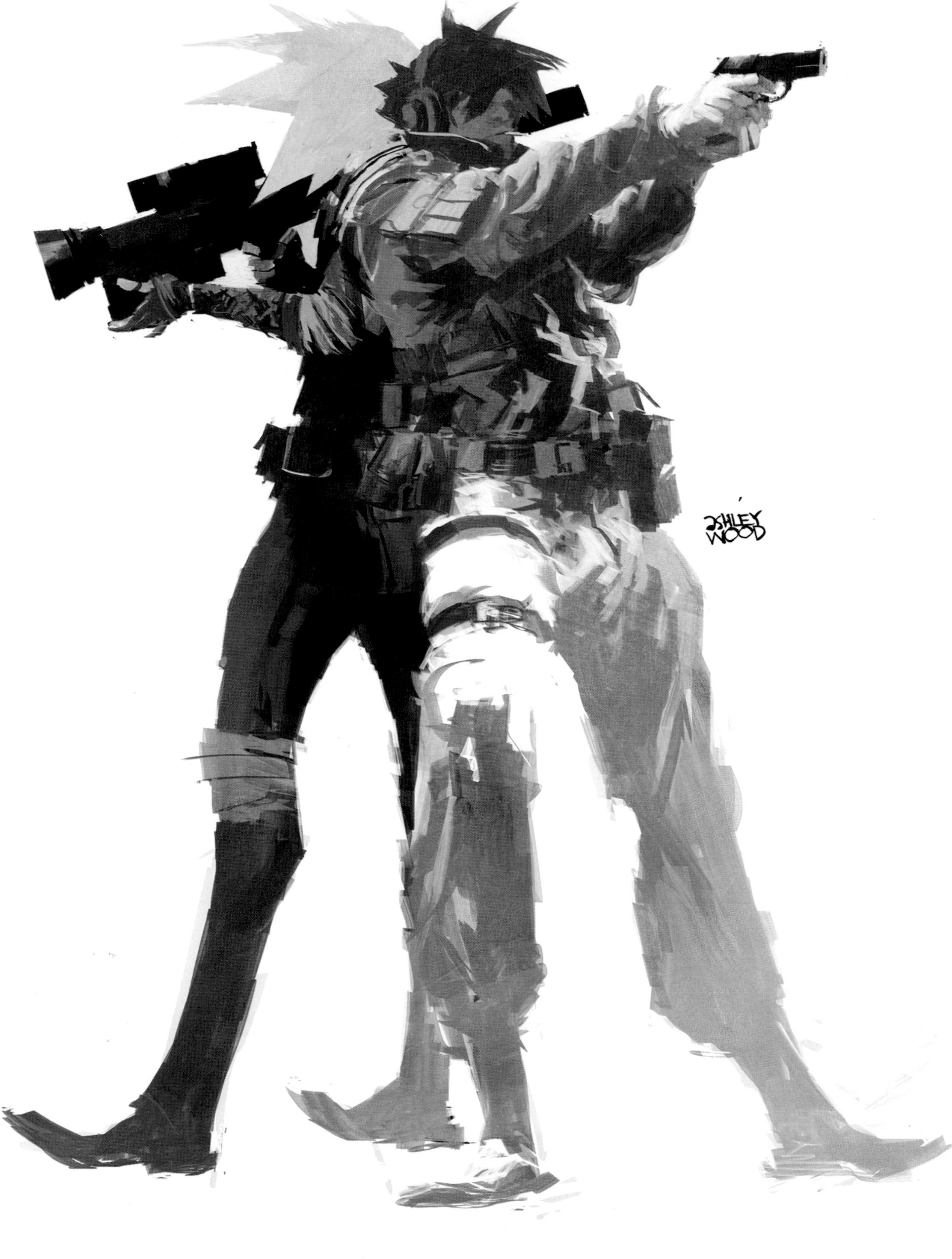
ASHLEY
WOOD

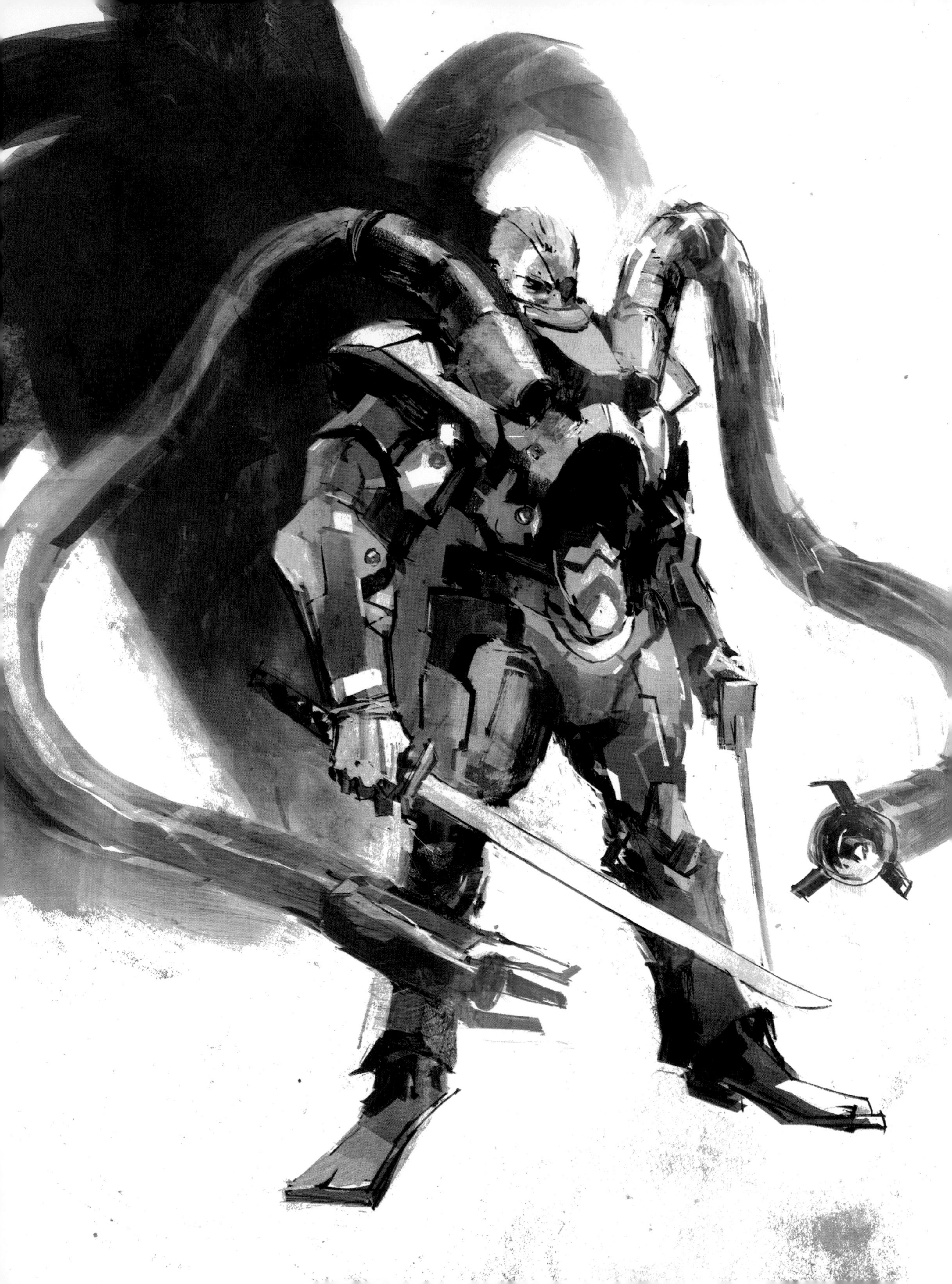

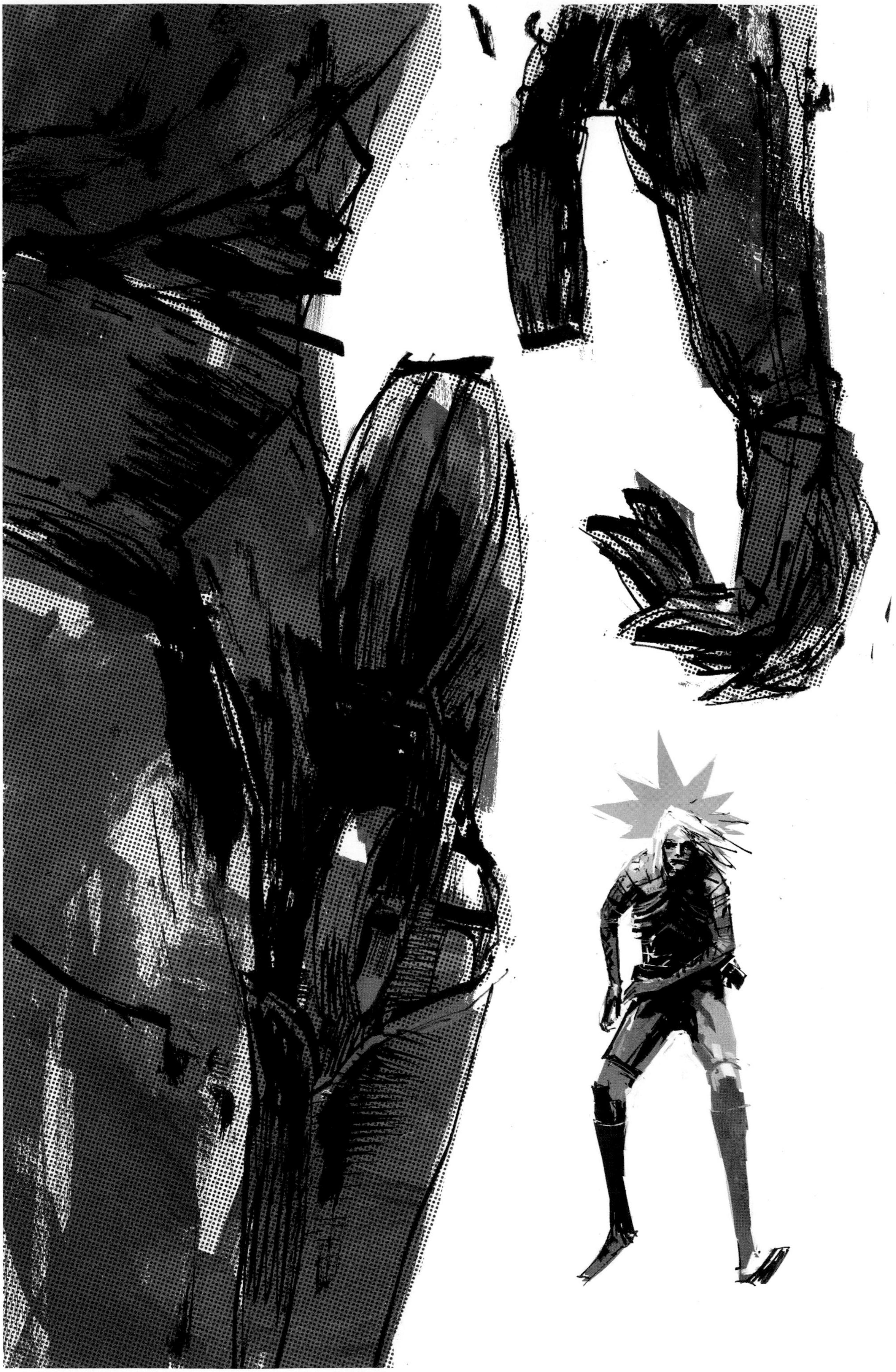

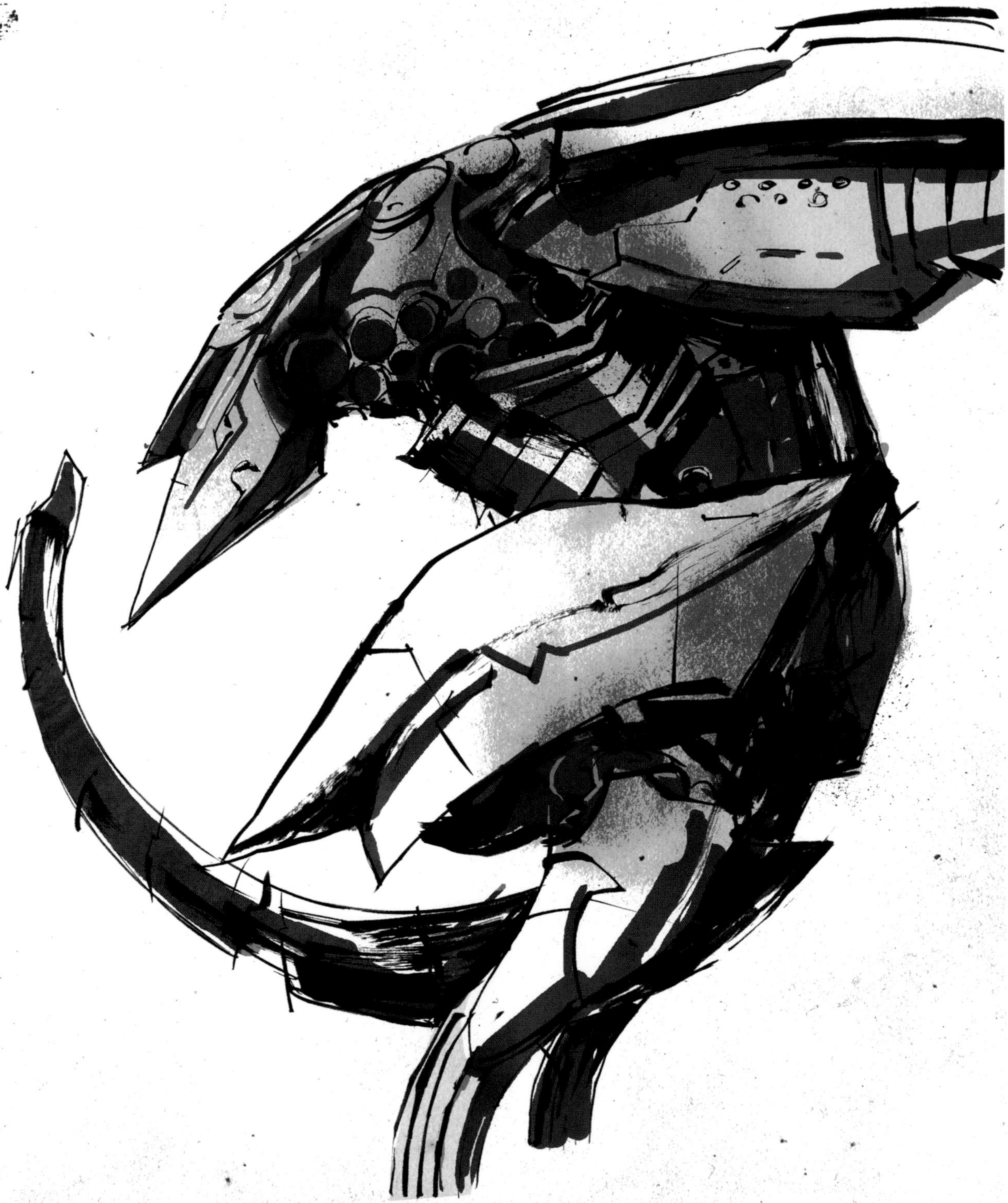

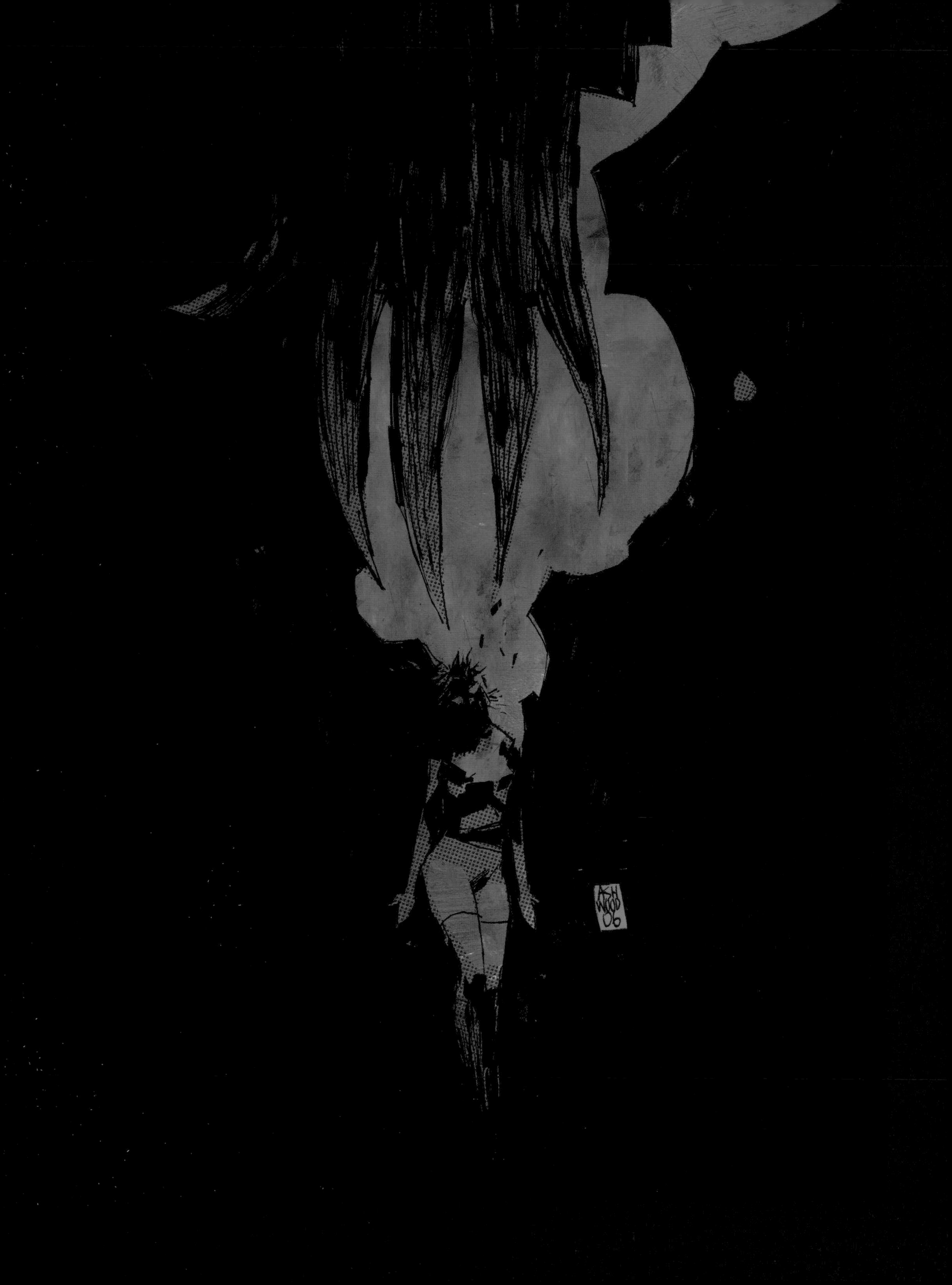
ASH
WOOD
06

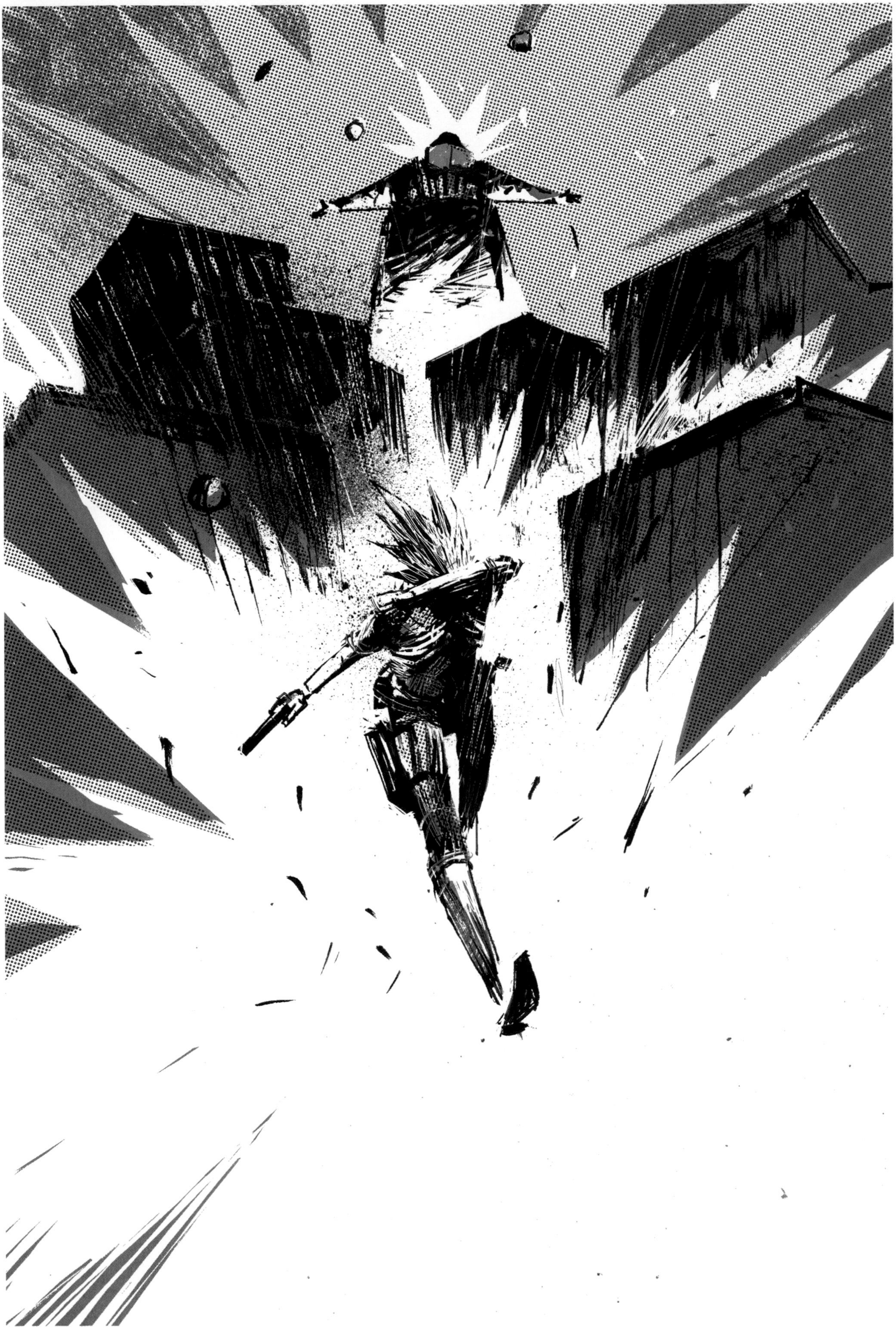

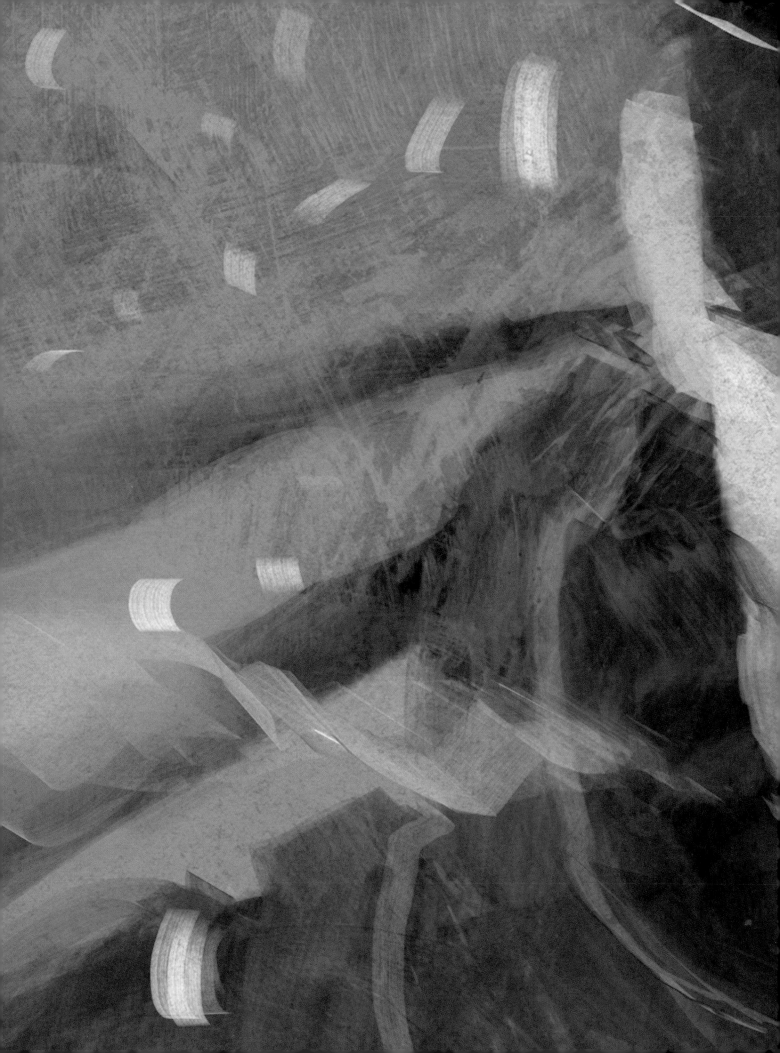

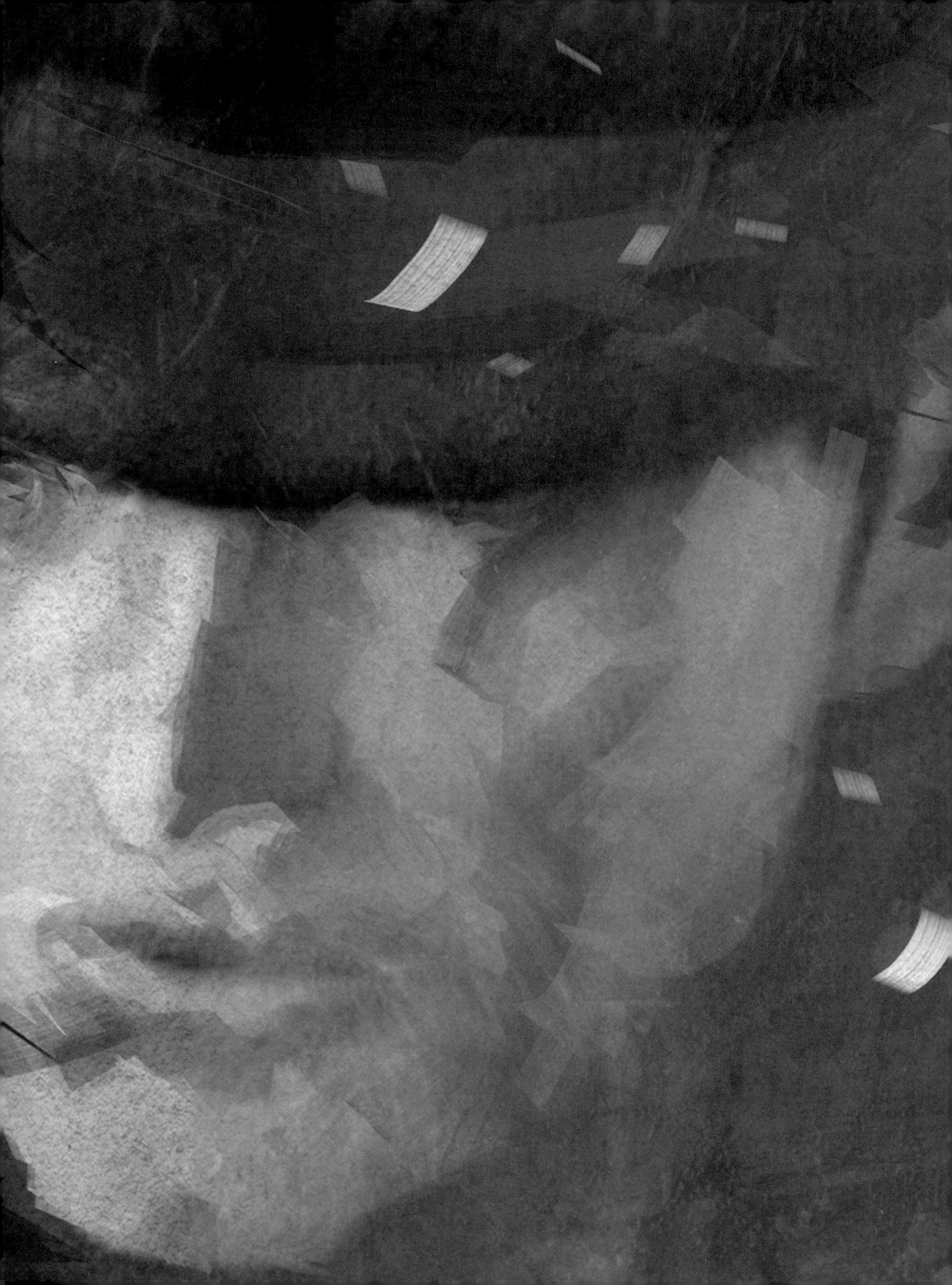

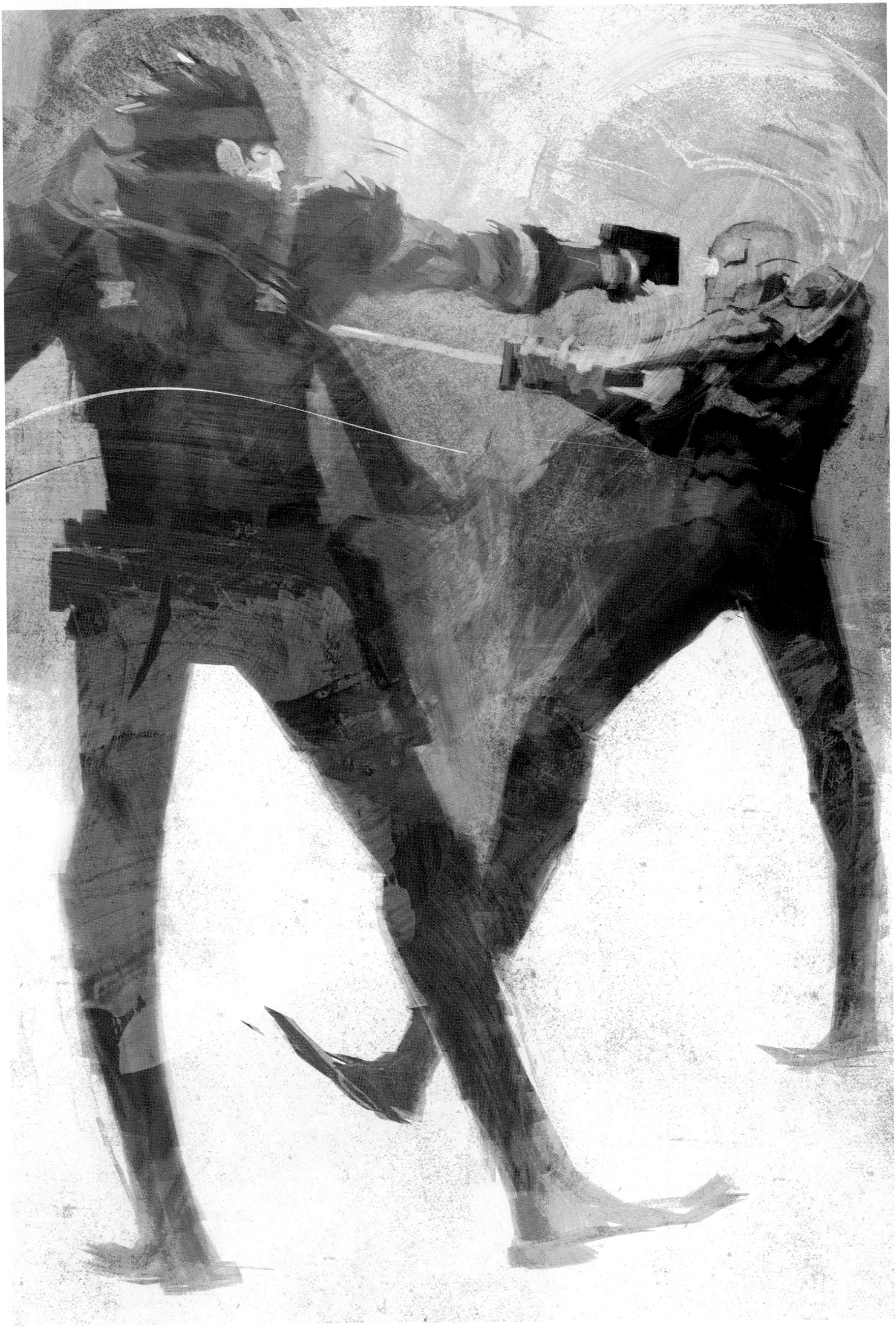

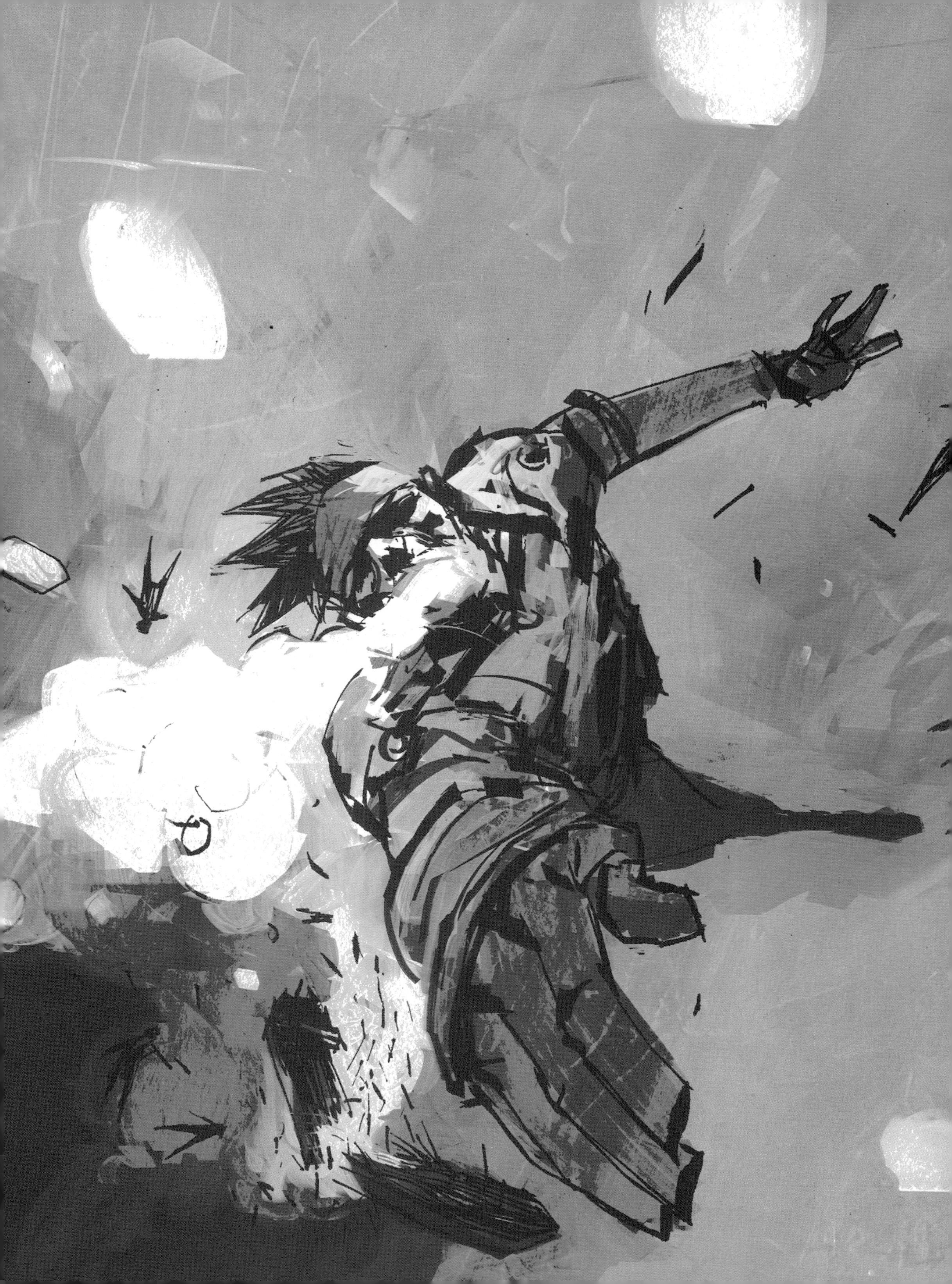

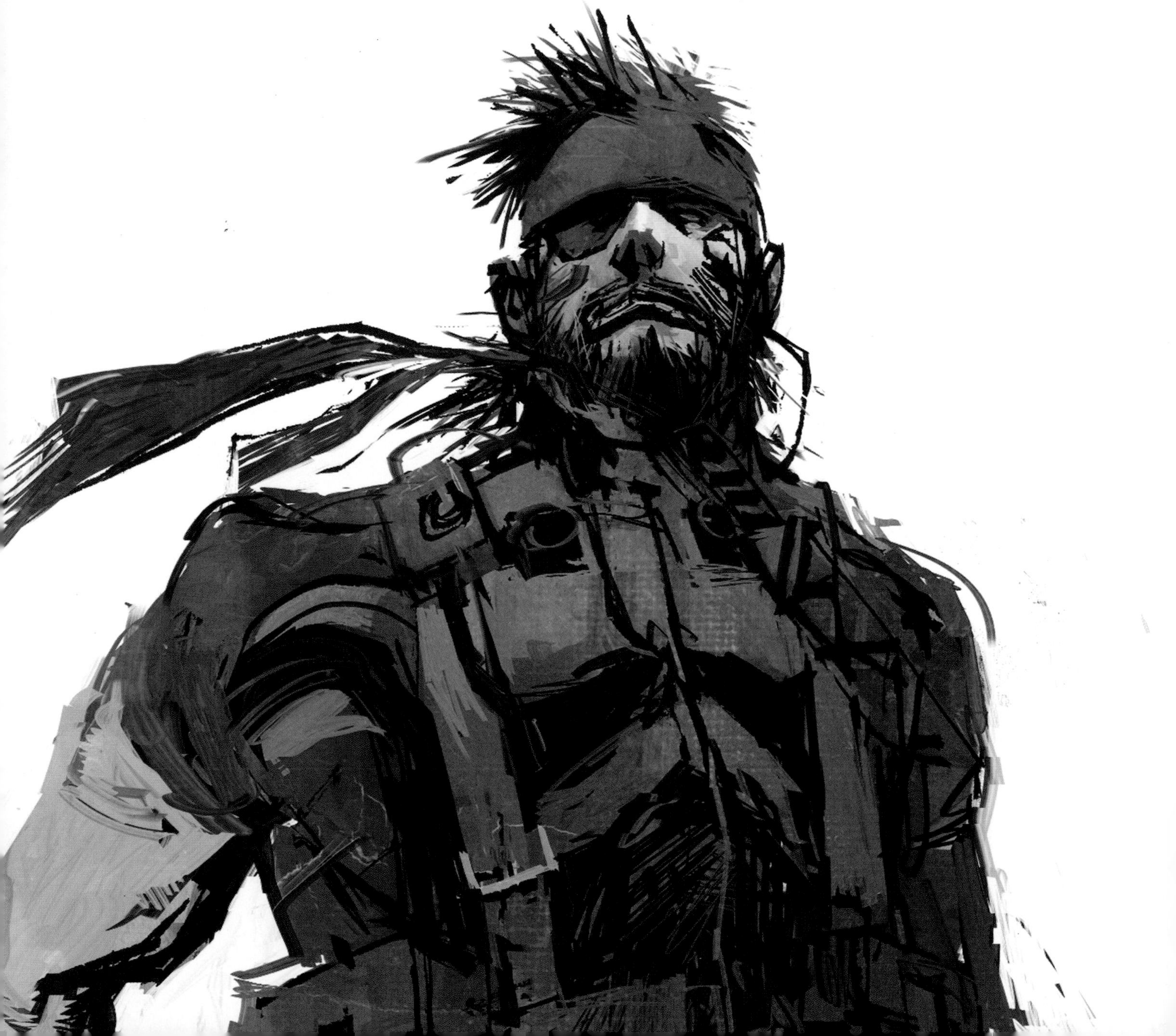

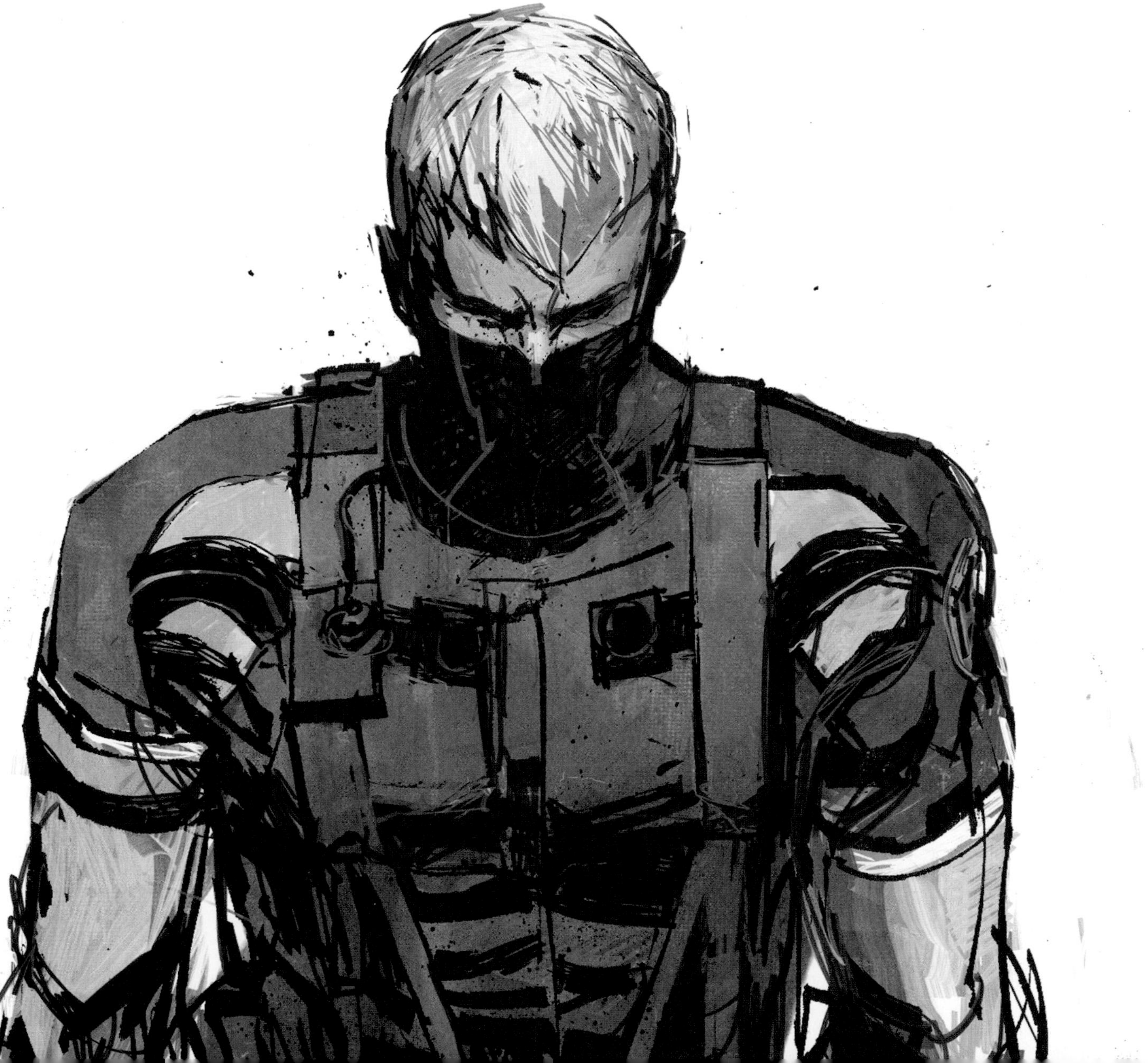

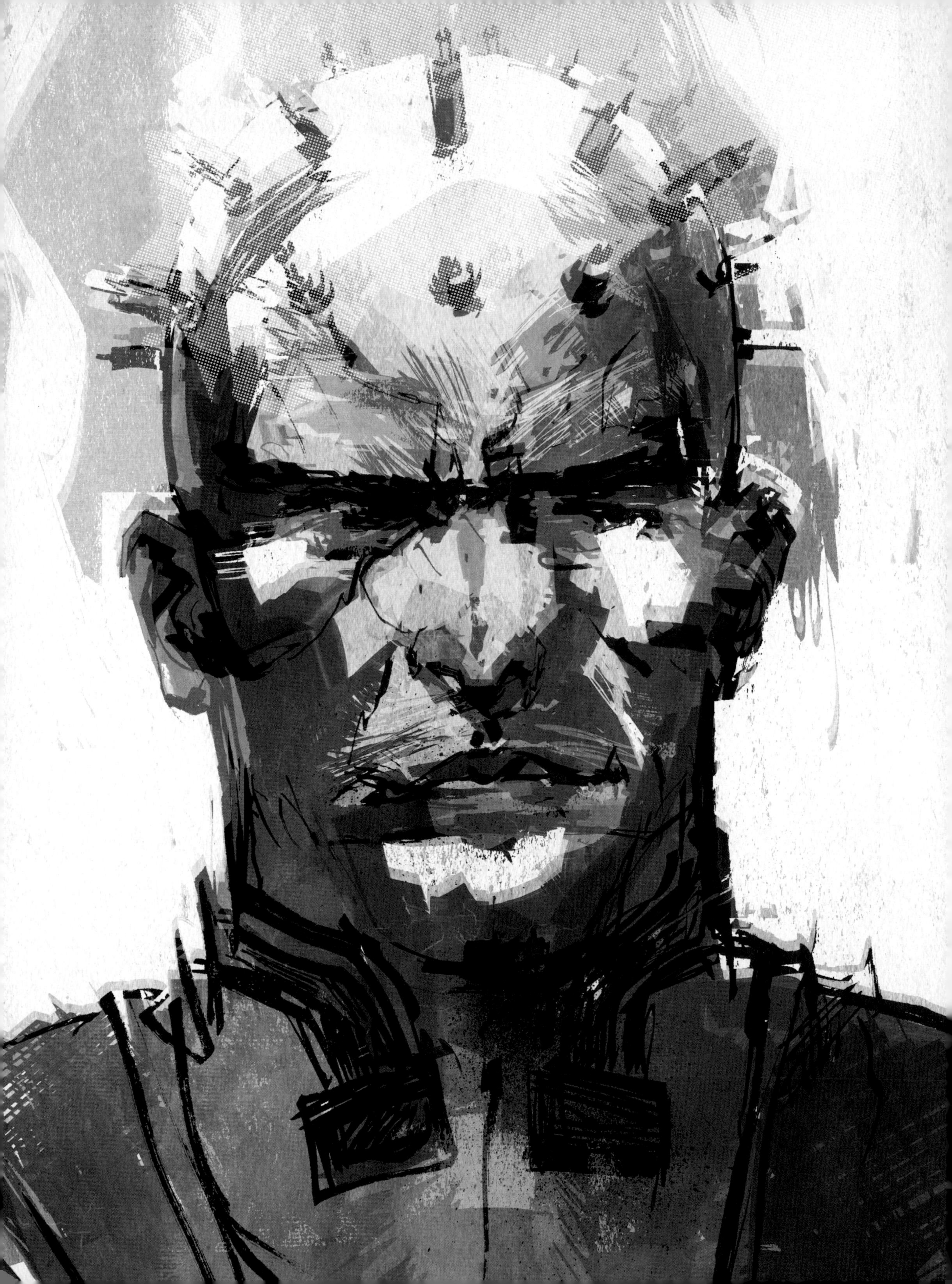

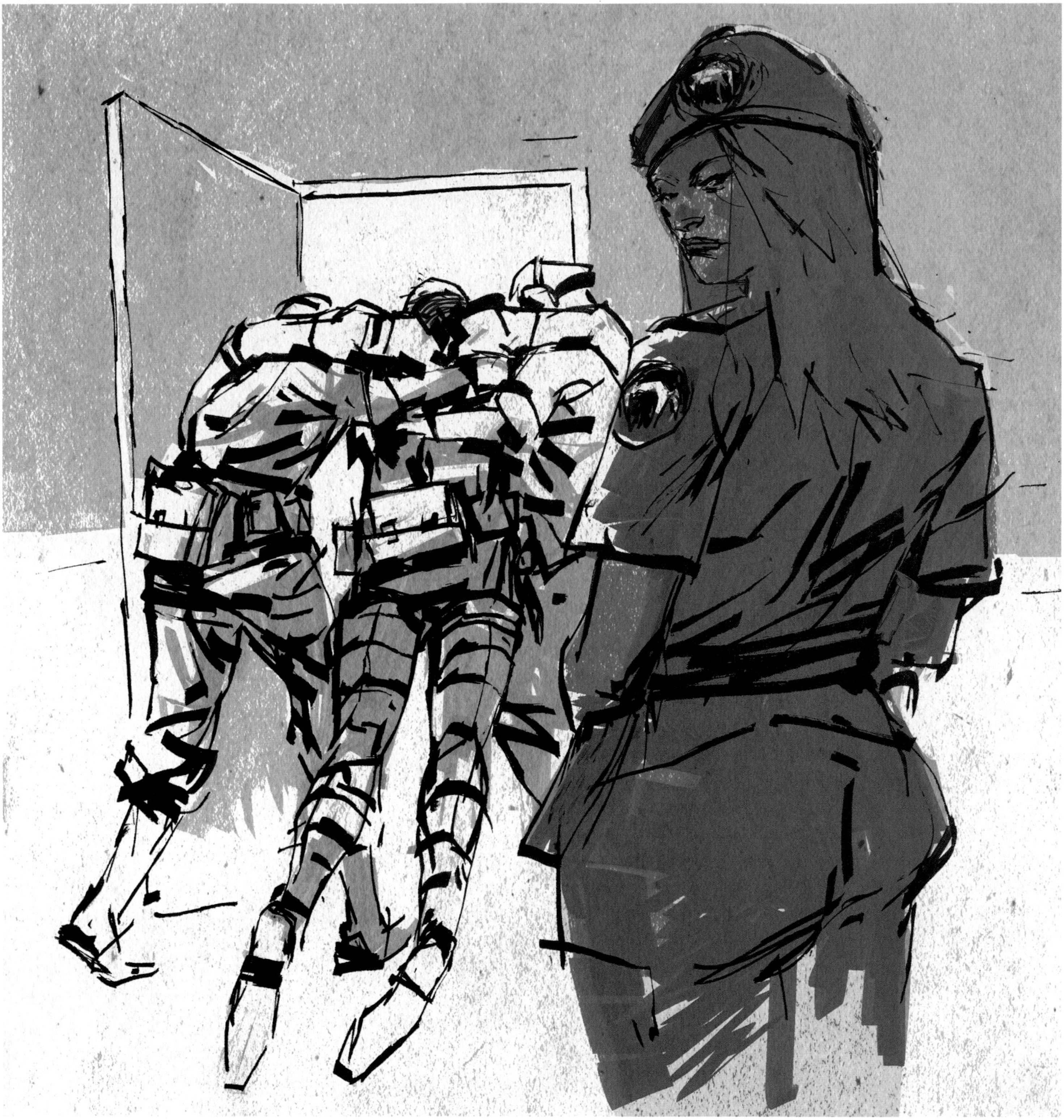

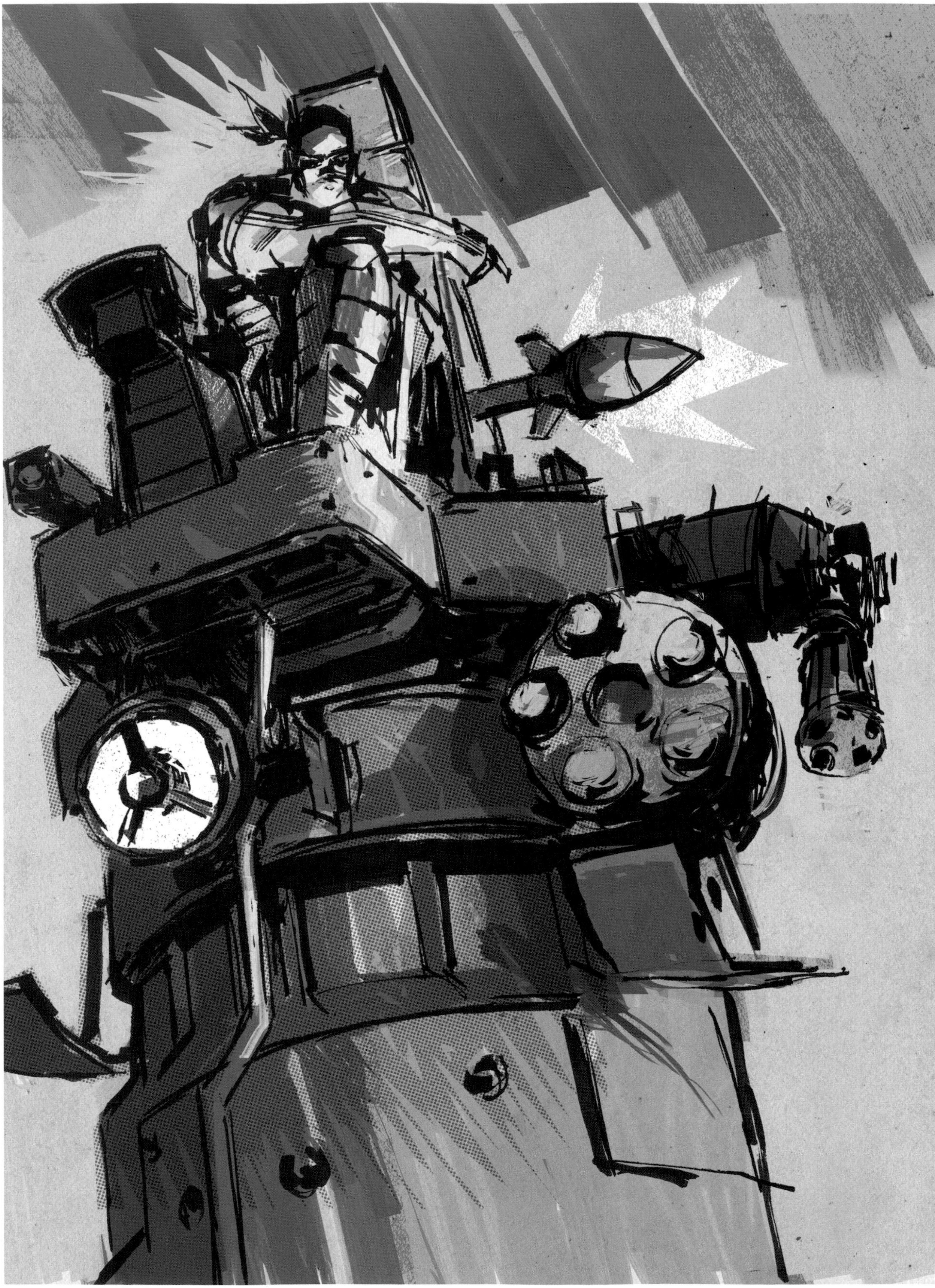

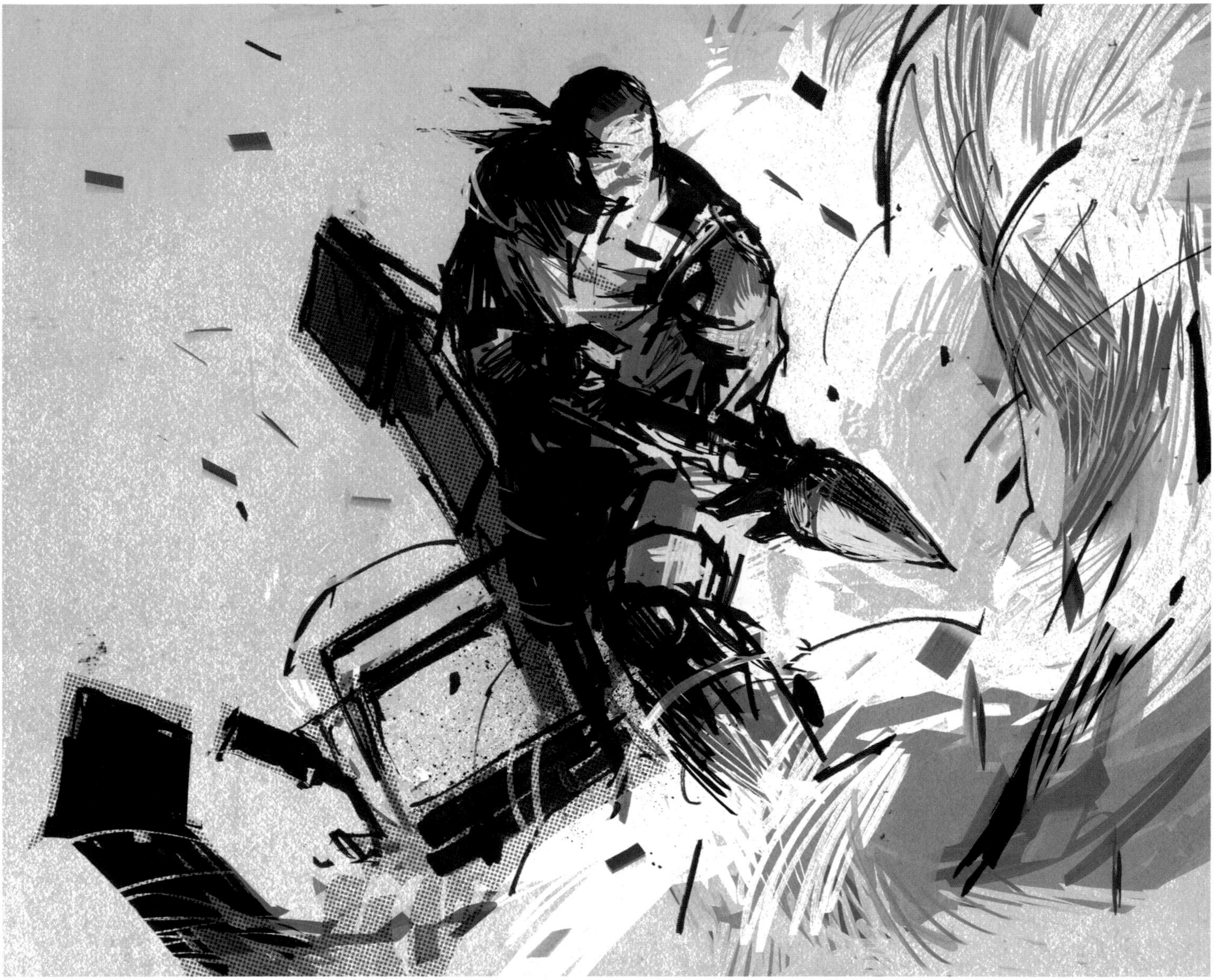

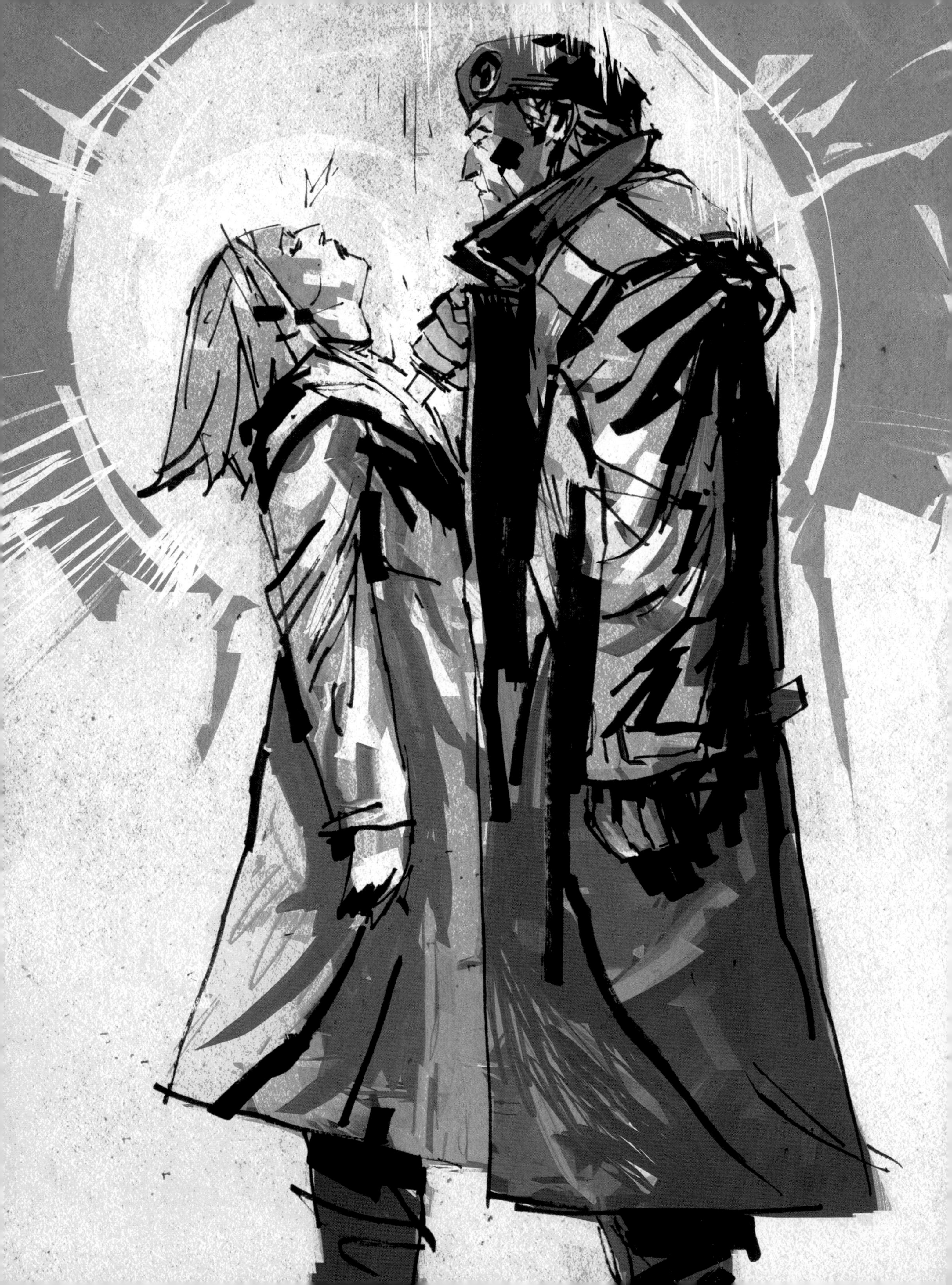

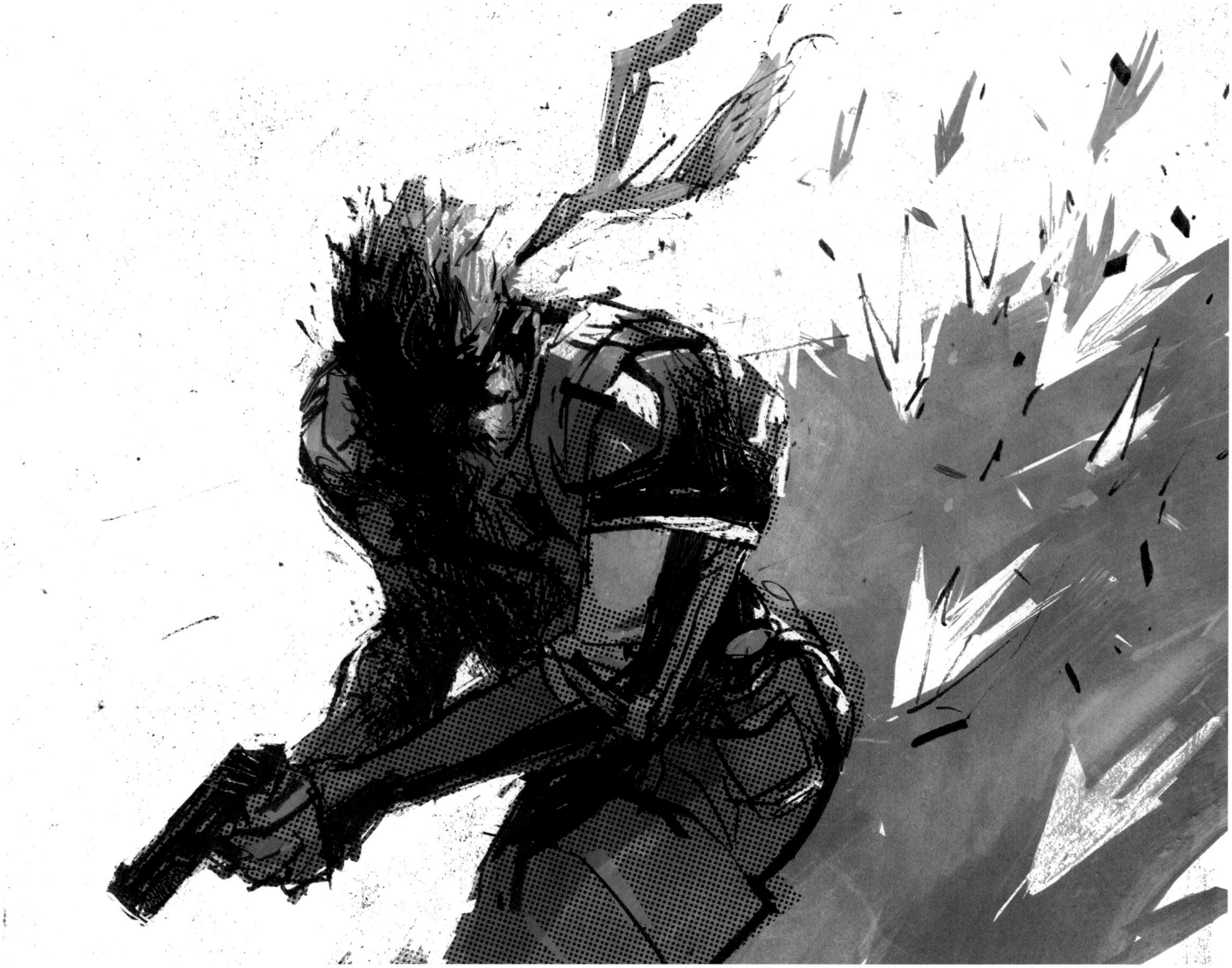

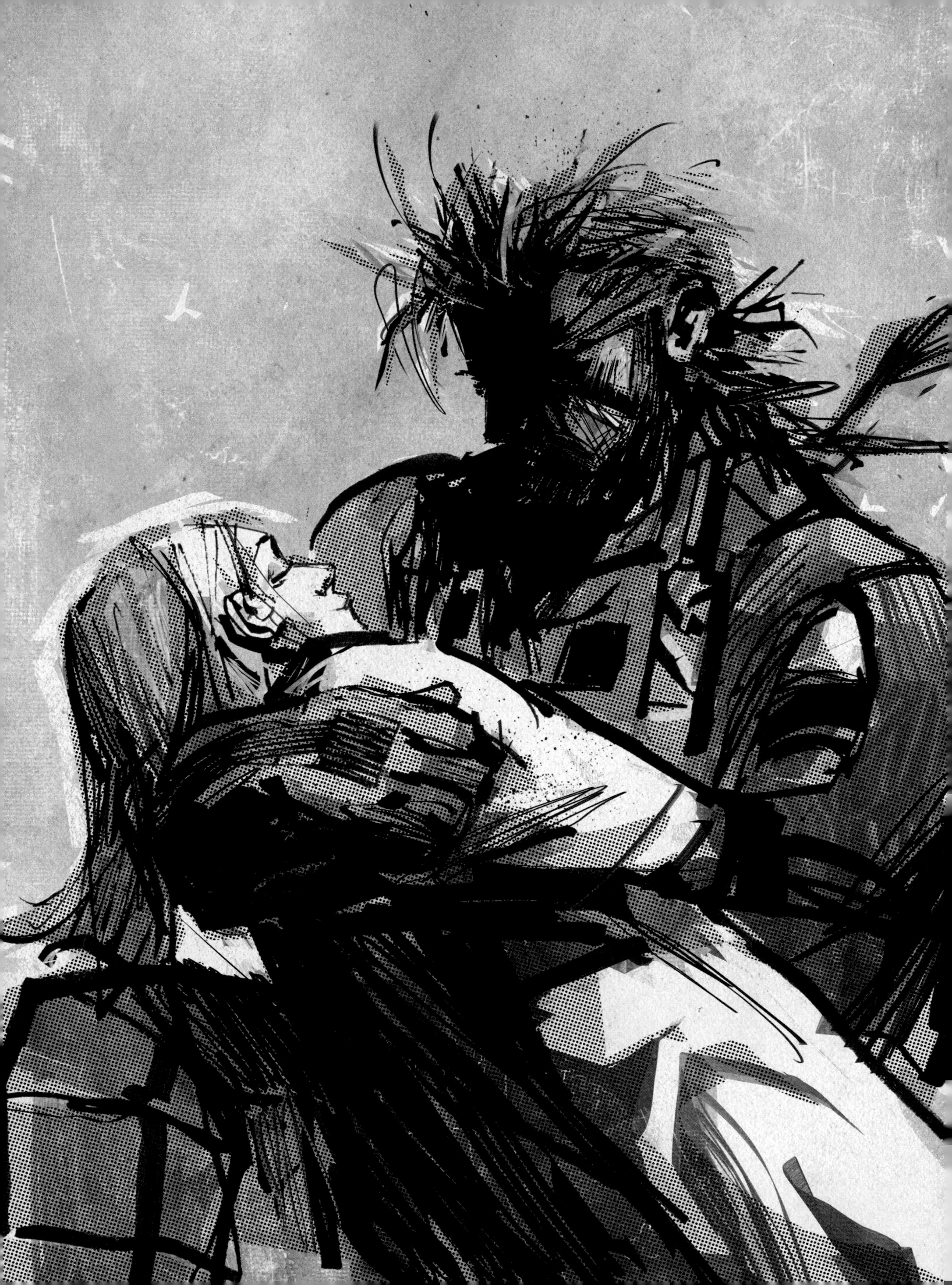

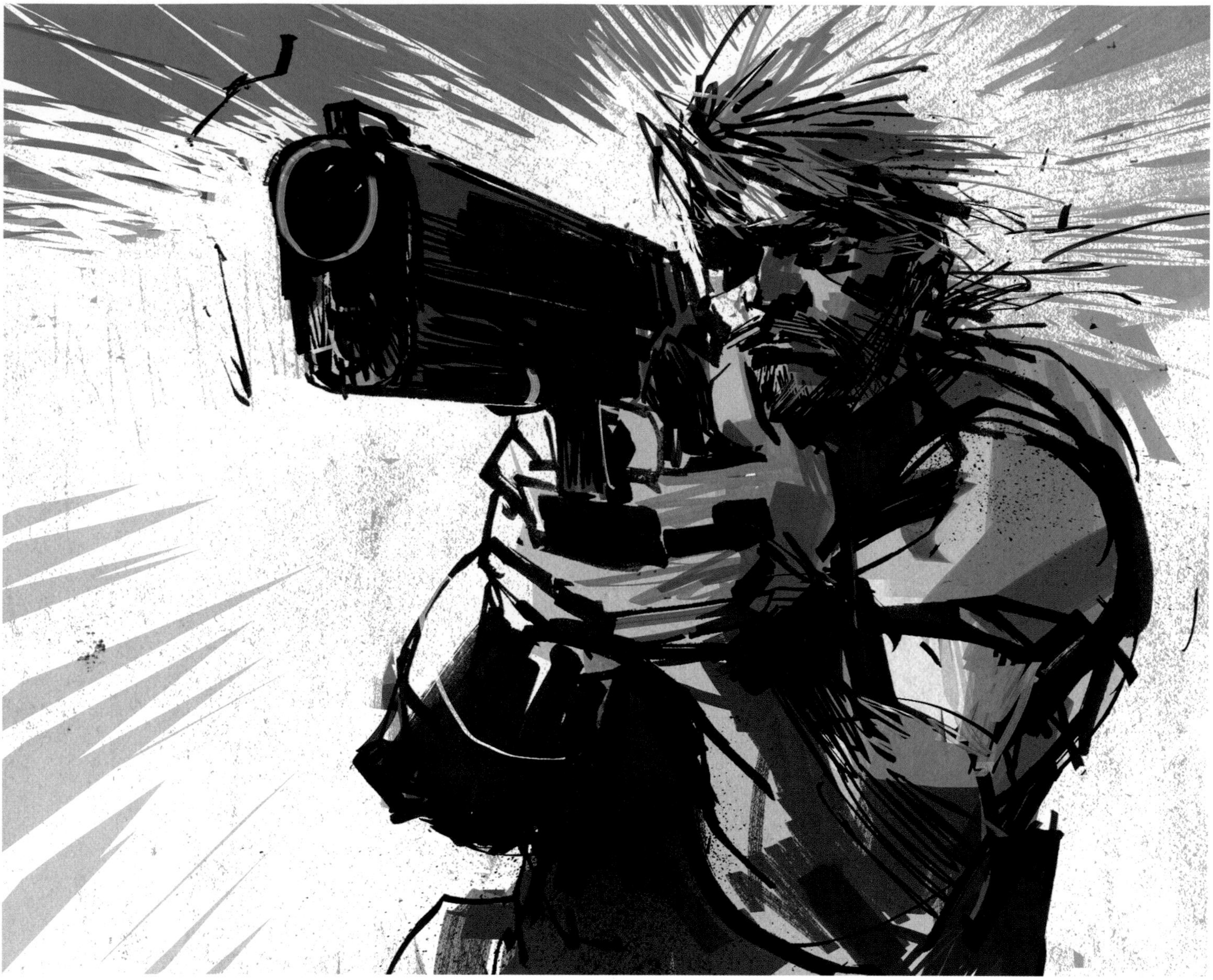

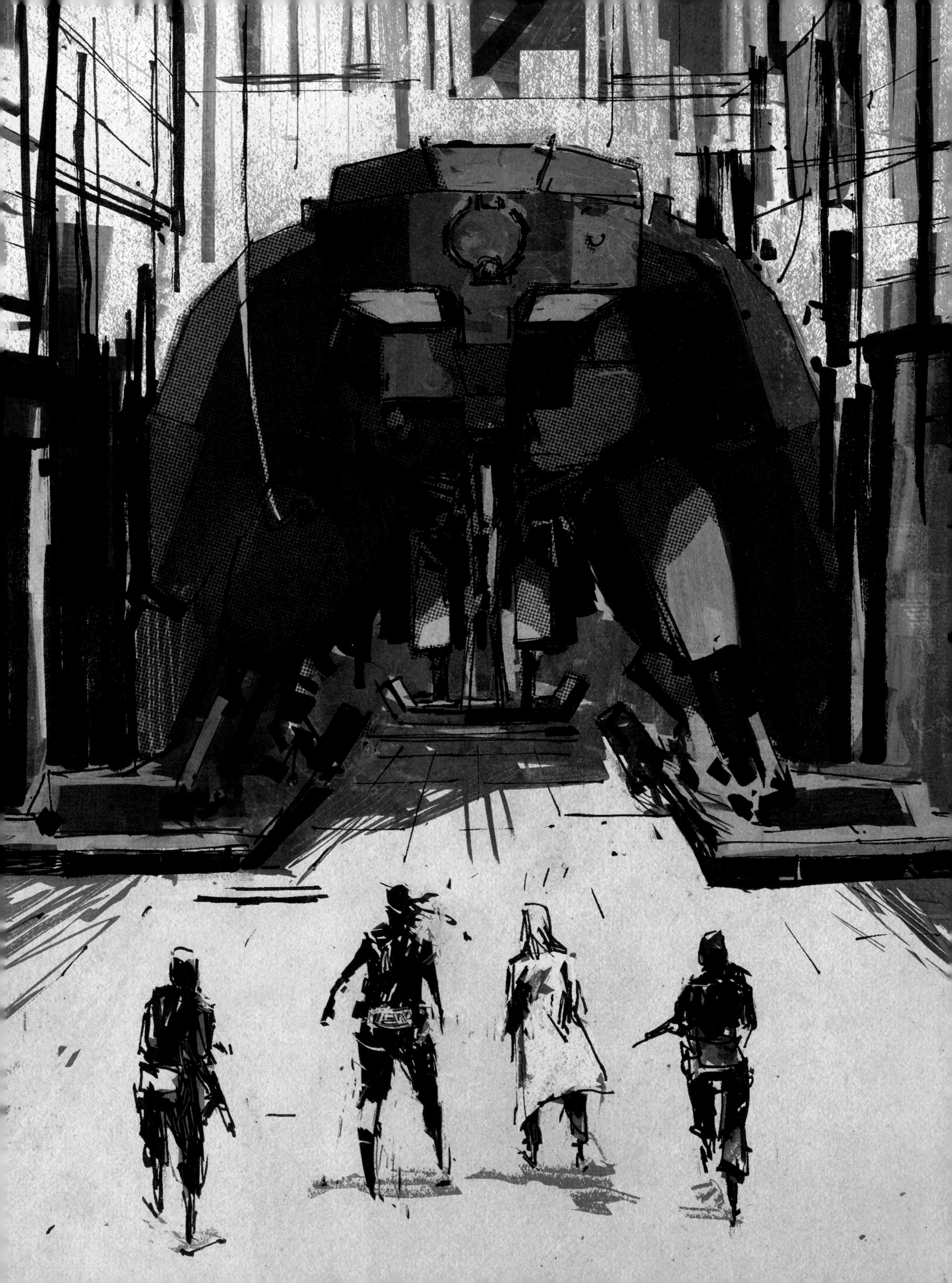

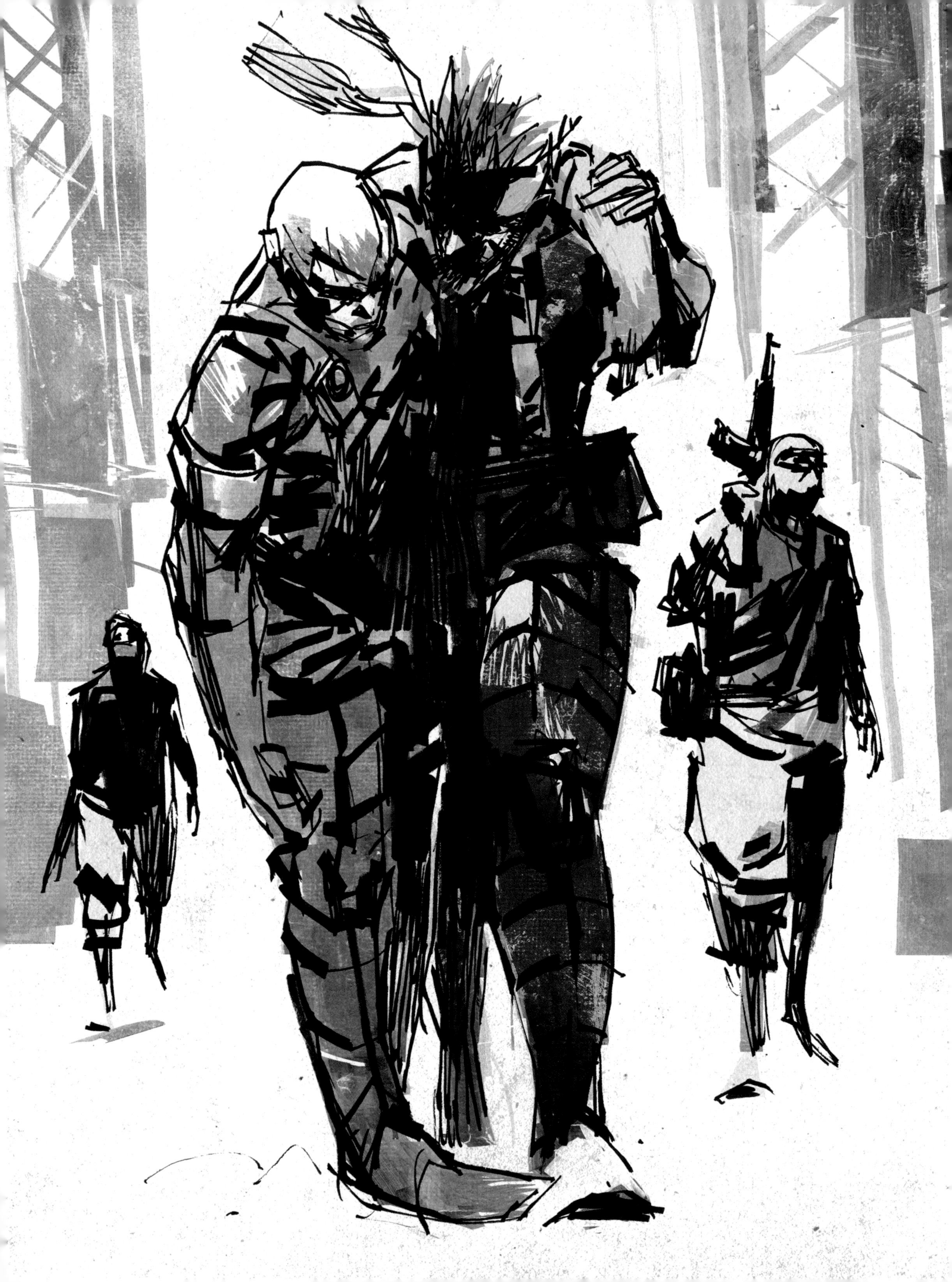

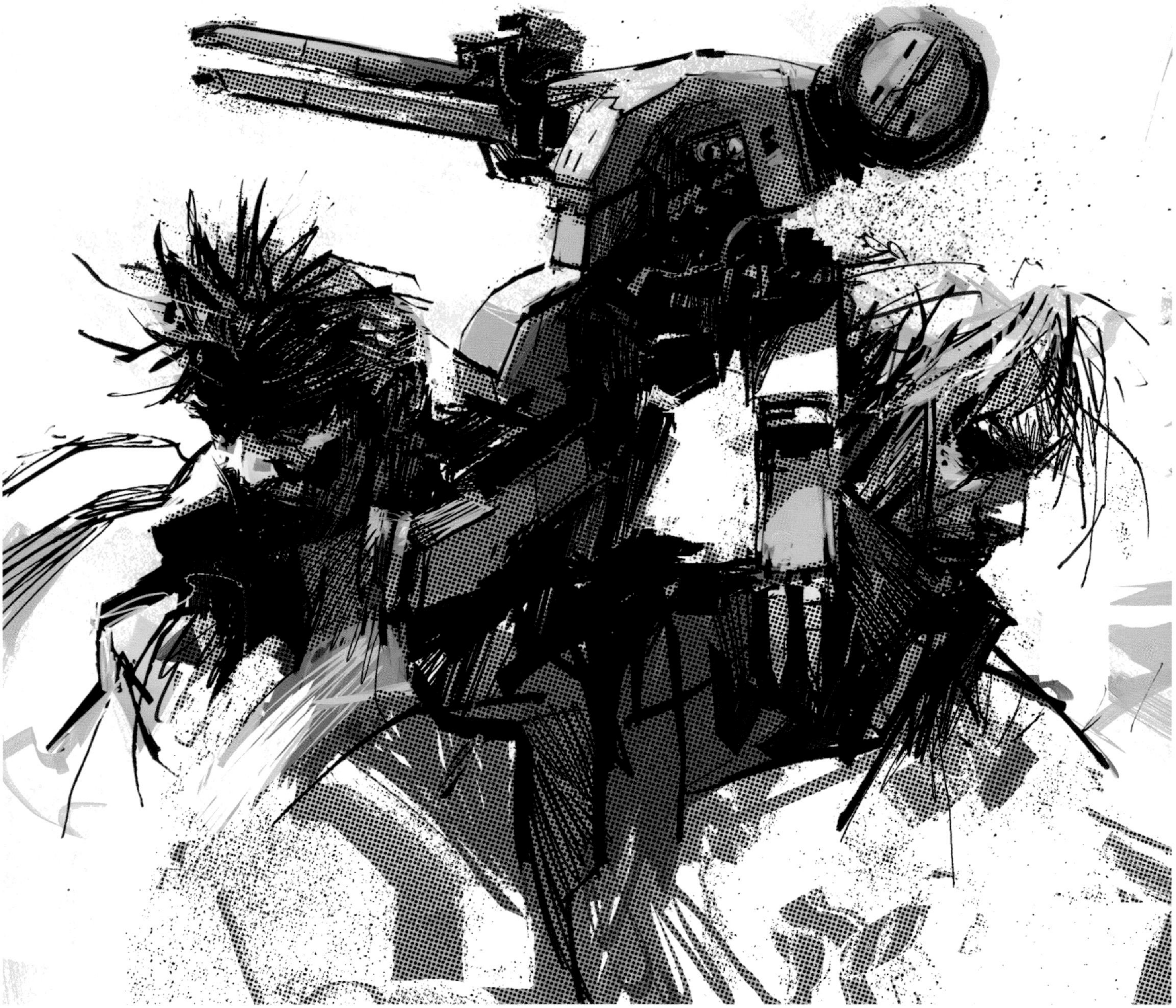

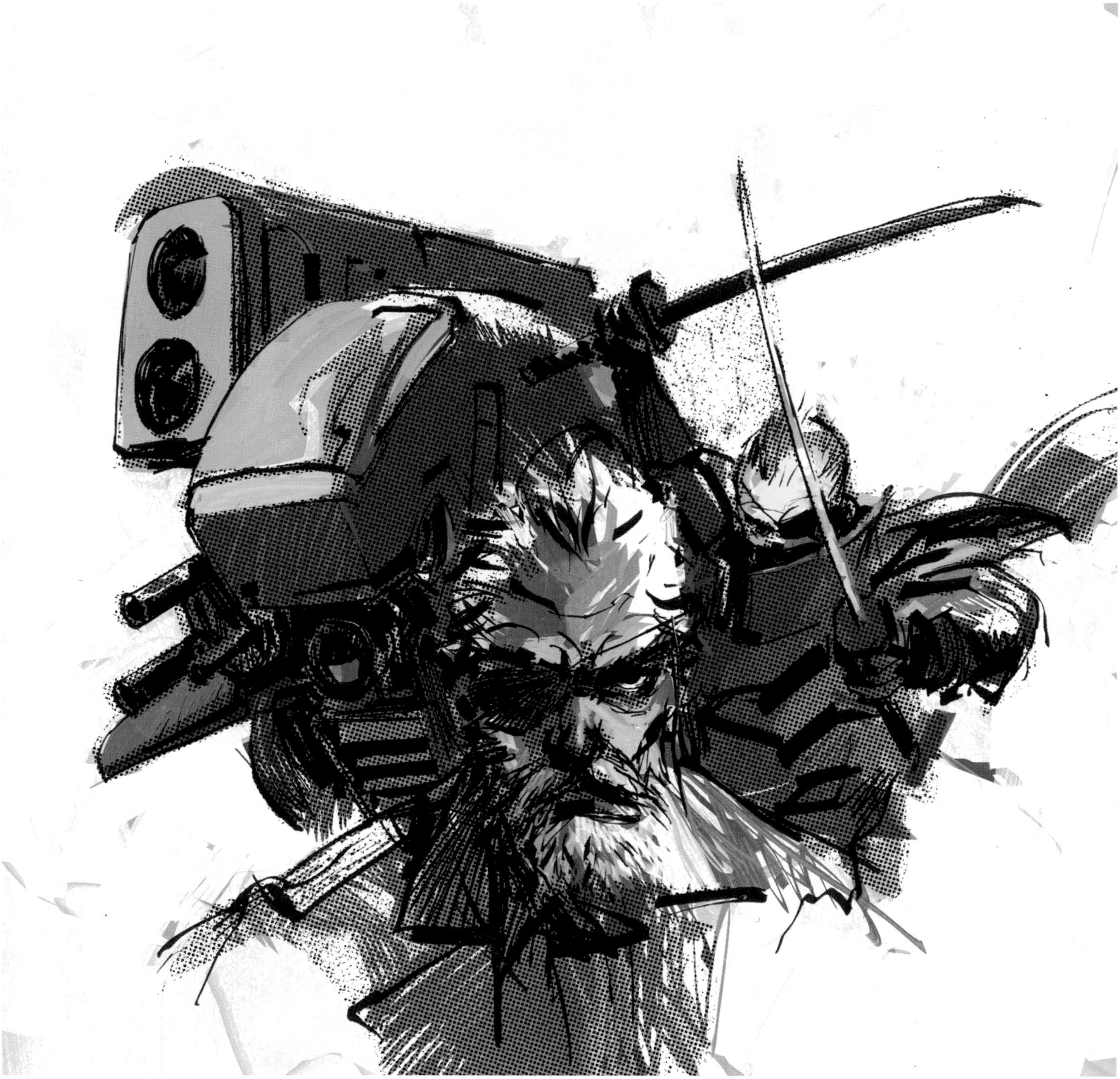

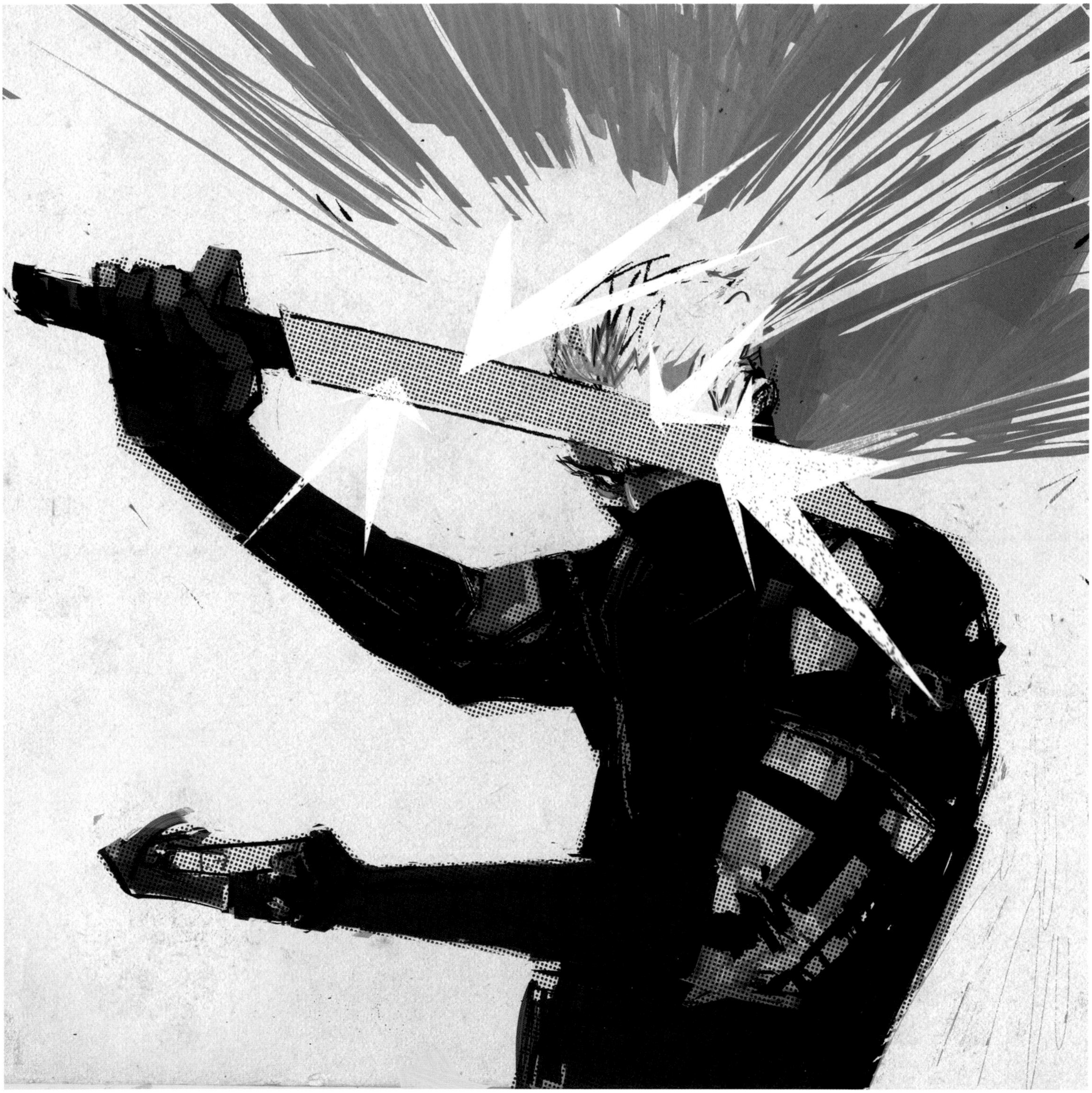

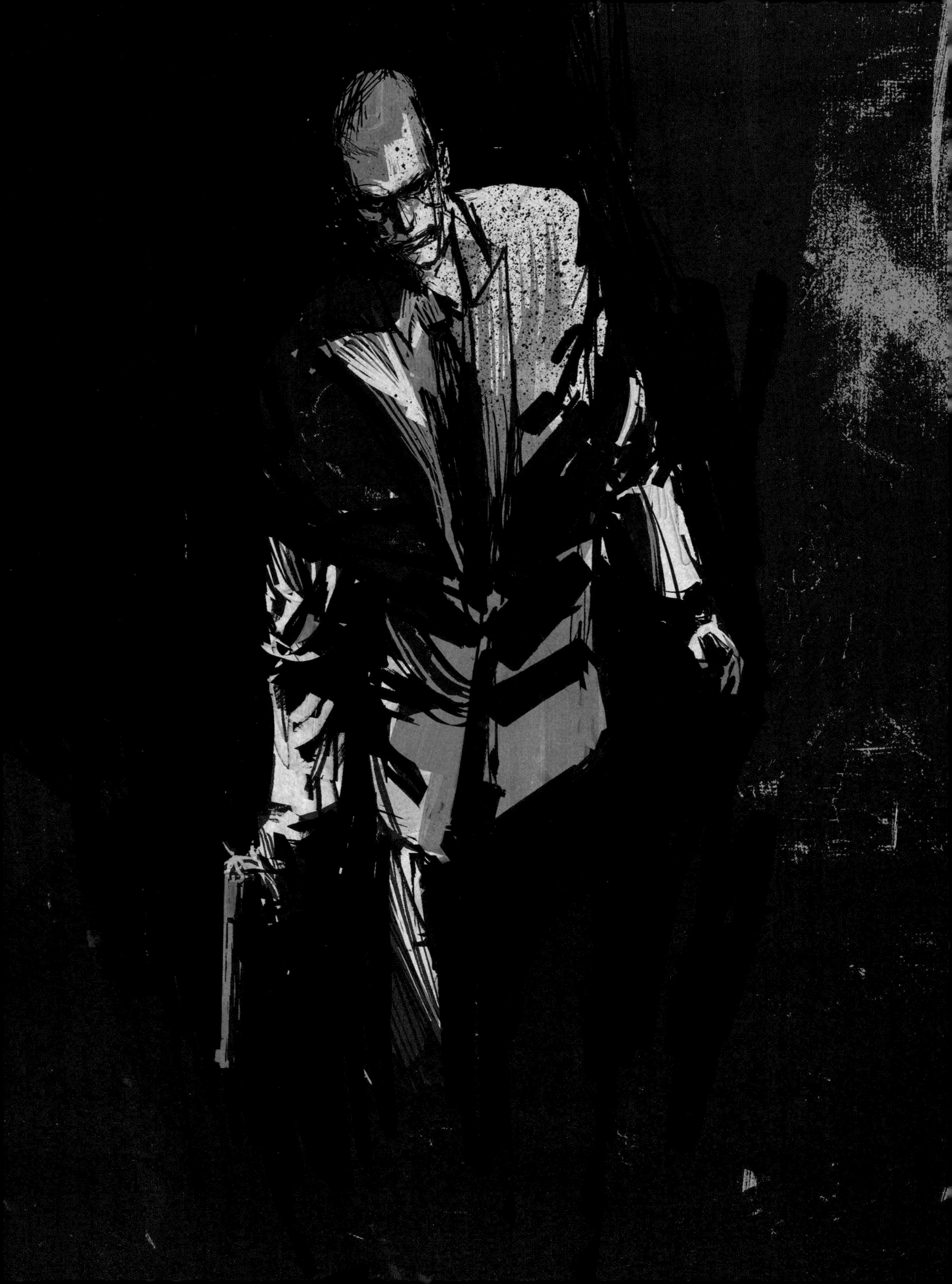

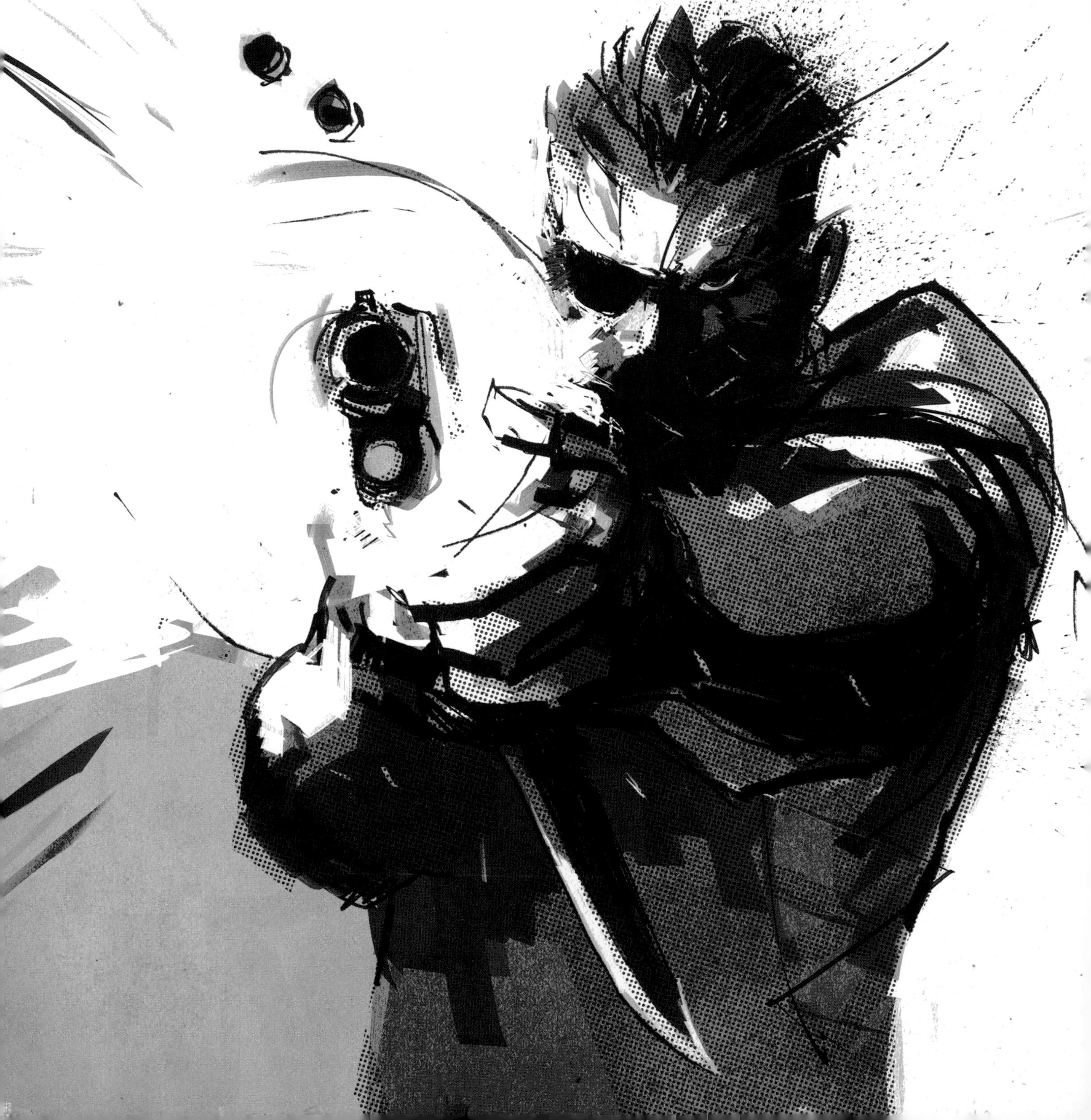

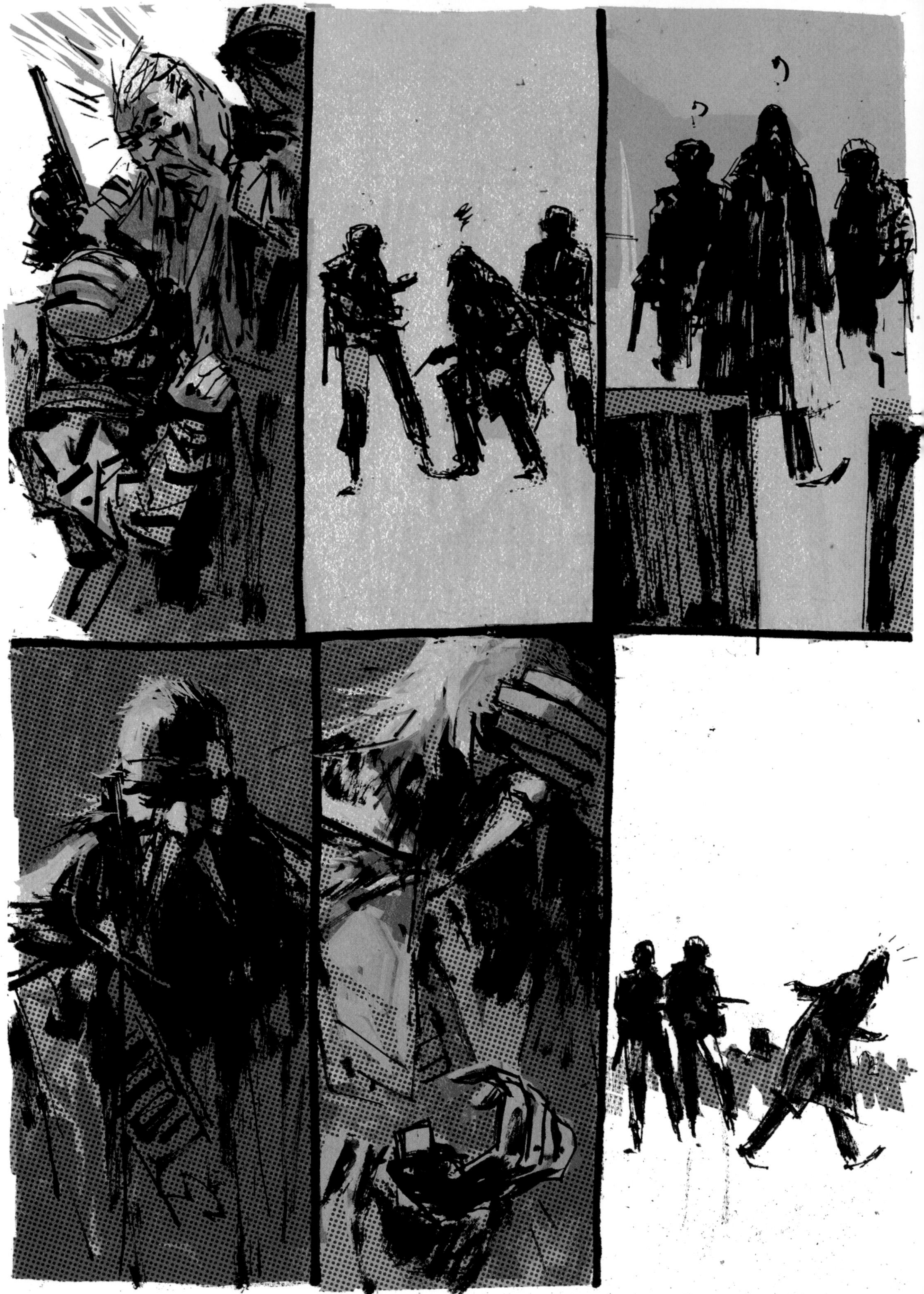

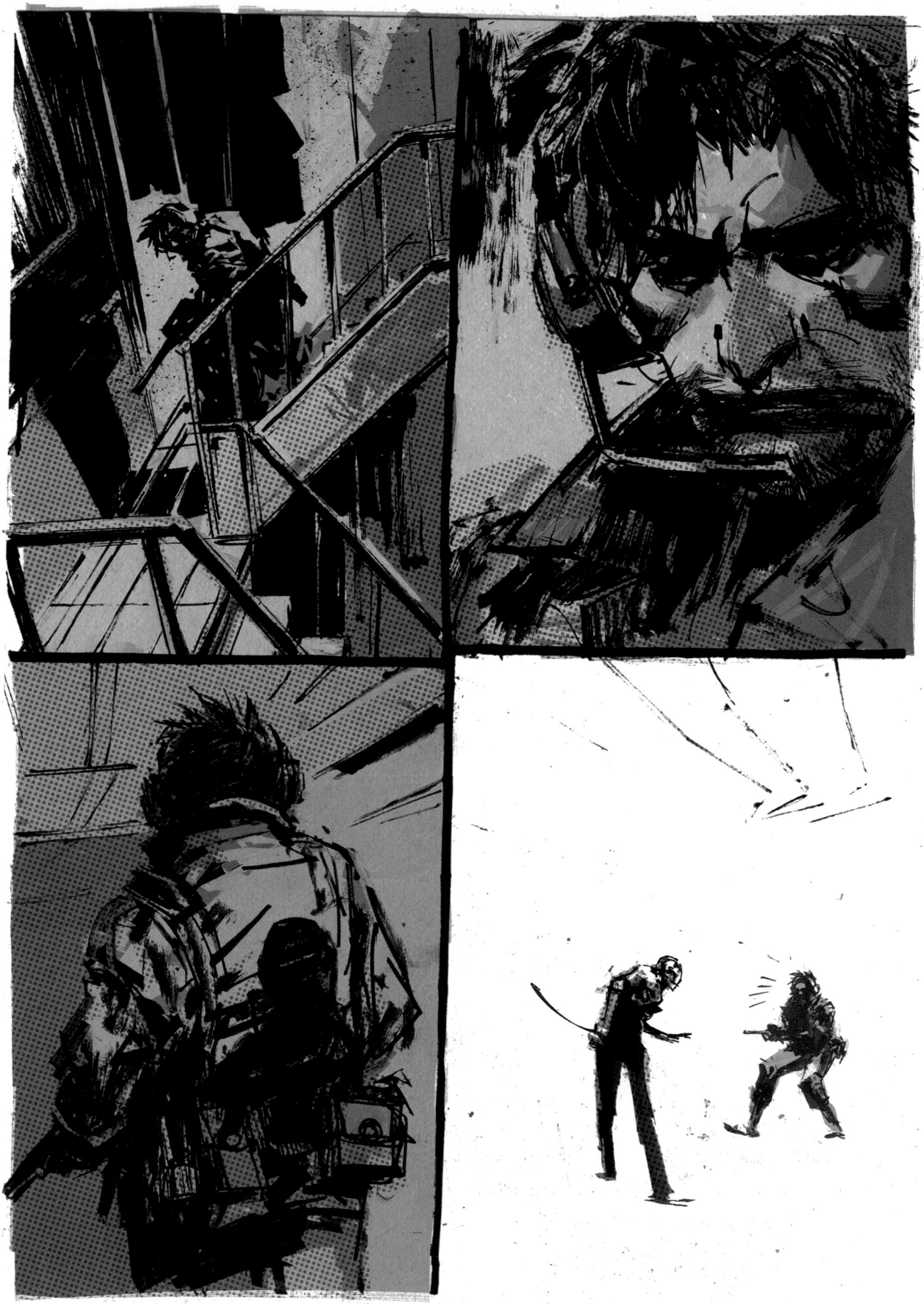

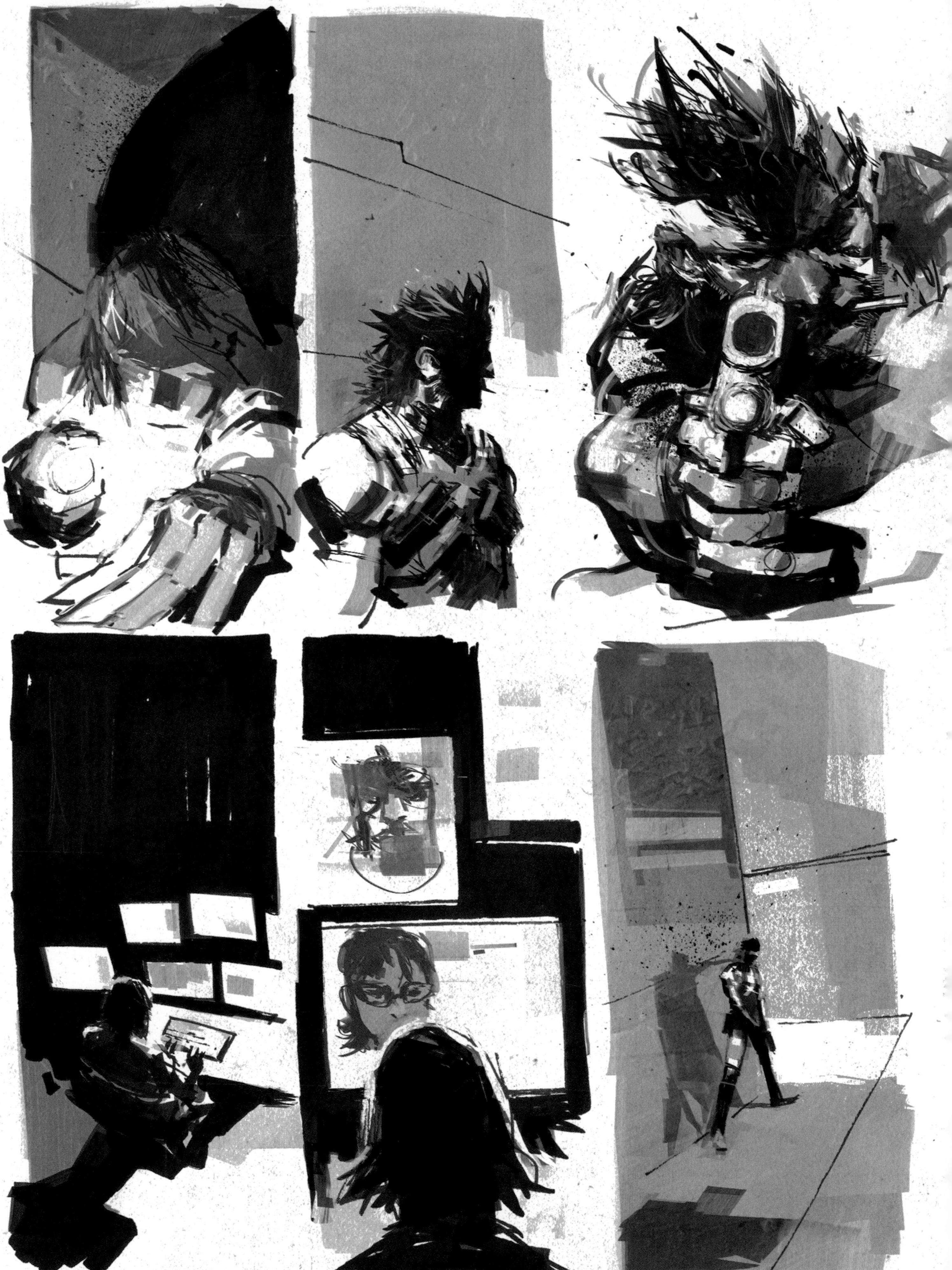

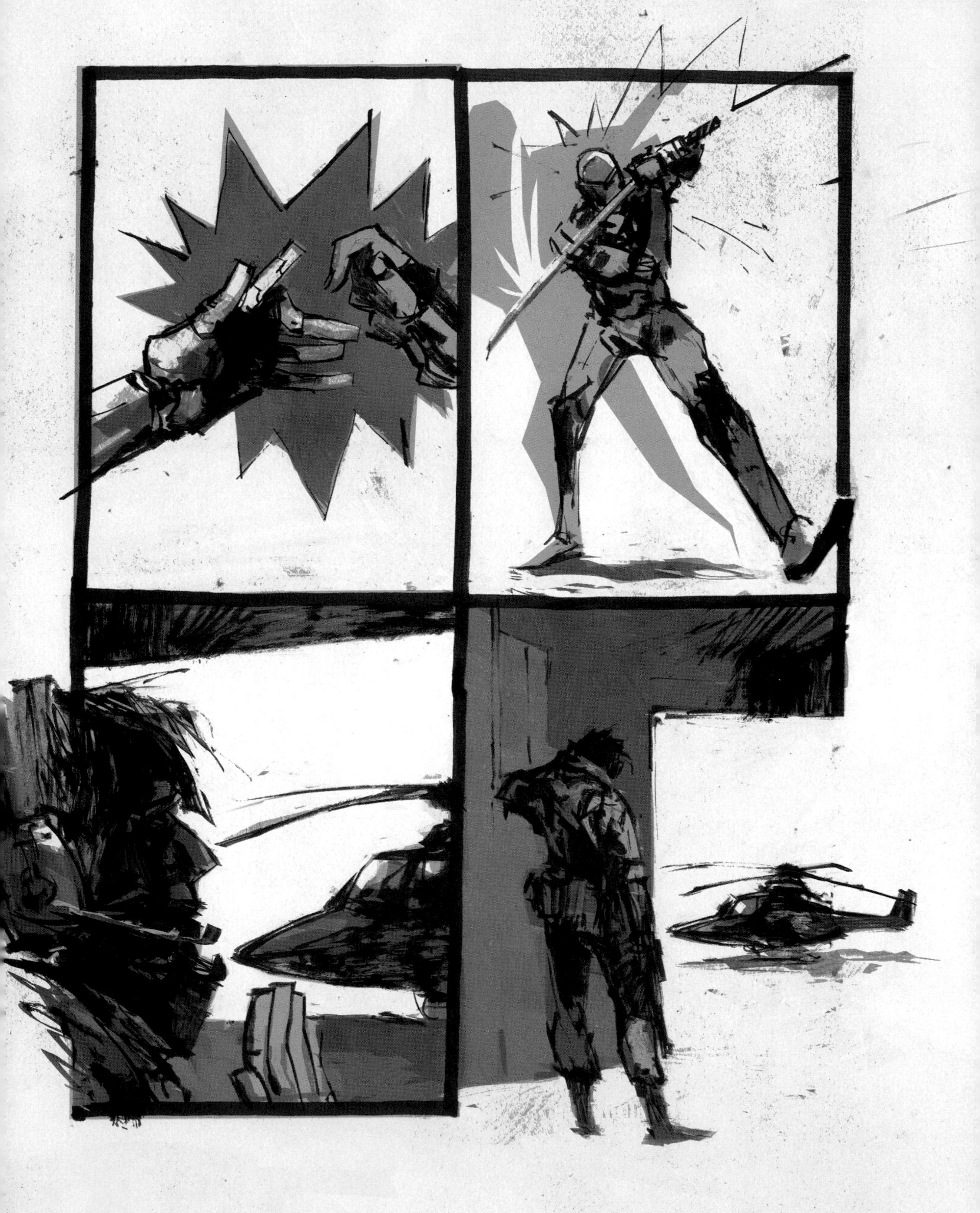

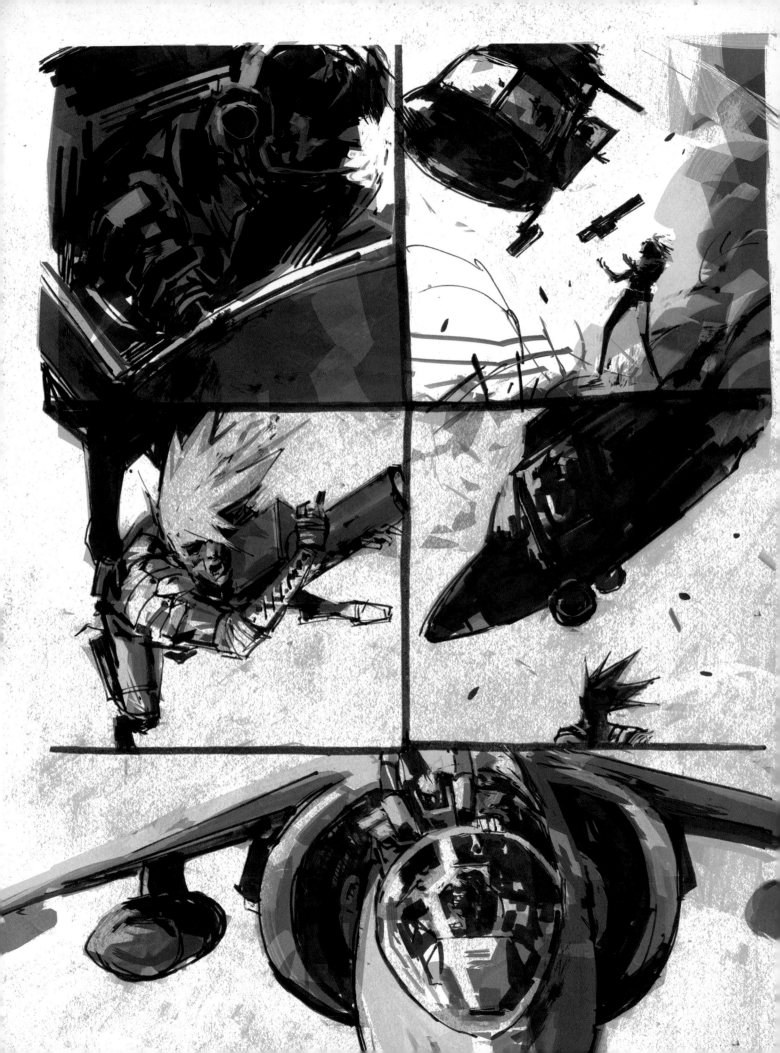

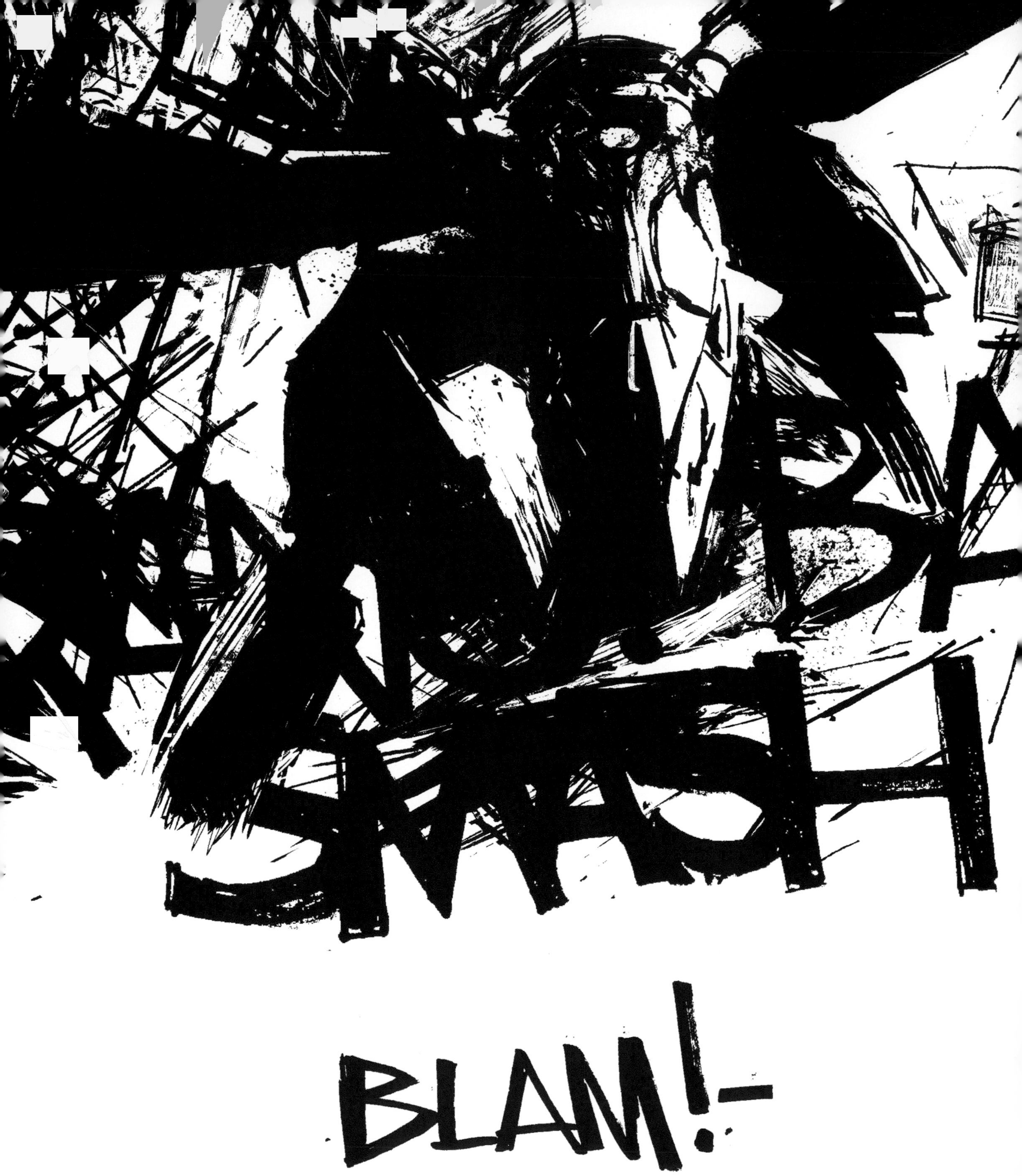
SMASH
BLAM!

ASHLEY WOOD'S ART OF METAL GEAR SOLID